BOUDICA

WOMEN IN ANTIQUITY

Series Editors: Ronnie Ancona and Sarah B. Pomeroy

This book series provides compact and accessible introductions to the life and historical times of women from the ancient world. Approaching ancient history and culture broadly, the series selects figures from the earliest of times to late antiquity.

BOUDICA

WARRIOR WOMAN OF ROMAN BRITAIN

Caitlin C. Gillespie

OXFORD
UNIVERSITY PRESS

Oxford University Press is a department of the University of Oxford. It furthers
the University's objective of excellence in research, scholarship, and education
by publishing worldwide. Oxford is a registered trade mark of Oxford University
Press in the UK and certain other countries.

Published in the United States of America by Oxford University Press
198 Madison Avenue, New York, NY 10016, United States of America.

Library of Congress Cataloging-in-Publication Data
Names: Gillespie, Caitlin C., author.
Title: Boudica : warrior woman of Roman Britain / Caitlin C. Gillespie.
Other titles: Boudica, warrior woman of Roman Britain
Description: New York, NY : Oxford University Press, [2018] |
Series: Women in antiquity |
Includes bibliographical references and index.
Identifiers: LCCN 2017050045 (print) | LCCN 2017053486 (ebook) |
ISBN 9780190609092 (updf) | ISBN 9780190875589 (epub) | ISBN 9780190875596 (oso) |
ISBN 9780190609078 (cloth : alk. paper) | ISBN 9780197503652 (paper : alk. paper)
Subjects: LCSH: Boadicea, Queen, -62. | Great Britain—History—
Roman period, 55 B.C.-449 A.D. | Great Britain—History, Military—55 B.C.-449 A.D. |
Queens—Great Britain—Biography. | Romans—Great Britain. |
Iceni—History. | Women in antiquity.
Classification: LCC DA145.3.B6 (ebook) | LCC DA145.3.B6 G55 2018 (print) |
DDC 936.2/04092 [B]—dc23
LC record available at https://lccn.loc.gov/2017050045

1 3 5 7 9 8 6 4 2

Printed by Sheridan Books, Inc., United States of America

To my parents, Joan and Dennis

Contents

Preface

In AD 60/61, Rome almost lost the province of Britain to a woman. Boudica, leader of the Iceni, joined with the Trinovantes and other allies in a swift revolt that reduced three sites to ash, destroyed part of a Roman legion, and caused the deaths of an untold number of Roman veterans, families, soldiers, and allied Britons. Fearlessly defending her daughters and her people, Boudica fomented a rebellion that proved catastrophic to Camulodunum, Londinium, and Verulamium, but resulted in the massacre of her own people. In the end, her vision of freedom was destroyed, and the Iceni never rose again. The Romans rebuilt their urban centers and continued to expand their empire.

The dramatic story of Boudica's rebellion attracted the attention of two ancient authors, Tacitus and Cassius Dio, whose narratives constitute the only ancient literary sources for the existence of Boudica, and range from a sympathetic portrait of a mother to a fantastic image of a vengeful, savage barbarian. Their portraits have inspired numerous biographies, histories, novels, plays, film adaptations, children's stories, and artistic renderings. Our modern impression is influenced by Boudica's extensive afterlife, especially in her adoption as a symbol of Victory, nationalist icon, and figurehead of resistance. Boudica has been abstracted into a malleable idea, altered to suit a number of competing contexts.

John Opie's *Boadicea Haranguing the Britons* (1793) provides an example: Boudica stands above her Britons in a white tunic bound at the waist and a brilliant red cloak, a bright figure in a dark world. In addition to her feminine garb, she wears a helmet, signifying her military role. She protects her daughters with her left hand, raising her right hand in a manner reminiscent of an ancient orator as she addresses her men. Opie's Boudica is a symbol of the fight for freedom. She is an adaptation of Tacitus's noble mother, her thoughts far from those of the murderous barbarian presented by Cassius Dio. The artist has manipulated her image in accordance with contemporary artistic trends and impressions: she belongs in a gallery among his portraits of British aristocrats, not on a first-century battlefield. Opie's portrayal might suit his eighteenth-century outlook, but it does little to inform us about the real Boudica.

In this book, I interrogate the ancient evidence in order to elucidate Boudica's unique identity. I illustrate her utility in the works of Tacitus and Dio by showing how these men manipulated Boudica's story and character in pursuit of their own literary themes. Tacitus and Dio have different agendas, and the reader must proceed with caution. Both see Boudica through Roman eyes: she is a figure of resistance to Roman cultural norms, whose actions demonstrate an extreme example of the dangers of putting women in positions of power. However, she has positive qualities of leadership as well: she has the family, wealth, moral character, and intellect to garner the respect of her people. Furthermore, she is aligned with literary models of Republican womanhood as a chaste mother who condemns luxury and avarice.

This book presents a comparative literary biography of Boudica, juxtaposing her different characterizations in our ancient authors and setting her beside other women and rebel leaders. Boudica becomes a useful screen against which contemporary attitudes toward women in power play out, and a tool to discuss the role of Britain in the Roman Empire. Yet the real Boudica remains elusive, her life story punctuated by moments of high drama, rage, pain, and war. Her response to Roman rule held up a mirror to Rome, demanding justification for imperialist policies and poor governance at the end of the Julio-Claudian era. As mother, warrior, and leader, Boudica's unique ability to unify disparate groups of Britons cemented her place in history. While the historical Boudica remains tantalizingly out of reach, her literary character still has more to say.

Acknowledgments

My thanks go to Ronnie Ancona for inviting me to contribute to this series, and to Ronnie and Sarah Pomeroy for their guidance on my initial proposal. I have benefited from the scholarship of the other contributors to the *Women in Antiquity* series, whose works have been instrumental for my own.

My interest in Boudica was sparked during graduate school at the University of Pennsylvania and continues to grow thanks to the encouragement of friends, family, and peers. I am indebted to a number of colleagues for their support in the completion of this project. My deepest gratitude goes to Cynthia Damon, for setting a standard of intellectual and academic rigor worthy of lifelong emulation. Jen Gerrish and Nell Mulhern commented on early drafts, and I have been aided by their erudition and judgment. Colin Gillespie provided welcome editorial advice in the production of the final text. The arguments concerning Boudica's speeches in Tacitus and Dio developed from a talk presented at the annual meeting of the Society of Classical Studies, later revised and published in *Classical World*. My thanks go to Lee Pearcy and Robin Mitchell-Boyask for their editorial expertise and for permission to recast some of that material here. Special thanks are owed to Eric Adler, Liz Cottam, Philip Crummy, John Davies, Joseph Farrell, Lee Fratantuono, Stephen Heyworth, James Ker, Myles Lavan, Marian Makins, Brian Rose, Julia Wilker, and Emily Wilson, for reading portions of the text, responding to inquiries and specific intellectual issues, and assisting in the acquisition of images.

At Oxford University Press, Stefan Vranka has been encouraging at every stage of the process, and I thank him and my anonymous referees for their considered responses to the manuscript. John Veranes has been a powerful force in assisting this book on the way to production. I thank Richa Jobin and the production team for bringing this book to completion. All errors or inadequacies remain my own.

This book has benefited from the assistance of the Loeb Classical Library Foundation as well as the Stanwood Cockey Lodge Fund at Columbia University. A research stay at the Fondation Hardt in Vandœuvres, Switzerland accelerated the completion of the project.

Final thanks go to my friends and family, who provide constant sources of artistic and intellectual inspiration. I owe thanks to my siblings, Ian, Colin, Fran, and Chas, who motivate me daily with their unique excellences, and to the residents of Elizabeth House, who provided a space for me to write. Danny Moffat has been an eager partner in my search for Boudica, and his love has sustained me throughout the journey. This book is dedicated to my parents, Joan and Dennis Gillespie, my ideal readers.

Texts and Abbreviations

This book uses Heubner's 1994 edition of Tacitus's *Annals*, Woodman's 2014 edition of Tacitus's *Agricola*, and Boissevain's edition of Cassius Dio's *Roman History* (1895–1969). Other quotations follow the texts listed in the bibliography or those used by the Packard Humanities Institute (*PHI*). Abbreviations used for names of ancient authors and their works are those of S. A. Hornblower, A. Spawforth, and E. Eidinow, eds., *Oxford Classical Dictionary*, 4th edition (2012), with a few exceptions. Authors and works abbreviated or otherwise cited in the text are listed below.

I. Greek and Roman Authors and Works

App.		Appian
	BCiv.	*Civil Wars*
Ath.		Athenaeus, *Deipnosophists*
Aug.		Augustus
	RGDA	*Res Gestae Divi Augusti (The Deeds of the Divine Augustus)*
AWP		Hippocratic Corpus, *On Airs, Waters, and Places*
Caes.		Caesar
	BGall.	*Gallic War*
Cic.		Cicero
	Att.	*Letters to Atticus*
	Cael.	*Pro Caelio*
	Rep.	*De republica*
	Fam.	*Letters to His Friends*
	Phil.	*Philippics*
	QFr.	*Letters to His Brother Quintus*

Dio	Cassius Dio, *Roman History*	
Diod. Sic.	Diodorus Siculus, *Library of History*	
Dion. Hal.	Dionysius of Halicarnassus, *Roman Antiquities*	
Hdn.	Herodian, *History of the Roman Empire*	
Hdt.	Herodotus	
Hist.	*Histories*	
Hom.	Homer	
Il.	*Iliad*	
Hor.	Horace	
Carm.	*Carmina* or *Odes*	
Joseph.	Josephus	
AJ	*Antiquitates Judaicae*	
Livy	Livy, *History of Rome*	
Per.	*Periochae*	
Luc.	Lucan, *Pharsalia*	
Mart.	Martial, *Epigrams*	
Plin.	Pliny the Elder	
HN	*Natural History*	
Plut.	Plutarch	
Ant.	*Life of Antony*	
Caes.	*Life of Caesar*	
Cor.	*Life of Coriolanus*	
Mor.	*Moralia*	
Pomp.	*Life of Pompey*	
Pompon.	Pomponius Mela, *De chorographia*	
Prop.	Propertius	
Carm.	*Carmina* or *Elegies*	
Sen.	Seneca the Younger	
Apocol.	*Apocolocyntosis*	
Clem.	*De clementia (On clemency)*	
De ira	*On anger*	
Dial.	*Dialogi*	
Ep.	*Epistles*	
Phaed.	*Phaedra*	
Serv.	Servius, *Commentary on the* Aeneid *of Vergil*	
SHA	Scriptores Historiae Augustae	
Sev.	*Life of Septimius Severus*	
Stat.	Statius	
Silv.	*Silvae*	
Strabo	Strabo, *Geography*	
Suet.	Suetonius	
Aug.	*Life of the Deified Augustus*	

	Calig.	*Life of Caligula*
	Claud.	*Life of the Deified Claudius*
	Iul.	*Life of the Deified Julius Caesar*
	Ner.	*Life of Nero*
	Tib.	*Life of Tiberius*
	Tit.	*Life of the Deified Titus*
	Vesp.	*Life of the Deified Vespasian*
Tab. Sul.		*Tabulae Sulis*
Tac.		Tacitus
	Agr.	*Agricola*
	Ann.	*Annals*
	Germ.	*Germania*
	Hist.	*Histories*
Val. Max.		Valerius Maximus, *Memorable Deeds and Sayings*
Vell. Pat.		Velleius Paterculus, *Roman History*
Verg.		Vergil
	Aen.	*Aeneid*

II. *Works of Secondary Scholarship*

ABC	Cottam, E., P. de Jersey, C. Rudd, and J. Sills. 2010. *Ancient British Coins.* Chris Rudd: Aylesham.
CIL	*Corpus Inscriptionum Latinarum.*
OLD	Glare, P. G. W., ed. 1968–1982. *Oxford Latin Dictionary.* Oxford: Oxford University Press.
RE 1	Mattingly, H. 1976. *Coins of the Roman Empire in the British Museum.* Vol. 1, *Augustus to Vitellius.* London: British Museum Press.
RIB	*Roman Inscriptions of Britain.*
RIC 1	Sutherland, C. H. V., and R. A. G. Carson, eds. 1984. *The Roman Imperial Coinage.* Vol. 1: Augustus–Vitellius (31 BC–AD 69). London: Spink & Son Ltd.
VA	Van Arsdell, R. D. 1989. *Celtic Coinage of Britain.* London: Spink & Son Ltd.

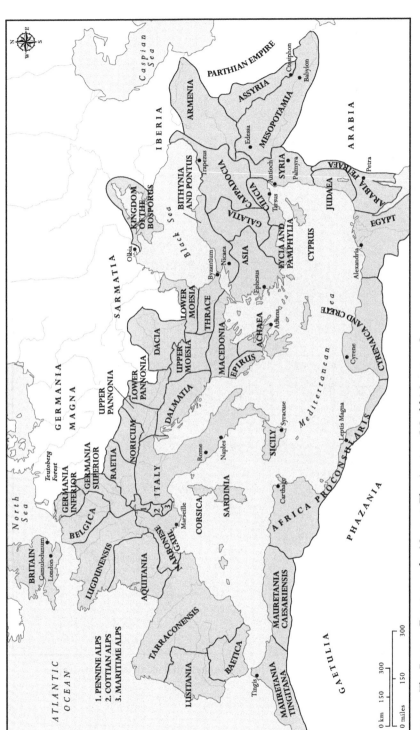

MAP 1. The Roman Empire under Nero. © The Ancient World Mapping Center 2003.

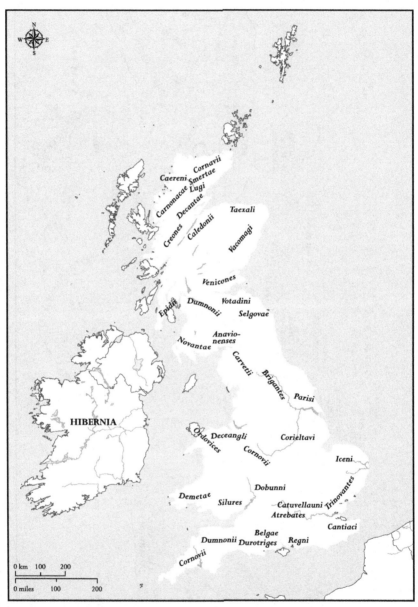

MAP 2. Peoples of Britain in the Roman period, based on Ptolemy (after Mattingly 2006, figure 3).

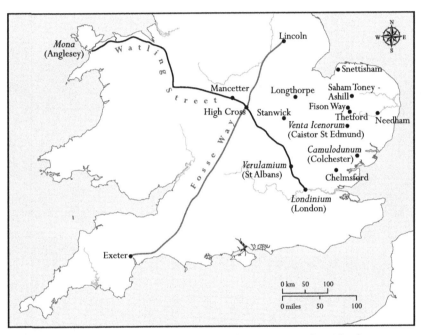

MAP 3. Sites important to the Iceni and to the narrative of Boudica's rebellion.

Introduction

Boudica, warrior woman of the Iceni, has been celebrated for centuries as the first female freedom fighter in Roman Britain. Her leadership of a revolt in AD 60/61 resulted in the burning of Camulodunum, Londinium, and Verulamium (modern Colchester, London, and near present-day St Albans, respectively). After this destruction, she spoke among her troops, her daughters before her, victims of Roman lust. Eyes glancing fiercely, golden hair cascading down her back, she grasped a spear and struck awe in all who beheld her as she captivated her audience and urged them to defeat the greedy tyrant, Rome. Although her army was quashed in a single battle against the Roman general Suetonius Paulinus, her legend lived on.

Boudica, whose name is spelled variously in ancient and modern texts (Boadicea, Boudicca, among others), is derived from a Celtic word *bouda*, meaning "victory."[1] Boudica comes closest to an ancient Celtic spelling.[2] The Roman historians Tacitus and Cassius Dio made her famous, although neither witnessed the rebellion.[3] Their opposing images form a core dichotomy in representations of Boudica. Whereas Tacitus heightens the glory of the woman warrior and celebrates her motherhood and noble fight for freedom, Dio's sensational portrait highlights her non-Roman appearance and the brutality of her actions. Tacitus's and Dio's texts have been supplemented by an increasing number of archaeological discoveries that allow us to fill in some of the details about Boudica's life and times. But many questions remain. The depictions of Boudica in Tacitus and Dio, and the archaeological evidence of early Roman Britain, give varying impressions of Boudica as a powerful woman of late Iron Age and early Roman Britain. Given such contrasting impressions, how do we understand Boudica as a historical figure? Should we see her as a barbarian woman, the ultimate "other" in the Roman imagination? Should we compare her to other rebels, symbols of freedom and the opposition to tyranny? Was she a prophetess, similar to the Druids? Or should we imagine her as a model mother, caring for her daughters above all?

In order to appreciate Boudica's central place in the history of Roman Britain, we must canvas her various identities. At different stages of their accounts, the ancient authors describe Boudica as a wife, mother, queen, warrior, rebel, or religious figure, connecting her to other such figures throughout the history of the Roman Empire. As such, she has a particular narrative utility in the histories of Tacitus and Dio. In this book, I aim to elucidate each of Boudica's roles by drawing together literary and material evidence for women in the domestic, political, and military spheres in late Iron Age and early Roman Britain. The importance of her characterization and her actions gains further prominence when placed beside historical comparisons. Throughout this work, comparative sketches are drawn between Boudica and others who garnered the interest of the ancient historians as positive or negative moral models. Veleda, another prophetess, was revered as almost divine; Caratacus and Calgacus, other rebels in Britain, are glorified for their devotion to freedom; additionally, several Roman leaders provide inspiration for the characterization of Boudica, from the noble Brutus to the courageous Cloelia of Livy's history. Antimodels include Cartimandua, queen of the Brigantes in Britain, the immoral wives of Claudius, Messalina and Agrippina the Younger, and the emperor Nero, who preferred the lyre to the sword. Through comparing Boudica to these other figures, a fuller portrait of the Icenian woman and her place in historiography emerges.

While Tacitus's Boudica represents Roman Republican values of motherhood and freedom, and demonstrates how the Romans encroached upon native independence, Dio utilizes Boudica to examine the place of women in leadership positions and to condemn the negative models among the imperial family. In the Roman imperial system, there was no room for institutionalized power for women—no place for an empress with a shared role in ruling the Empire. Boudica allowed Roman historians to explore a culture with a different gender ideology than their own and to illustrate the consequences of such an ideology.[4] Historical comparisons allow us insight into which aspects of Boudica individuate her and which traits characterize her as a stereotypical female barbarian, as seen through Roman eyes. While many details of Boudica's life may never be resolved, comparisons better equip readers to understand her importance in the ancient texts.

The majority of modern scholarship has focused on establishing the details of Boudica's revolt, but it often fails to critique thoroughly the literary accounts or to analyze archaeological evidence with equal rigor.[5] Several authors have addressed the differences in Tacitus and Dio, interrogating these texts for authorial bias, or examining the ways in which Boudica narratives represent ancient perceptions of women in power and views on the position of Britain in the Roman Empire.[6] Archaeologists have considered the material relating to Boudica in order to describe the lifestyles of the Iceni as moneyers and crafts people living in proto-cities and farming settlements, and to suggest ways in which the Roman Empire impacted local identities.[7] Material evidence allows us to flesh out our perception of women and family life in Roman Britain without imposing a Romano-centric view.[8] Reception studies, especially that of Hingley and Unwin, have outlined how Boudica's image has been manipulated throughout history, providing a warning to readers about how modern representations unfailingly alter our understanding of the historical figure and the events in which she was involved.

Despite her immediate impact on the Romano-British landscape and her everlasting fame as a rebel, literary accounts of Boudica are sparse. Those who study Boudica are faced with a lack of contemporary literary accounts, as well as biases in the sources that remain. A brief background to Tacitus and Dio, their styles, and historical contexts assists in guiding readers toward a critical perspective of the literary evidence for early Roman Britain, as presented through a Roman lens. These ancient authors may have used the same original sources for their narratives, including a possible memoir of the Roman governor, Suetonius Paulinus, as well as the eyewitness account of Tacitus's father-in-law, Agricola, and the narratives of other historians of the time, including Cluvius Rufus, Fabius Rusticus, and Pliny the Elder.[9] However, differences in their narratives suggest that, even if the two men had access to the same works, they prioritized them differently.[10] Some have argued Dio did not read Tacitus at all for his account.[11]

Gaius (or Publius) Cornelius Tacitus was born in AD 56/57 to an equestrian family in Gallia Narbonensis (modern Provence in southern

France). He was celebrated for his oratorical skill and received senatorial status under the emperor Vespasian.[12] He proceeded to climb the *cursus honorum* (sequence of offices), holding the positions of quaestor, tribune of the plebs or aedile, and praetor. During the reign of Domitian, he was a member of the *quindecimviri sacris faciundis*, a college of fifteen men tasked with sacred duties. Tacitus married the daughter of Julius Agricola and was abroad when his father-in-law died in AD 93, although he does not say where.[13] He gained the consulship in AD 97. His early works include a dialogue on oratory, an ethnographic study of the Germanic peoples, and a biography of Agricola, all published around AD 98. He then wrote a history of the period after the death of Nero, published around AD 107, and the *Annals of Imperial Rome*, a history from the death of Augustus in AD 14 to the death of Nero in AD 68.[14]

Tacitus recounts the revolt of Boudica in both the *Agricola* and the *Annals*. The *Agricola*, a biography of Tacitus's father-in-law, challenges ancient concepts of this literary form by including sections that read more like an ethnography, history, encomium, funeral laudation, or *apologia*.[15] Within the *Agricola*, Boudica's revolt is part of the historical background of the Roman presence in Britain prior to Agricola's governorship. Agricola served in Britain under the governor Suetonius Paulinus from AD 58–61, during the time of Boudica's revolt, and was likely an eyewitness. The rebellion brought Agricola experience, whetting his appetite for further military glory.[16] Boudica's literary character is comparable to those of the rebels Caratacus and Calgacus, and her actions serve as an exposition to the theme of freedom versus servitude that runs throughout the text. Agricola later became governor of Britain in AD 77 and served for seven years. He annexed the territory of the Brigantes and pursued further conquest to the north against the army of Calgacus. According to Tacitus, his military success was balanced by his honest governorship. He was considered kind toward the local populations, and he promoted their adoption of Roman cultural practices. However, Tacitus represents Roman interventions in native cultures as a form of servitude, leading readers to question the aims and results of imperial expansion, as observed and promoted by Agricola himself.[17] Agricola gained triumphal honors for his defeat of Calgacus at the battle of Mons Graupius in AD 83 but was recalled to Rome before he completely subdued the northern peoples.[18] He failed to receive further appointments and died from a mysterious illness. He may have been poisoned on orders from Domitian.[19]

In the *Annals*, Boudica's revolt is the centerpiece of book 14, a book framed by the emperor Nero's murder of his mother, Agrippina the Younger, and his murder of his wife and stepsister, Octavia. Within this context, Boudica emerges as a strong, exemplary mother, who acts in defense of her daughters' lost chastity (*pudicitia*). Her opponent in Britain, the governor Suetonius Paulinus, is in a contest for glory with Gnaeus Domitius Corbulo, a successful general in Armenia.[20] Boudica is an integral figure in Tacitus's representation of the failures of Nero and his mismanagement of provincial rule, as well as his presentation of powerful women of the early empire.

Our second literary source appears a century after Tacitus. Lucius Cassius Dio was a native of Bithynia and relative of the orator Dio Chrysostom.[21] Like Tacitus, he was an imperial senator from the provinces. He was born to a Roman senator, Cassius Apronianus, in the middle of the second century AD, and came to Rome after his father's death. He was in Rome by the time of Commodus's accession in AD 180.[22] After witnessing the cruelty of the emperor Commodus and the contested rule after his death, Dio attained the office of praetor under Septimius Severus, who brought with him an era of hope and renewal.[23] Dio enjoyed a prestigious career and held various political offices during the Severan dynasty, serving as consul twice, as proconsul of Africa, and as governor of Dalmatia and Upper Pannonia, before retiring to his native Nicaea.[24] His account of Boudica is within his eighty-book *Roman History*, now fragmentary, which began with Aeneas and ended with Dio's second consulship in AD 229. Boudica appears in the epitome of book 62, compiled by Xiphilinus, an eleventh-century monk living in Constantinople.[25]

Writing almost a century and a half after Boudica's revolt, Dio has a different perspective from her nearer contemporaries, and he uses Boudica to reflect upon politics in Rome under a tyrannical emperor, as well as the politics of empire on the whole. Within his history, Dio tells of Nero and Domitian, despots also known to Tacitus, as well as Commodus and Caracalla, drawing out a lineage of cruel failures of dynastic succession. In Dio's lifetime, Britain was once again a site where imperial power was contested. The emperor Septimius Severus died in Britain in AD 211, where he was campaigning for the continued expansion of the empire.

In reading Tacitus and Dio, it is useful to keep in mind several interlocking ideas of the purpose of history and the task of the historian, as defined by the ancient sources. According to Tacitus, history is intended to be both pleasurable and useful.[26] However, ancient texts demonstrate that authors disagreed on the prioritization of each. The historian is responsible for recording events factually, but he must choose which version (or versions) to include, how to use sources, and what additional information or background is necessary to complete the picture of a given historical moment. Historians may create memorable characters, models of particular virtues or vices, provide practical advice (such as battle strategy), and include observations on human nature. Scenes should be memorable, crafted with force and vividness through interweaving description, narration, and discourse. Tacitus notes the exemplary nature of history and suggests that history can have a moral function as well as a political one: notable individuals illustrate conduct worthy of imitation or avoidance, and the lessons of history can make readers better Romans.[27] He observes that the task of the historian is to commemorate good deeds and virtuous behavior, but also to include perverse words and actions so as to create a deterrent.[28] As Luce has argued, Tacitus does not advocate simplifying history into a set of positive and negative moral models for a general audience, nor does he suggest that easy labels of virtues and vices may be attached to his characters. His portrait of Boudica connects to his theory of exemplarity in history, challenging the reader to analyze her character for both positive and negative attributes. She also provides a counterpoint to his portraits of the leading men and women of Rome. Such characterizations allow readers to intuit Tacitus's negative view toward the principate, the form of rule by an emperor that began with Augustus: his message is primarily directed toward an audience of the elite senatorial class, for the principate brought with it a lack of *libertas*, the senatorial freedom vital to maintaining a balanced political climate.[29] This was especially true under emperors like Nero. The elderly Nerva, who ruled from AD 96–98, was the first to combine *libertas* (freedom) and the principate, allowing Tacitus to speak.[30]

Dio did not suffer from the same fear regarding his freedom of speech, nor does he make any concrete statement concerning the function and nature of *exempla* (role models) or declare that his aim is to write an exemplary history. However, he clearly evaluates his characters, especially senators and emperors, as well as the women associated with them, thus providing role models for his senatorial readership.[31] Augustus is his model leader, who established the paradigm for his Severan present.[32]

Audience and style must be considered when comparing our historians' accounts of Boudica. Tacitus acknowledges that some of his inclusions may seem trivial or insignificant, but he suggests that seemingly inglorious moments give rise to great events.[33] His work is characterized by variation in syntax, conciseness of expression, and an ambiguity that allows for multiple interpretations.[34] Dio, on the other hand, argues that anecdotes and details should give way to larger aspects and the significance of events.[35] His style seems modeled primarily on that of the fifth-century BC Greek historian, Thucydides, although this does not necessarily extend to his political views.[36] As a rhetorician, Dio tends to adorn or modify facts so as to create a more dramatic presentation. His details can be scanty or impressionistic, and neither he nor Tacitus is very precise on battle formations or attack strategy, including those of Boudica.

Recent scholarship on Roman imperialism has centered on the ways in which Roman historians denigrate non-Romans, whether consciously or unconsciously. Boudica was an obstacle to the continued Roman expansion into Britain, and so her literary portrait must be scrutinized for Roman stereotypes that cloud our view of historical events.[37] Neither Dio nor Tacitus was a contemporary of Boudica, nor did they ever go to Britain; thus, their images of Boudica must be at least partially conjectural. Both use Boudica as an emblem of barbarian otherness, with attributes commonly used by Roman authors who presuppose that non-Romans are by nature inferior and in need of Roman rule.[38] Her narrative reflects an assumption that all peoples of Britain operate similarly and have the same laws, rituals, and power structures, an assumption readily disproven on closer examination. Boudica is the "other" to the Roman "self" in these texts: she allows historians to hold a mirror to their own society, to compare the customs, values, and characters of others to themselves, to consider what it means to be Roman, to reveal the power dynamics of Rome and perhaps to critique these dynamics as well as the failing morality of Roman society.[39]

Boudica's method of warfare, rituals, family values, and views on luxury and freedom all reflect on Roman practices and the power of the imperial family, leading to conclusions on what separates the "self" from the "other" and what draws them together. This is especially true in the speeches Boudica gives before her troops. Tacitus and Dio use the speeches of foreigners, including Boudica, to comment upon Roman imperialism and society, particularly in the realms of morality and justice.[40] Boudica's speeches echo those of many freedom fighters, as she condemns the avarice and moral inferiority of the Romans.[41] Her speeches provide an opportunity for each author to give insight into the politics, power, and the position of women in the early empire, as well as in their contemporary worlds.

Whatever the gaps in the literary sources, coins and other archaeological material provide evidence for the rebellion and its impact on the landscape of southeast Britain.[42] Material evidence of late Iron Age and early Roman Britain continues to divulge new information about the experiences of real women of Boudica's time, including female leaders and warriors, providing insight into family life, wealth and status, religious practices, and concerns with death and memorialization among the Iceni and neighboring peoples.[43] While numismatic evidence advertises power relationships and possible dynasties, torcs (a type of metal band worn around the neck) and other ornamentation provide indices of wealth and status. A compact level of burnt debris known as the Boudican destruction layer confirms the devastation or partial devastation of Camulodunum and Londinium, two sites attacked by Boudica's army; material from within, above, and below this deposit allows us a glimpse into the development of these towns and the lives of their inhabitants before and after the revolt. A composite analysis of visual and literary evidence allows us to understand the revolt as a reaction against cultural shifts already in motion at the end of the Iron Age.[44]

Both literary and archaeological sources point toward broader issues inherent in the clash between Roman and native cultures. Evidence of the development of towns, trade, and networks of power disrupt literary claims concerning the uncivilized state of those the Romans wished to conquer. Boudica cannot be studied in isolation from the history of Romans in Britain and the continued expansion after Claudius's invasion in AD 43. The impact of the Romans on native populations depended on a number of factors, especially location. Boudica attacked three sites central to Roman control.

Analyzing the relationship between Rome and Britain in the time of Boudica is rife with difficulties. The literary evidence is one-sided—there are no contemporary literary sources by the conquered Britons—and varied theoretical approaches have been applied to the evidence that exists. This book does not employ the term "Romanization," which was used formerly to define the ways in which local populations adopted, adapted, or otherwise aligned themselves with the Romans in language, material culture, art, urbanization, government, religion, and land holdings, among other aspects.[45] Scholars have rejected the term as problematic, as it implies a deliberate policy of the Romans towards the conquered, including the straightforward adoption of a "Roman" way of life.[46] However, "Roman" cannot be identified with a unified, homogenous set of practices and ideas capable of being transmitted from Rome elsewhere.[47] Boudica lived in a time of shifting local and regional identities, influenced by contact with the Roman world, but the Roman influence is hardly without tension or evenly visible among different peoples and across social classes. Binary oppositions between Roman and native, cultured and uncultured, fail to depict accurately the realities of life in Britain, and scholars continue to question whether local populations intended to adopt Roman practices or to adapt, and how they continued to assert their own identities. Some have suggested local elites first mimicked Roman practices as a response to their changing political realities, which then filtered through society as an emulation of the elites by nonelites.[48] Scholars fluctuate between interventionist and noninterventionist models, and they debate the degree of agency local peoples had in their cultural transformation.[49] As Mattingly suggests, the idea of "pro-Roman" attitudes should be described as "opportunistic or pragmatic": the adoption of aspects of Roman culture is integrally bound up with power, status, and the new construction of elite identity within their own societies.[50] Alternative models to "Romanization" include creolization, hybridization, pidginization, bricolage, and discrepant experience, a term borrowed from Edward Said.[51] Rogers uses the model of a critical biography to reexamine the archaeological evidence and understand local identities.[52] Revell examines the intersection of age, gender, status, ethnicity, occupation, wealth, and other factors present in the archaeological record that are relevant to the expression of individual identity.[53] Such methodologies investigate the types of interaction and the manifestation of sociocultural change in Roman Britain, and they attempt to analyze the processes of power and its negotiation between Rome and her subjects.[54]

Further complications arise from the use of the term "tribe" to describe the social organization of different societies present in Britain at this time. This term has been critiqued by anthropologists but still emerges in many archaeological studies of Roman Britain.[55] The ancient texts use several words with varied connotations to describe the peoples of Britain: while Julius Caesar uses *civitates* (states), Tacitus shifts between *civitates, gentes* (clans, peoples), and *nationes* (nations, kingdoms), and Cassius Dio refers to groups by name, such as the Iceni.[56] The Latin terms point toward the emergence of various social and political entities in Britain in the late Iron Age, while illustrating that it was not always clear what the name of a group demarcated, or if that group would identify themselves in the same way. The Romans did not necessarily recognize the complexities of those living in Britain, and they assumed that these names indicated distinct groups whose society was organized hierarchically and who exercised political control over a defined geographical area.[57] Such assumptions fail to consider the level of flexibility in political hierarchies and attribute territories to named leaders that are more extensive than the evidence suggests. "Tribe" is both an oversimplification of late Iron Age social formation, as well as an ambiguous term that could imply ethnicity, political or social structures, territory claims, or a combination of these. Moore observes that replacing "tribes" with "peoples" or "kingdoms" does not clarify whether names such as Iceni indicate social or political structures or communal identities.[58] Such titles also fail to take into account the degree of flux or fluidity between social groups and power regimes by too often assuming a rigid, unchanging power structure. Lacking more precise terminology, this book refers to named groups as "tribes" or peoples, while recognizing the difficulties in categorizing the Iceni and others in Britain at the time of Boudica's revolt.[59]

This study examines the experience of one woman surviving under the pressures of Roman rule, and it attempts to uncover the various aspects of her identity that impacted her individual relationships with those in power and those around her. Boudica lived in a time of social and cultural transformation that was neither standardized nor predictable. She occupied a rare position as the wife of a client king, but this social bond with Rome was broken after the death of her husband. She is the object of male authorial bias and a member of a society with a distinctly different gender ideology than that of Rome. Boudica was involved in the politics of provincial governorship and suffered from the abuses of power-hungry provincial administrators. The study of Boudica allows us to see the impact of imperialism and urbanism on family life with reference to an individual woman of consequence. Her story gives us insight into various elements of her identity, including her sense of place, kinship group, gender identity, and status. As a wealthy, elite wife and mother with a possible religious or political role, Boudica offers a particular view on life in early Roman Britain.

The literary portrait of Boudica is most profitably studied in conjunction with the archaeology and history of Roman Britain, ideas about non-Roman female leaders, and literary representations of native revolts against Rome and the impact of Roman imperialism more generally. Due to the dearth of factual information about Boudica, this book does not follow a straightforward chronological organization. Boudica's story unfolds step by step over the course of the work, as each chapter tackles a central theme, elaborating upon Boudica's actions and motivations within a broader sociohistorical context.

Chapter 1 establishes the historical timeframe for Roman Britain and places Boudica's revolt in the context of Roman imperial expansion. The early history of Roman Britain shows the impact of the Romans from the time of Julius Caesar onward. After Claudius's conquest of Britain in AD 43, the Iceni rebelled unsuccessfully in AD 47/48. After the death of Boudica's husband Prasutagus, a number of issues combined to spark the revolt of AD 60/61. This chapter details the rebellion, focusing on discrepancies in the sources.

In chapter 2, I investigate Boudica's status and the lifestyle of the Iceni. Dio labels Boudica as a queen, using a Roman term with political implications that may be inaccurate. As the wife of a client king, Boudica may have been a Roman citizen, but her political authority is ambiguous. Archaeological evidence indicates how different peoples experienced the Roman presence: the land of the Iceni and the three sites Boudica destroyed represent four separate types of interaction between Romans and Britons. The question of status is relevant for the causal factors of revolt and the events leading up to Boudica's final battle.

Chapters 3 and 4 analyze Boudica's prebattle speeches as the focal point of her characterization in both Tacitus and Dio. Chapter 3 addresses Tacitus's enduring image of Boudica as a mother who is able to lead a revolt through appealing to family values and attaching them to the ideal of freedom (*libertas*). Boudica's cry for freedom is intimately connected with her motherhood and the theme of chastity (*pudicitia*). Tacitus draws upon numerous historical figures in order to align these two concepts and to contrast Boudica's values of chastity and parenthood with the violence, licentiousness, and greed of the Romans. Chapter 4 discusses Dio's representation of Boudica as a powerful woman in appearance and speech. Boudica's fearsome visage opens the conversation. I then focus on Boudica as an internal commentator on the failures of Nero's regime and the lack of imperial models of traditional Roman morality. Dio's Boudica states the models she is working against, culminating with Nero, whose effeminate actions negatively impact the manliness of all Romans.[60] Through drawing upon these models, Dio connects moral failures in Rome to revolt in Britain.

From antimodels and prebattle speeches, I turn to military and ritual action during the revolt and in its immediate aftermath. I examine Tacitus's image of Boudica as a warrior in chapter 5 and Dio's image of Boudica as a religious figure in chapter 6, and I consider the challenges she poses to Roman conceptions of masculinity. In Tacitus's interpretation, Boudica is a commander woman (*dux femina*), comparable to Vergil's Dido. Several models and antimodels emerge from Roman history and myth to color a Roman reader's interpretation of Boudica as a *dux femina*. Unlike other female leaders, Boudica inspires men to prove their masculinity. Boudica's revolt becomes an insurrection not only against servitude, but also against leadership without morality, and a lifestyle that prized wealth and leisure above family and a warrior ethic. Dio questions Boudica's morality through critiquing the religious rituals of her Britons. Boudica's revolt has been interpreted as a reaction against the destruction of the center of Druidic worship at Mona, and Boudica is involved in two rituals during the revolt. While her role as a diviner receives praise, her army's treatment of their captives is soundly condemned. Boudica's death provides a final opportunity for ritual celebration.

The final chapter places Boudica's revolt in the context of other native revolts against Rome in order to demonstrate both similarities between provincial uprisings as well as the uniqueness of Boudica as a warrior woman. While Dio connects Boudica to the Illyrian Rebellion in AD 6–9, Tacitus aligns Boudica with Arminius and his destruction of Varus and his three Roman legions in AD 9. The memory of Varus reminds us that Boudica's revolt could have lost the Romans full legions and an entire province. However, readers must question Boudica's lasting memory in light of her ultimate failure to stem the imperial progress of the Romans. The epilogue turns to her reception, where Boudica has been adapted to suit a variety of contexts. Her importance lies in her adaptability to be presented as a model queen, rebel, mother, and warrior.

1

Britain

The Final Frontier

At the time of Boudica's revolt, southeast Britain was a recent addition
to the Roman Empire, her geography vague and her peoples barely differentiated from one "tribe" to the next.[1] Our ancient sources betray
an ignorance of cultural practices, social expectations, and gender
roles among the various inhabitants of Britain, as well as an overarching view of Roman imperialism and superiority that inherently justi-
fied the desire to transform Britain into a Roman province. Literary
sources reveal discrepancies with archaeological evidence that add to
the difficulty in separating stereotype from reality. This chapter provides an overview of the history of the Romans in Britain from the time
of Julius Caesar to the period following Boudica's revolt, highlighting
trends in how Britain is presented in our literary evidence.[2] I outline the
revolt, note inconsistencies in the sources, and address the immediate
aftermath. While Boudica had little lasting impact on the expansion of
Roman rule, she remained a cultural reference point for questions of
gender and the negotiation of power in the Roman Empire.

Romans in Britain: Dispelling the Myth

Although the Romans were aware of its existence, Britain went unex-
plored until the end of the Republic.[3] The island was a land of mystery
and the marvelous.[4] Situated at the outer limits of the known world,

it was, in some ways, more an idea than a place.[5] Despite stories about early Greek, Phoenician, and continental merchants, no general had attempted to cross the Ocean and breach her shores.[6] In the first century BC, Britain remained one of few locales not yet under Roman control.[7] Julius Caesar took on the challenge.

Caesar recounts his successive journeys to Britain in 55 and 54 BC in his commentary on the Gallic Wars.[8] The expedition of 55 BC occurred late in the campaign season and served as an exploratory journey in preparation for the next year's invasion. Caesar's motivations are not altogether clear. He may have hoped to gain wealth and knowledge of the natural resources that could present commercial possibilities, or he may have wished to prevent armies of Britons from crossing the channel to assist the Gauls and Germanic peoples in their resistance to Rome. He may have been fascinated by Britain as an isolated, unconquered, unknown land. As Dio notes, he may have "desired the island" for himself.[9] Whatever the reason, his first campaign succeeded in proving Britain's existence and little else. After occupying a beachhead in the area of Kent after several battles, Caesar made peace with those he conquered and demanded hostages before departing to winter on the continent.[10] Only two peoples sent the requisite hostages; nevertheless, the Romans lauded Caesar as a conqueror and voted a thanksgiving of twenty days.[11] When he returned to Gaul, a few elite Britons approached Caesar as allies, including Commius of the Atrebates and Mandubracius of the Trinovantes, whose ruling father had been killed by Cassivellaunus, king of the Catuvellauni.

The following year, Caesar mounted an expedition with five legions, including a number of horsemen, across the Thames and into the land of the Catuvellauni, but failed to establish a lasting foothold. The locals were superior at using guerilla-style tactics and light, two-wheeled chariots that were easy to maneuver, even on the beach. His chief adversary was Cassivellaunus, who had gathered various peoples of southeast Britain under his leadership. These groups began to defect to Caesar, including the Trinovantes. At the end of the campaign, Cassivellaunus capitulated. Commius mediated the peace and was appointed king of the Atrebates by Caesar for his efforts. Caesar demanded hostages, yearly tribute, and forbade war between Cassivellaunus and the Trinovantes. He installed Mandubracius in his father's place as king and sailed back to the continent.[12] Caesar's forays into Britain suggested the island was worth further exploration, but his immediate impact was negligible. He was prevented from returning by the revolt of Vercingetorix in Gaul and never resumed his conquest. Tacitus succinctly defines Caesar's role: "First of all Romans, the deified Julius entered Britain with an army. Although he alarmed the inhabitants by a successful battle and controlled the coast, he seemed to have pointed it out to those who came after him, but not to have handed it over."[13]

In his narrative, Caesar creates Britain as a desirable territory, even though isolated and distant, and the Britons as a worthy enemy. His account of the peoples he encountered reflects preconceived notions about the barbarians of the north.[14] As early as the fifth century BC, the author of the ethnographic treatise *On Airs, Waters, and Places* characterized the people of Europe as courageous and willing to enter battle, as well as savage, antisocial, and wild.[15] Centuries later, Caesar echoed these sentiments. According to Caesar, "tribes" in Britain were primarily warrior aristocracies whose lives centered on agriculture and the defense of their territory. They coexisted in peace or as enemies and were unable to form a unified army. Caesar attaches transferable motifs from the Gauls to the Britons, perhaps implying that, since their cultures are similar, they must also be conquerable. They stand out for their skill at fighting from chariots and the bluish appearance of their woad-dyed warriors, but they are faithless and irrational.[16] Nevertheless, they honor the Druids, and Caesar claims Druidism was devised in Britain and brought to Gaul.[17] They believe in life after death and the transmigration of the soul, and this removes the fear of death and allows for their courage in battle.[18] Their domestic lifestyle is confounding: Caesar claims they shared wives between them, even incestuously.[19] His attestation has no factual basis but reflects a common critique of non-Roman peoples who practiced greater gender parity than the Romans, including the Amazons, the Spartans, and even the Etruscans.[20]

Although Caesar fell short of dominion over Britain, his impact was felt in a number of ways. Caesar's contemporary Cicero describes Britain as a land of chariots and warriors, but not learning. Without gold or silver, the island had little to offer for trade, aside from slaves.[21] Due to its isolation, it posed no threat to Rome, so no immediate military action was necessary.[22] Free from the threat of war, other types of interactions developed. Direct and indirect Roman contact is evident in the patronage of individual leaders and embassies to Rome, as well as in an increase in trade and the variety of goods present in southeastern Britain from the time of Caesar onward.[23] The Gauls traded wine, pottery, metalwork, ivory, and amber for corn, cattle, leather, gold, hunting dogs, and slaves from Britain.[24] An economy based on agriculture and war was strengthened through trade, as were the cultural connections between Rome and Britain, via Gaul. This impact was primarily felt in southeastern Britain. By the early first century AD, Camulodunum had become the center of exchange.[25]

Trade was one of many factors that influenced an ongoing process of social change in late Iron Age societies, especially among the upper classes. Elites became wealthier, increasing the social stratification of their people. *Oppida* (centers of habitation or ceremonial power, but not necessarily towns) developed into new economic centers, and those in positions of power found ways to articulate their authority through material goods.[26] Coins minted from the second century BC onward demonstrate contact between Gauls and Britons, as well as the increased wealth of several local kings.[27] Coins were used to advertise positions of power and individual authority, and they could create links in political families through denoting father and son relationships.[28] The appearance of Latin on coinage, including the term *REX* (king), lineage claims, and place names suggest some leaders were recognized by Rome and maintained friendly relations.[29] The type of leadership denoted by *REX* is not clear. Many kings were probably more like elected chiefs rather than monarchic dynasts. For some peoples, the idea of kingship shifted in the first century BC and into the first century AD, as kings formed client relationships with Rome. Through using Roman terms, coins communicated the power structure of a given people with their allies and trading partners; the message was intended for those with knowledge of Latin, whether elite Britons educated in Rome or non-indigenous consumers.[30] Coin obverses usually display implements, religious iconography, or animals important to culture and trade; some mints began to use Roman motifs, such as the symbol of Victory. Coins thus indicated a combination of cultural values of the local population with iconography understood by Roman merchants. These were portable symbols, markers of power as clear as the gold torc worn by a regent.[31]

From the time of Caesar, a campaign to conquer the island seemed inevitable, yet the Romans did not make further inroads for several generations.[32] Octavian planned three campaigns but was waylaid by insurgencies in Gaul and Spain.[33] His interest seems to have peaked around 27 BC, when Octavian first adopted the title of Augustus and was striving to replace the memory of recent civil war with victory over external enemies.[34] The idea of conquering Britain faded as his reign as first emperor progressed. Augustan poets such as Horace note that the Britons and Parthians are the only two peoples left for Rome to subdue.[35] While Augustus succeeded in establishing peace with the Parthians and acquiring the standards lost by Crassus after the battle of Carrhae in 53 BC, Britain remained a remote, unknown, untamed place, ruled by the Ocean if ruled at all.[36] Disruptions elsewhere in the empire also dissuaded the emperor from attempting a campaign into Britain. These rebellions are discussed in chapter 7 as comparative material for Boudica; foremost among them was the Varian Disaster (*clades Variana*) of AD 9, when the rebel Arminius and his Germanic allies ambushed three Roman legions under the command of Publius Quinctilius Varus in the Teutoburg forest. Arminius's effective annihilation of the Romans provided a stark warning against attempting to defeat those adept at guerrilla tactics and temporarily halted Roman expansion to the north.

Although Augustus did not travel to Britain or adopt any formal policies of trade or taxation, several Britons sought alliances with the *princeps*, and local leaders may have sent their sons as *obsides* (usually translated as "hostages," but similar to foster-children) to be educated in Rome. Two such foreign princes appear in the Imperial procession frieze on the Ara Pacis, one of whom is thought to be from the east, and the other from the west.[37] In Britain, Camulodunum grew as a center of cultural contact, as indicated by burial evidence such as the tumulus at Lexden, whose grave goods include a medallion comprised of a silver coin of Augustus from around 17 BC.[38]

After the death of Augustus, the emperor Tiberius adopted a policy of neglect, and Caligula failed to follow through on an invasion planned for AD 40.[39] Around this time, the death of Cunobelinus offered an opportunity for Roman advancement. Cassivellaunus, Tasciovanus, and Cunobelinus spanned the century from Caesar to Claudius as rulers of the Catuvellauni. Tasciovanus's center of power was located at Verlamion (Roman Verulamium). After Tasciovanus's death around AD 10, Cunobelinus ruled from Camulodunum. Gold staters of Cunobelinus, such as figure 1.1, celebrate the center of his power with the legend CAMV for Camulodunum. Suetonius calls Cunobelinus the "king of the Britons," and although the label is contestable, Cunobelinus was the local leader most visible to the Romans.[40] After his death around AD 40, his sons Caratacus and Togodumnus

FIGURE 1.1. Gold stater of Cunobelinus. Linear type. Early first century AD. *ABC* 2774, *VA* 1925, *BMC* 1772–83.

Image © Chris Rudd Ltd. www.celticcoins.com.

divided the kingdom between them, while his son Adminius fled to Gaul and sought Roman protection. Verica, leader of the Atrebates, went to Rome to escape Caratacus and his attempts to expand the power of the Catuvellauni. Verica's plight gave the emperor Claudius an excuse to invade.[41]

In AD 43, Claudius sent Aulus Plautius and his four legions to campaign in Britain, and they defeated Caratacus at a decisive battle at Medway.[42] Togodumnus's fate is unknown. Claudius, together with a transport of elephants, joined Plautius shortly before his assault on Camulodunum. Although he only remained for sixteen days, he captured this center of Catuvellaunian power. The emperor left Plautius to conquer the rest, and Plautius remained in Britain as governor until AD 46.[43] Despite the nature of his focused attack, Claudius was declared victor over the entire island and celebrated a triumph in Rome in AD 44. Triumphal arches were set up in his honor, one in Rome and one at Gesoriacum (Boulogne) in Gaul, the site of his army's departure from the continent.[44] Figure 1.2, a Roman aureus of this period, depicts the triumphal arch in Rome with the legend DE BRITANN on its architrave, surmounted by an equestrian statue of Claudius situated between two trophies; the coin obverse portrays the laureate head of Claudius, his laurel wreath a symbol of his position as emperor. The inscription on the Claudian arch in Rome proclaimed the surrender of eleven "tribes" and commemorated Claudius, who "first brought the barbarian peoples across the Ocean under the authority of the Roman people."[45] Although the names of the "tribes" and their leaders do not remain, the Iceni,

FIGURE 1.2. Roman aureus of the emperor Claudius. AD 46–47. *RIC* 1 33, *RE* 1 32.
Image © The Trustees of the British Museum/Art Resource, NY.

Brigantes, Catuvellauni, and Trinovantes may have been among them; these four groups are central to Boudica's narrative.

Claudius's invasion proved consequential for solidifying his reign and his legitimacy as an emperor.[46] Although contact between Romans and Britons had been increasing over the past century, AD 43 has been heralded as the definitive end of the late Iron Age and beginning of a Roman Britain. Much of southeastern Britain was considered part of the Roman province. Roman rule was split between a governor, who oversaw the military, and an imperial procurator, who was in charge of taxes and provided a safeguard against the governor becoming too powerful. Camulodunum became a legionary fortress after the conquest. Around AD 49 the fortress became a *colonia*, the capital of the province and a settlement for veterans.

Roman Imperialism in Theory and Practice: Camulodunum

While Caesar conquered the myth of Britain, Claudius made it a province. The Romans then encountered a period of rebellion so disastrous that the emperor Nero considered abandoning the island altogether, but he gave up the idea because it may have diminished the glory of his stepfather Claudius.[47] Before discussing the failures of leadership that provided the impetus for Boudica's revolt, it is important to consider the nature of the Roman imperial mission, and the Romans' approach toward the establishment and maintenance of the empire.[48]

The Romans, as stated by Cicero, viewed their rule as in accordance with nature: the Romans were morally superior and ruled in the best interest of their subjects.[49] Dionysius of Halicarnassus defined Roman superiority as encompassing war, justice, piety, and self-control.[50] The Roman imperial mission is memorialized in Vergil's *Aeneid*. As Aeneas views the parade of heroes in the underworld, his father, Anchises, states, "Remember, Roman, to rule the nations with your power (these will be your skills) and to combine civilization with peace, to spare the defeated and battle down the proud."[51] Vergil's ideal Roman is a man of mercy and justice, devoted to the pursuit of peace. It follows that Roman rule should be comparable to patronage rather than the tyrannical exploitation of native inhabitants and their resources.[52] The exchange is of course one-sided: the Roman mission is to impose their own notion of culture and civilization on the conquered landscape, without adopting or adapting any native customs themselves.

Whereas Caesar provided an overall perspective on the similarities between Britons and Gauls, Tacitus clarifies how these parallels relate to the readiness of Britain for Roman imperialism. In a digression on ethnography in the *Agricola*, Tacitus describes Britain and her peoples, noting their possible autochthonous as well as foreign origins, as deduced from their varied physical characteristics: indigenous, Spanish, Gallic, and Germanic peoples all contributed to the current inhabitants of Britain.[53] The Gauls are most similar to the Britons, perhaps due to climate, and share the same language, religion, and boldness of spirit, but the Britons are bolder because they have not been enervated by a lengthy peace.

At the end of his characterization, Tacitus delineates the political structure that allowed the Romans to conquer: the Britons were once ruled by kings, but are now divided by chieftains and partisan factions.[54] Furthermore, the Britons fail to take counsel in the public interest, and rarely do multiple "tribes" come together to overthrow a common danger. Such failures are especially helpful to the Romans who oppose them. Tacitus concludes, "Thus they fight singly, they are all conquered."[55] Tacitus suggests geographical determinism while acknowledging disparate origins, and asserts similarity between the Gauls and Britons in religion, character, and the slothful effects of life without war. Physical descriptors are subordinated to moral judgments and observations on culture and the warrior class, culminating in a critique of political organization and an inability to unite against the common enemy: Rome.

Tacitus implies a connection between morality and origins, and outlines the cultural and architectural impact of Rome in his biography of his father-in-law, the *Agricola*. Agricola was a member of Suetonius's army during Boudica's revolt and returned to Britain almost twenty years later as governor. After a mass slaughter in AD 78, Agricola uses almost the same words as Vergil's Anchises as he turns to forgiveness and the enticements to peace:[56]

> In order to accustom a people scattered and uncultivated and thus prone to war to rest and leisure through pleasure, he urged privately and assisted publicly that they build temples, fora, and homes, by praising the eager and by reproving the lazy. Thus honor and rivalry replaced compulsion.[57]

Agricola describes the positive impact of the Romans in Britain. Agricola assumes Roman customs are superior, implying that the Britons lacked a civilized lifestyle prior to the conquest. Although Agricola's reforms occur almost twenty years after Boudica's revolt, the Roman impact is similar. Agricola introduces and encourages the adoption of Roman building projects, the Latin language, Roman dress, and Roman education. The native elites are supposed to gain social cohesion through urban life, engage in public duties through visiting temples and marketplaces (*fora*), and alter their domestic lifestyles through moving to homes in town. Tacitus also notes that Agricola encouraged the education of the sons of the elites, including learning Latin, and that the Britons have more natural ability than the Gauls. As the Britons learn to desire the eloquence of Latin, they also desire the honor of the toga, a social marker implying they could become Roman citizens.[58] Such transformations suggest the natives are naturally inferior, and Agricola becomes both conqueror and civilizer.[59] However, the natives are also drawn to the vices of the bath and fine dining, and they may have been tempted to the immoral actions aligned with such markers of luxury.

Tacitus concludes his depiction of Agricola's impact with the biting observation, "And this was called *humanitas* among the ignorant, when it was part of their servitude."[60] *Humanitas*, often translated as "civilization," is a merit imposed upon the Britons that indicates progress but also causes concern. In ancient texts, it includes the idea of a shared humanity as well as respect of Roman societal structures.[61] In Woolf's formulation, *humanitas*, "encapsulated what it meant to be a Roman" and embodied "concepts of culture and conduct that were regarded by the Romans as the hallmarks of the aristocracy in particular, yet also appropriate for mankind in general."[62] Although understood as the purview of the elite, any man could aspire to the moral and intellectual ideals suggested by *humanitas*. In his *Natural History*, written several decades before Tacitus's *Agricola*, Pliny the Elder claimed it was part of Rome's place in the world to confer *humanitas* upon mankind.[63] In Tacitus's text, the outward appearance of the Roman ideal is subverted into a type of domination that compels the Britons to adopt Roman ideas of culture and civilization.

Although it has been popular to claim that Claudius's conquest of Britain in AD 43 marked the end of the Iron Age, this claim overlooks the developing interactions between foreign and indigenous peoples from the time of Caesar onward and fails to consider the gradual cultural shifts already in process, especially in southeastern Britain.[64] The influx of Romans after the invasion may have sped up a cultural transition, but it was built on an ongoing trend. The local populations reacted against land confiscations and overwhelming financial obligations toward Rome. Tacitus notes, "The Britons readily endure conscription and taxes, as well as other duties imposed by the Empire, if there are no injustices."[65] The native elite depended upon a differentiation between subjugation and enslavement. Camulodunum became the nexus of that contrast.

The focus of Claudius's campaign was Camulodunum. This *oppidum* (plural, *oppida*) was on the land of the Trinovantes, a tribe that had been friendly to the Romans from the time of Caesar. As an *oppidum*, Camulodunum was an area of concentrated settlement, but not necessarily a town.[66] Around AD 10, this area became the center of power for Cunobelinus of the Catuvellauni. After the Roman invasion, instead of returning Camulodunum to the Trinovantes, Claudius ordered the construction of a fortress for the Twentieth Legion. The fortress then became a veteran colony, and the surrounding land was appropriated for veteran soldiers. Tacitus records the colony was established both to protect against revolt and to familiarize the allied Britons with Roman law.[67] First-century evidence suggests an amalgamation of local and Roman practices in housing, food, hygiene, religious rituals, mortuary practices, and other cultural concerns. Imported goods from around the Mediterranean attest to the increased wealth of the area, including containers for wine, olive oil, and *garum* (fish-sauce).[68] Evidence of toilet items suggests a shift in attitudes about hygiene and an attention to the maintenance and presentation of the body.[69] Within the veteran colony, Roman construction projects arose. Dio mentions a theater, senate house, and statue to Victory. A temple to the divine Claudius was built and maintained by local funds, and priests appointed from the native population imposed taxes for its upkeep. They themselves grew accustomed to luxury, sloth, and the exploitation of the locals, and thus represent the worst outcome of the Roman presence in Britain: assimilation to immoral, greedy victors. To the native population, the temple came to represent the end of freedom.

The Character of the Iceni

The Iceni were the neighbors of the Trinovantes to the north. They lived in East Anglia, occupying areas of Norfolk, northeast Cambridgeshire, and the northern parts of Suffolk.[70] They may be the same as Caesar's Cenimagni, interpreted as the Iceni Magni, or "great Iceni," one of five "tribes" that submitted to Caesar after the Trinovantes came under his protection.[71] The Iceni appear to have been a wealthy people interested in metalware and horses.[72] Archaeological finds of horse-related objects are common, while weapons and imported pottery are rare. Icenian coinage was minted in three phases from about 50 BC to AD 50 and developed clear denominational groupings, including gold staters, quarter staters, silver units, and even fractional units, indicating a complex monetized economy.[73] Silver coins dating from c. 50–15 BC display a female head wearing a diadem (perhaps a lunar crown) on the obverse, and a horse on the reverse, as in figure 1.3.[74] This may be the earliest coin type of the Iceni.

Coins featuring women and horses have been used to suggest the presence of female warriors among the Iceni and others, as well as the importance of horses.[75] The earliest coins securely identifiable as Icenian date from about 10 BC and are similar to those of Tasciovanus. Gold staters and common silver units of c. AD 20–50 from East Anglia may indicate a tribal federation through the legend ECEN or ECE (for Iceni), as in figure 1.4. After this period, Icenian coinage was replaced by that of Rome, although hoards of mixed Icenian and Roman coinage have been found in East Anglia, suggesting the Iceni continued to use both coinage several decades after the Roman invasion.

FIGURE 1.3. Silver unit of Norfolk diadem type (Bury B). *ABC* 1501.
Image © Chris Rudd Ltd.

FIGURE 1.4. Silver unit of Ecen corn ear type. *ABC* 1657. *VA* 730.
Image © Chris Rudd Ltd.

After Claudius's conquest, the Iceni became allies of Rome. They were allowed to retain their land, have their own ruler, and mint their own silver coins, rather than use the coinage of their conquerors. Despite this alliance, the Iceni and their neighbors revolted in the winter of AD 47/48 after Aulus Plautius had left for Rome and his replacement, Publius Ostorius Scapula, had not yet arrived. Scapula was responsible for appropriating the land around Camulodunum from the Trinovantes and distributing it to Roman military veterans. Camulodunum, named for the Celtic war god Camulos, was renamed the Colonia Claudia Victricensis (the colony of Claudius the Victorious).[76] Furthermore, Scapula forbade all Britons, including allies of Rome, from carrying arms aside from hunting weapons. The Iceni revolted, along with the neighboring Coritani and Catuvellauni, but were quickly suppressed by Scapula and a small force of auxiliaries.[77] Notably, all of these "tribes" had formed alliances with Rome. They revolted against harsh measures taken against them, not against the Roman presence on the whole. Tacitus records that Scapula invaded the territory of allies (*agrum sociorum*), perhaps that of the Dobunni.[78] In AD 52, Scapula died and was replaced by Aulus Didius Gallus. Prior to his death, he was able to arrest Caratacus and send him to Rome for punishment. Too old for bold action, Gallus left much of the governance to his underlings. Quintus Veranius replaced Gallus in AD 57 or 58, but died within the year. Gaius Suetonius Paulinus replaced him and split the governance with the procurator Decianus Catus. Suetonius had served as praetor in AD 40 and as governor of Mauretania in AD 41, where he suppressed a revolt and was the first general to explore the land across the Atlas Mountains.[79] He arrived in Britain looking for further glory.

During this period, Prasutagus became a client king of Rome. This is the first indication of the political organization of the Iceni. They may not have had a king prior to Prasutagus, but were ruled by a confederation of communities or another form of social organization.[80] One mid-first-century coin type of the Iceni has a Roman-style head, pointing toward an alliance with Rome, or at least an attempt for recognition by the Romans.[81] This type bears the Latin legend, SUBRIIPRASTO, and has been suggested as a coin of Prasutagus.[82] However, more legible coins from the Fincham hoard (Norfolk) read SVB ESVPRASTO, suggesting a different name.[83] This type is represented in figure 1.5. As

FIGURE 1.5. Esuprasto silver unit. *ABC* 1711, *VA* 780.
Image © Chris Rudd Ltd.

such, we have no clear verification of Boudica or Prasutagus from coins of the first century, forcing us to rely on the Roman written record for their existence and for their names. Furthermore, we are unsure where his center of power was located and where his family lived.

The Revolt

After Prasutagus's death in AD 59 or 60, the alliance between the Iceni and Rome fractured. Accounts of Boudica's revolt differ, rendering a straightforward narrative impossible. The exact timing and length of the revolt remains unclear. Some argue that the revolt was condensed into a single year, with Boudica gathering forces and revolting in the summer of AD 60. Others suggest Boudica spent AD 60 gathering forces and that she attacked in AD 61.[84] By the end of the year, the scattered remnants of the rebel army were hunted down and either captured or killed. Writing tablets found at Bloomsbury, London have been used to argue for the earlier date: tablets dating as early as AD 62 suggest a trade network was already in place between Verulamium and Londinium, implying the towns had suffered little or had been swiftly rebuilt after Boudica's revolt.[85] Later chapters develop the thematic import of the revolt; what follows here is the outline of her actions and those of her allies and enemies that provides the basis for later interpretations.

Numerous factors contributed to the growing tensions between the Iceni and their allies against the Romans. For Dio, the primary issue concerns money: the procurator Decianus Catus confiscated the money Claudius had given to the elite Britons, and Seneca, tutor and adviser to Nero, demanded the return of the 40 million sesterces he had loaned to local leaders at high interest, doubtful of his investment.[86] Tacitus does not mention the loans, although he mentions Seneca loaning money elsewhere in his *Annals*.[87] Rather than financial concerns, Tacitus asserts other causal factors led to revolt, including legal, ethical, religious, and political failures. Tacitus's account centers on the death of Prasutagus that dissolved the client king relationship with Nero. In his will, Prasutagus bequeathed half of his kingdom to Nero and the other half to his two daughters; however, Decianus Catus failed to ensure the will was followed. The Romans beat Prasutagus's wife, Boudica, raped his daughters, enslaved his relatives, and took command of his ancestral territory. The governor Suetonius Paulinus was 250 miles away on the island of Mona (modern Anglesey), attacking the center of Druidic power. The Druids had gathered in the sacred groves on Mona with those who had supported Caratacus and refused to submit to Rome. The Romans, usually tolerant of the religious practices of others, eliminated them.

In various measures, the recalling of loans, the appropriation of lands, the actions of Scapula, Decianus Catus, and Suetonius Paulinus, the seizure of the Icenian property, and violence against the family of Prasutagus, the mistreatment of the Druids and disrespect of sacred sites, an overwhelming sense that nothing was safe from Roman greed and lust, and the growing inevitability of the native population's descent into servitude, fueled the revolt. In addition, the Trinovantes had been planning to rebel and were ready for an alliance.[88]

In both Tacitus and Dio, numerous portents warn of the approaching conflict. The Victory statue at Camulodunum turned its back as if in surrender; frenzied women cried out that ruin was at hand, imagining that the theater resounded with wailing and the senate with foreign shouts; women envisioned an overthrown city reflected in the Thames; the ocean appeared bloody and left traces of human bodies in the tide. All of these signs gave the Britons hope and the veterans dread.[89] While portents are a standard feature of conflict narratives, the citation of specific buildings and structures emblematic of Roman power, entertainment, and urbanism speaks to the purpose of the rebellion as a political and cultural opposition to Rome.

Tacitus provides a summary of the actions of Boudica and her allies in his *Agricola*. The Britons unite and inspire each other through airing their grievances, and then, "with Boudica as their leader, a woman of royal descent (for they do not distinguish between the sexes in their command), they rose up together in war."[90] Boudica's revolt occurs in three main stages: the destruction of Camulodunum, the burning of Londinium and Verulamium, and the final battle. Both Dio and Tacitus name Boudica as the general, and her gender does not factor into her ability to lead an army. Dio calls her a queen, while Tacitus avoids the title, suggesting she was not recognized as a regent by Rome. Nevertheless, her people followed her command. Dio claims she had as many as 120,000 troops, although this number is surely exaggerated.[91] In the first stage, the army of Britons marched (perhaps from Thetford) to attack Camulodunum.[92] The procurator Decianus Catus sent two hundred poorly armed men from Londinium to assist the Romans, and the legate Quintus Petillius Cerialis brought his Ninth Legion, perhaps from the area around modern day Lincoln or the fortress at Longthorpe; however, Cerialis and his Roman column did not reach Camulodunum in time.[93] After a two-day siege, the *colonia* was engulfed in flames, and those who sought shelter in the temple complex were burned along with the citadel. Burn evidence from the Boudican destruction layer suggests a widespread fire, but few skeletons have been found, suggesting the bodies were removed and properly cremated by the survivors.

Boudica capitalized on the momentum from the destruction of the *colonia*. Her troops ambushed Cerialis's men on the road from Camulodunum and almost completely annihilated them. The few survivors retreated. The rebels advanced upon the trading settlement at Londinium (near where London Bridge stands today), perhaps destroying minor settlements en route.[94] Suetonius Paulinus heard of the devastation at Camulodunum, and, leaving a garrison at the defeated Mona, advanced ahead of his Fourteenth Legion, detachments from the Twentieth Legion, and auxiliary infantry and cavalry.[95] Tacitus claims that without his swift action Britannia would have been lost to the Romans.[96] Decianus Catus fled to Gaul. Poenius Postumus, acting commander of the Second Legion in Exeter, refused to send any forces or to join Suetonius in Londinium. Thus, with no walls to protect them and fewer than ten thousand troops, Suetonius advised everyone to abandon the city.[97] Suetonius and his troops retreated with the refugees from Londinium along Watling Street. The rebels killed those that remained. Tacitus succinctly personifies the Britons's cruelty toward the conquered: "Rage and Victory omitted no kind of savagery that exists in barbarian temperaments."[98] Dio details the horrific treatment of the bodies of captured women, mutilated and impaled on stakes as part of a celebration of thanks to the goddess of victory, Andraste.[99]

From Londinium, Boudica's army continued on their destructive path to Verulamium, a possible *municipium* (free town) of Rome and former center of Catuvellaunian power.[100] This is the "tribe" that seized Camulodunum from the Trinovantes; the rebels attack a local enemy as well as one enjoying a special alliance with Rome. As a *municipium*, Verulamium would have been allowed a degree of self-government, and those holding official positions may have had the possibility of becoming Roman citizens. This site suffered because of its pro-Roman sentiments. Dio mentions two sites, whereas Tacitus mentions three, and there is some doubt as to the level of destruction of this third destination.[101]

Burn evidence is not as clear as at Londinium and Camulodunum. Some have argued certain places indicative of the Roman influence were targeted, such as shops with imported goods, rather than the entire town.[102] Between the three sites, Tacitus declares some 70,000 Roman citizens and allies fell, although Mattingly estimates the death toll was closer to half of that number.[103]

In the meantime, Suetonius Paulinus formulated a plan. Although wildly outnumbered, lack of food and the approach of the enemy forced him to engage in battle. Dio claims Boudica's numbers had swelled from 120,000 to 230,000 Britons, while Tacitus claims an "unprecedented" number of forces.[104] Webster qualifies the ancient sources and estimates as many as 100,000 Britons and 11,000–13,000 Romans, including the Fourteenth Legion and parts of two others, as well as several thousand auxiliaries and cavalry on the wings of the battlefield.[105] The location of the final battle is debatable. Tacitus records that Suetonius chose a strategic location, a narrow pass cut off by a forest at the back. Among modern scholars, Mancetter in North Warwickshire, and High Cross in Leicestershire, the crossroads of Watling Street and Fosse Way, are favored possibilities.[106] After rousing their armies with exhortations, Boudica and Suetonius clashed. As the Britons rushed forward, letting out piercing battle cries, the Romans stood silent, waiting for them to advance within reach of their javelins. The battle is portrayed as a confusion of weapons and men. The rebels rush into battle with the sound of the war horn (*carnyx*), fighting without armor, protected only by oval shields that stretched from chin to knee. They rode forth in chariots and leapt off to attack with spears and flat, double-edged swords. The Romans, on the other hand, wore helmets and body armor and carried javelins and short swords. The Romans advanced in a wedge-shaped formation, cutting through the rebel lines in hand-to-hand combat, their cavalry on the wings. Roman archers proved ineffective. The Britons became caught in the narrow defile and could not use their long swords.[107] When the Britons retreated, they were hemmed in by the women they had placed in wagons on the edges of the battlefield to watch the assumed victory.

In a single conflict, the Britons were almost completely obliterated due to their overconfidence in superior numbers, disorganization, and the absence of a common training or military discipline. The Romans pursued them into the forest, killing many and capturing others.[108] Tacitus claims eighty thousand Britons and four hundred Romans were killed in the battle, although these numbers are certainly exaggerated in order to highlight the overwhelming defeat of the rebels and their inability to combat the Romans.[109] Those who escaped rallied to fight again, but Boudica died in the meantime. According to Tacitus, she poisoned herself so as not to become a Roman captive, while Dio records she died from sickness. She was given a lavish burial, and the remaining Britons scattered, regarding themselves as defeated.[110]

Post Mortem

Dio's account ends with Boudica's death. Tacitus reports some of the aftermath. After the Roman victory, the Fourteenth Legion was named *Martia Victrix* (martial and victorious), and the Twentieth Legion was called *Victrix* (victorious). Poenius Postumus, who had ignored Suetonius's request for assistance, fell on his own sword.[111] The Roman army remained in the field and was supplemented by two thousand replacements from the Ninth Legion, and the auxiliary forces were increased by eight cohorts and two *alae* (cavalry units) from Germany, some perhaps led by the future emperor Titus.[112] The Romans routed the remaining barbarians, burning settlements, killing rebels, and taking slaves. Famine destroyed many more. Boudica's army had deprived the area of much of its agricultural produce, and the local inhabitants had failed to plant, harvest, and store up supplies for winter in the year of the revolt. Hoards of coins, precious metalware, jewelry, and other items were buried perhaps by those fleeing death who never returned. Suetonius Paulinus stamped out all remnants of the revolt, but his vengeance was regarded as excessive. The procurator Gaius Julius Classicianus replaced Catus and advised Nero to consider replacing Suetonius.[113] Nero sent the Greek imperial freedman Polyclitus to investigate. Suetonius was held responsible for the loss of a few ships and crews, and ordered to hand over his army to Petronius Turpilianus. Petronius concluded his consulship and arrived as the new governor in AD 61, but proved unassertive. Tacitus's account ends with a terse critique, describing him as a man who, "without provoking the enemy and unprovoked, imposed the honorable name of peace on slothful inactivity."[114]

Boudica's revolt was not the last act of defiance in Roman Britain.[115] After her death, the Romans sent reinforcements and solidified their holdings, but Roman expansion ceased until the end of Nero's reign.[116] Camulodunum was rebuilt twice as large with a defensive ditch and thick defensive wall. The reconstructed Temple of Claudius remained a symbol of Roman authority for the next 350 years. While Camulodunum provided the religious center of Roman Britain, the capital of the province was moved to Londinium. Construction began at Londinium and Verulamium, and both cities would grow and thrive for centuries to come.[117] The Iceni and Trinovantes never reached prominence again. Venta Icenorum, "marketplace of the Iceni" (modern Caistor St Edmund), a town with a distinctly Roman appearance, from its amphitheater to regular street grid, was built on Icenian land around AD 70 as a *civitas* capital, the administrative center of the region. New forts were established to allow for the increased numbers of legions and auxiliaries, as well as roads and other military buildings. Relations between Britain and Rome remained tense.

Boudica's revolt occupies a pivotal moment in late Iron Age and early Roman Britain, after the invasion of Claudius and prior to the advances of Vespasian and Agricola, between the insurrections of Caratacus and Calgacus. Boudica's ability to unify thousands betrays an overarching disquietude with the Roman presence, and her revolt provides an opportunity for reflection on the impact of the Roman incursion into Britain. Tacitus and Dio allow Boudica to voice her concerns as an elite, foreign, female leader observing the transformation of her society a century after the first Roman military expedition onto her island. Their narratives represent the culmination of what the Romans learned, assumed, or guessed about the land beyond the Ocean. Surprisingly, little seems to change between Tacitus and Dio. Some of Boudica's views seem anachronistic, suited to the time of Tacitus's or Dio's composition, but these in turn provide invitations to reflect on the ways in which Roman authors represented non-Romans to their readership. Despite Boudica's failure to stem the Roman advance into Britain, the warrior woman occupies a central place in the history of Roman Britain as a model of strength and authority.

2

Wife, Queen, Roman?

Boudica was born during a period of cultural and political transformation in East Anglia.[1] We do not know where she was born and raised, or whether she was a member of the Iceni by birth or by marriage. Although the details of her life are scarce, ancient narratives and material evidence allow us insight into the organization of her people, the importance of status and wealth, and the place of women among the Iceni. In the first century, relationships between communities in southeast Britain were constantly shifting,[2] and growth in trade and wealth was creating increasingly visible distinctions between classes.[3] Daily life was also changing, especially for those who moved from unfortified settlements and complexes housing multiple generations to houses in towns, where rectangular dwellings emerged next to traditional roundhouses and additional Roman architectural forms displaced earlier buildings. East Anglia, a land of largely undefended agricultural settlements, lay open to attack.[4]

In her adolescence, Boudica witnessed the upheaval caused by the Claudian invasion. She would have been aware of the influx of soldiers into southeast Britain, the swift transformation of Camulodunum into a Roman provincial capital, and the rise there of Roman buildings and cultural mainstays, including a theater, baths, and the Temple of Claudius, the central symbol of Roman rule. Londinium, no longer a backwater village on the Thames, grew as a center of commerce, and Verulamium benefitted through trading for items from around the Mediterranean. The Iceni seem to have rejected such developments. Few imported objects have been found in East Anglia, suggesting the Iceni did not adopt the Roman habits of drinking wine, using olive oil, or cooking with Roman-styled pottery.[5] Late Iron Age material from East Anglia is distinctive for its high proportion of horse-related material, lack of weaponry, and lack of continental imports, leading to questions about the relationship between the Iceni and Rome. This relationship became increasingly complicated due to issues in the governance of the province. The Romans governed Britain by dividing responsibilities between a procurator and a governor. The former was in charge of taxation and the latter controlled the army. Both asserted unwanted control over local inhabitants and disrupted alliances formed between kings and the emperor in Rome.

Boudica is introduced by Tacitus as a woman of noble ancestry and as the wife of the client king, Prasutagus. We know little about Prasutagus aside from his status and his family wealth. When Prasutagus died, he left his property to Nero and his two daughters, but the transference of power is unclear. Boudica may have become the sole ruler of the Iceni; however, at this time, the Iceni may have been plagued by power struggles between those who aligned themselves with the Romans, such as Boudica's husband, and those who did not. Prasutagus's property and people became vulnerable after his death. The Romans descended on his property and annexed his kingdom. Boudica, then in her thirties, took control.[6]

Queen?

Narratives of Boudica focus on the last year of her life. The literary sources portray Boudica as a powerful woman, while questioning her claims to her husband's throne. Her main role is to unite the Britons and to provide an impetus to fight. Boudica's complex political position brings into sharp relief the unclear system of provincial governing in the decades following Claudius's conquest. While Dio refers to Boudica as a queen, Tacitus allows for more ambiguity in her political position. The idea of Boudica as regent has implications for her character and authority as viewed by her own tribe as well as the Romans. The title of queen implies legitimate, formal rights, and can be misleading in Boudica's case. Furthermore, the concept is fearsome and anxiety-producing for the Romans, especially if a queen rules alone.

Roman texts are replete with assumptions about a woman's inability to rule, and literary impressions of queens are almost uniformly negative. The historian Livy suggests monarchy is inherently dangerous, as it limits the freedom of the ruled. Queens are especially suspect, as they tend to care for themselves rather than their people, are insatiable in their greed and lust for power, and are willing to compromise their morality in order to achieve their aims. Livy's primary example derives from the regency of Servius Tullius, the sixth king of Rome, who reigned in the middle of the sixth century BC. Servius's elder daughter Tullia became desirous of her father's power and convinced her brother-in-law Lucius Tarquinius to bring about the deaths of their respective spouses so that they could marry.[7] Tarquinius eventually declared himself king, threw Servius down the senate house steps, and had him killed. Tullia ran over the murdered body with her chariot, which Livy denounced as a "horrible and inhuman crime."[8] According to Livy, worst of all was the fact that the couple had cut off the life of the one man who may have planned to end the monarchy and liberate Rome.[9]

Tullia's actions are typical of a violent, overbearing queen. Hostile foreign regents similarly display masculine strength or feminine licentiousness and immorality.[10] Amanirenas, a Meroitic queen who led a war against the Romans from 27 to 22 BC, is referred to by Strabo not by name, but by the title of Candace, and described as a "masculine sort of woman" with one eye.[11] The elegiac poet Propertius offers to teach his reader to fear the power of women and elaborates with mythological and historical figures from Medea to Penthesilea, Omphale to Semiramis.[12] Cleopatra, the last queen of Ptolemaic Egypt (ruled 51–30 BC), is his foremost model: not only was she masculine and immoral, but she also had the ability to control Jupiter (Julius Caesar) himself, and threatened the very future of Rome.[13] Rome feared Cleopatra because she challenged every aspect of Roman life, including religion, politics, and the military. It was the same threat the Romans posed to the cultures of those they conquered, including Boudica and her Iceni.

In 31 BC, under the leadership of the general Agrippa, the forces of Octavian defeated those of Antony and Cleopatra off the coast of Actium. This decisive battle was immediately mythologized as "the ultimate triumph of civilization over barbarism."[14] Cleopatra's defeat symbolically proved the superiority of the Romans and the viability of their mission to cultivate and conquer the world.[15] Propertius's contemporary, the poet Horace, celebrated the victory at Actium while recognizing Cleopatra's strength and fortitude in the face of loss. In his *Ode* 1.37, she is a "deadly monster" (*fatale monstrum*) who sought a noble death, choosing to drink in the poison of twin asps rather than allow herself to be demeaned and displayed in Octavian's triumph.[16] Thus while Propertius emphasized Cleopatra's use of her sexuality to gain influence over Roman men,[17] Horace suggests she gained honor in death.

Cleopatra, a non-Roman female leader, is memorialized as the ultimate "other" in the Roman imagination.[18] She was dangerous for her ability to entice men to act immorally, even the powerful Julius Caesar and the warrior Mark Antony, and for the threat she posed to Rome and its imperial mission.[19] As a queen, she was masculine, decisive, and cruel. However, her defeat helped bring about peace and reconciliation throughout the Roman world, and it initiated the golden age of Octavian, renamed Augustus. He allowed her full honors of burial and entombed her next to Antony.[20] Egypt was annexed as a Roman province. Cleopatra proved unable to save her kingdom or her family.[21] Almost a century later in Britain, Boudica tried to preserve both.

Cartimandua, Queen of the Brigantes

Roman assumptions about foreign queens color their perception of reality, especially when such queens have a relationship with those in power in Rome. Against this literary backdrop, Tacitus presents the stories of two female leaders of late Iron Age Britain: Boudica of the Iceni, and Cartimandua of the Brigantes. As leaders, Boudica and Cartimandua stand out from Roman women, who could not hold official positions of power, as well as women in their own societies.[22] Cartimandua was a client queen around the time of Boudica and one of few women recognized as a queen (*regina*) by Tacitus.[23] Her regency predated and extended beyond the revolt of Boudica, and her literary depiction presents an alternate view of a woman with authority.[24] Cartimandua is characterized as the personification of her name, "sleek filly."[25] She is an unbridled woman, whose immorality, licentiousness, feminine deception, lawlessness, corruption, and cruelty seem to be predetermined aspects of a foreign queen. She provides a literary foil to Boudica, and Tacitus may have intended to increase his audience's sympathies toward Boudica through this comparison.[26]

Cartimandua's actions and the reactions of her people encapsulate issues in the client regent system. Cartimandua was queen of the Brigantes, a "tribe" or a confederation of "tribes" in northern Britain.[27]

Her seat of power was likely at Stanwick in northern Yorkshire, whose imported goods from the time of Boudica suggest privileged connections with Rome.[28] She gained her position by birth, which implies the Brigantes could transfer power along the female line.[29] Cartimandua may have been queen at the time of Claudius's invasion, and at some point thereafter she established an alliance with Rome.[30] Her Brigantes were one of the groups that gave the governor Publius Ostorius trouble in the early years of Roman Britain, along with the Iceni and Silures. The Iceni were defeated and the Romans pursued the Decangi and others to the north, but were recalled by a dispute among the Brigantes. Tacitus describes the Brigantes as unique because their feuds seem to be among themselves more than against the Romans. Ostorius intervened, killing some and pardoning the rest.[31] The Silures, under the command of Caratacus, continued to resist the Romans but were defeated in AD 51.[32] Caratacus survived and sought the protection of Cartimandua, but Cartimandua handed him over to the Romans.[33]

Cartimandua's betrayal of Caratacus brought her increased power, wealth, and luxury. This betrayal also may have been the beginning of her client relationship with Rome, as it is unclear whether she had this privileged position prior to AD 51. By aligning herself with her conquerors rather than her fellow Britons, Cartimandua opened herself up to insurrection. Her husband Venutius raised an army against her after she divorced him and had his family killed. According to Tacitus, her personal attack on Venutius's family gave rise to civil conflict, and Venutius's army rallied around their aversion to rule by a woman.[34] Cartimandua was no warrior. She called on the Romans for protection, and a legion lead by Caesius Nasica championed her cause against her own people.[35]

Cartimandua failed as a moral model and noble leader at every turn. When she married Venutius's armor-bearer, Vellocatus, she lost the trust of her people. Tacitus records, "Immediately her household was shaken by this shameful act. On the side of the husband, the affections of the people; on the side of the adulterer, the lust and savagery of the queen."[36] More than a decade after his failed first invasion, Venutius attacked again.[37] The second revolt took place in AD 69, almost ten years after Boudica. The uprising indicates the local population was split in their opinion of who should rule, and whether they should strive for independence or obey a client regent of Rome. Cartimandua sought protection from the Romans, who sent their infantry and cavalry to battle Venutius's army for her and to remove her from harm. At the end of the revolt, Venutius replaced Cartimandua. Tacitus concludes, "The kingdom was left to Venutius, war to us."[38] Petillius Cerialis subsequently defeated the rebels in the early 70s. Cartimandua's fate is not recorded by Tacitus.

Tacitus's character assassination is precise. Cartimandua prefers wealth and luxury to cultivating leadership qualities and a warrior class. She is an immoral adulteress, disloyal to her husband and other Britons, and wholly dependent on Rome. Despite her noble birth, Cartimandua is deceitful, greedy, adulterous, lustful, and savage. She is a stereotypical *regina*, who preserves herself rather than working for the good of her people. Worst of all, she gives up her independence, and her allegiance toward Rome is an index of her servitude (*servitium*) rather than her loyalty (*fides*). Cartimandua's dependence on Rome suggests several ways a client regent could prove more harmful than helpful. Details in such relationships are key to understanding both Cartimandua's situation and that of Prasutagus and his Iceni.

Client relationships were established between the Roman emperor and an individual, not between Rome and a client kingdom. The relationship was intended to be mutually beneficial, although Rome held all the power.[39] A client regent was ideally regarded as a king and ally and friend (*rex sociusque et amicus*); as such, the regent was in a position similar to that of a client toward a beneficent patron. He may have been granted the rights of a Roman citizen. If so, this status likely extended to his wife and children.[40] From the time of Augustus, many future client kings spent their childhood in Rome as hostages. These hostages were similar to foster-children of the imperial family. The foreigners grew up and received their education in Rome, with the intention that they would learn Roman customs and become loyal to the imperial family. After reaching adulthood, these men might serve in the Roman military, and might be rewarded with a position in their homeland as king. The client king was thus able to keep the recognized method of government in his kingdom relatively unchanged. However, such kings were not always accepted among their own people, and generated resentment since they were appointed by the Roman emperor.[41]

In an ideal situation, under a client king there would not need to be as strong a Roman military presence as in an annexed kingdom, saving the Romans money and manpower.[42] The Romans were required to provide the king with military support and protection when necessary, as well as other aid, subsidies, and perhaps land. In return, the kingdom was taxed and became a source of wealth and resources for Rome.[43] The kingdom could also become "a focal point of allegiance to Rome and her empire."[44] This allegiance was apparent with Cartimandua, but not among her people. The Brigantes rejected the rule of a cruel woman and her reliance upon Rome.

Cartimandua proved that the client system, defined as a relationship between two individuals, was riddled with flaws. The system depended upon the local population's acceptance of the client ruler, as well as her ability and willingness to rule with Roman interests in mind. Cartimandua embodied the central problem of the client system: she gained a kingdom but lost her independence. Tacitus condemns the ability of a queen to deprive her people of freedom through cruelty and avarice, and her use of the Roman army to fight her civil war against her ex-husband. Through the narrative of Cartimandua, Tacitus identifies the innate paradox of the client regent as both master and slave, an "instrument of servitude" forever in debt to the emperor.[45]

Wife of a Client King

Cartimandua's client relationship with Rome binds her thematically to Boudica. However, Boudica was the wife of the client king, not the client regent herself. Readers cannot assume she had the same obligations as Cartimandua, or the same status. Among the Brigantes, it is clear that a queen could wield sole political power, hold property, and divorce and remarry of her own will.[46] The sources do not indicate whether women of the Iceni and the Brigantes had the same opportunities for political advancement, or if Boudica could have ruled after the death of Prasutagus. In either case, it is doubtful that the Romans would have recognized her as sole regent. Comparisons with the Brigantes allow us to view critically the relationship between the Iceni and Rome, the position of Prasutagus, and Boudica's role as his wife. The response of the Romans after Prasutagus's death illustrates further variability in the interactions between indigenous populations and the Romans, even after an alliance had been struck.

Cracks in the relationship between Rome and the Iceni began long before Boudica's rise to power. The Iceni are the first people mentioned in the revolt during the governorship of Ostorius. Due to continued uprisings among the native populations in the wake of Claudius's invasion, Ostorius wished to confiscate all of the arms of suspected persons and to control the local peoples with forts placed as far north as the rivers Trisantona and Sabrina.[47] The Iceni refused, and Tacitus describes them as "a powerful people not yet conquered in battle, since they willingly entered our alliance."[48] The Iceni were not as battle-worn as others, since they seem to have cooperated with Roman authorities after Claudius's victory. Under Ostorius, they reacted against the limitation of their right to have weapons, and others joined them in their resistance. However, they failed in their attack, and those debating whether to fight decided not to engage the Romans in battle.[49]

Boudica would have been in her late teens or early twenties at the time of the first revolt. Her Iceni emerge as a well-known, powerful people who had an alliance with Rome after Claudius's conquest. The form of the alliance is unknown, but it may have included an agreement for the cessation of hostilities in return for the payment of tribute or hostages. The alliance also may have created a client relationship between the Iceni and Claudius. It is unclear whether Prasutagus was king during the first rebellion. Tacitus records that he was a client king of Nero, who became emperor in AD 54. It is doubtful that Prasutagus was educated in Rome or ever went to the city. Complex relationships characterize the division of power between Prasutagus, the governor Suetonius Paulinus, and the procurator Decianus Catus: Prasutagus owed his allegiance to the emperor, but local magistrates held sway over the maintenance of the province, taxation, and the military. Local inhabitants were required to obey the Roman emperor, but their daily lives were affected by the decisions of the procurator and the governor. These concerns have led some to suggest that the client regent system was dying out by the time of Boudica's revolt, and all but disappeared by the reign of Vespasian. Client kings no longer functioned as intermediaries between their people and the emperor, and were rendered obsolete.[50]

The death of the client king exacerbated inconsistencies in the client system. Although client kingship was an official appointment confirmed by legal procedures, this position primarily depended on the individual relationship between a monarch and the Roman emperor.[51] Tacitus does not give evidence of the transfer of power from a client king to a spouse or children after death as a right based on formal legal rules.[52] Nevertheless, Tacitus speaks of Prasutagus's will, suggesting he had the right to make one, with the expectation that it would be respected.[53] Prasutagus's motivations are just as important as the contents of the will. Tacitus introduces his concerns in this way: "The king of the Iceni, Prasutagus, distinguished by his long wealth, had appointed Nero his heir and his two daughters, thinking by such indulgence both his kingdom and his own household would be far from injustice."[54] In Tacitus's estimation, Prasutagus was a man of ancestral wealth and power, who desired to leave his kingdom and household intact. It is impossible to know how exactly Prasutagus envisioned his wealth divided between Nero and his daughters. He may have intended for his daughters to take over the regency; however, his death dissolved the client relationship with Rome and left the status of the Iceni and his family indeterminate.[55] Prasutagus may have intended Nero as the heir to the kingdom, and for his daughters to be provided for in other ways.[56] Prasutagus's will suggests the Iceni recognized wealth and the maintenance of ancestral land as expressions of status and power. The directions of the will also imply Icenian women could inherit their father's wealth and property.

Prasutagus's expectation that naming the emperor as partial heir would protect his family from injury and injustice connects Tacitus's portrait of the Briton to his depictions of Roman men that tried to accomplish a similar goal. In his *Agricola*, Tacitus outlines the negative implications of appointing the emperor as one's heir. Agricola dies after a protracted illness, and the emperor Domitian attempts to hide his joy at the death, as well as his fear that others may suspect his involvement. Agricola's will is interpreted as a subtle insult to the emperor: "It was known well that, after reading the will of Agricola, in which he appointed Domitian as coheir with his excellent wife and most dutiful daughter, he was delighted just as if it conferred an honor on him."[57] Tacitus continues, "His mind was so blind and corrupted by continuous flattery that he did not know that only a bad emperor would be appointed an heir by a good father."[58]

In this instance, Domitian failed to understand the proper behavior of a good emperor, and he accepted an inheritance from a man who left behind surviving children.[59] As a client king, Prasutagus was not necessarily expected to make a will. However, through describing two wills with similar contents, Tacitus aligns Prasutagus and Agricola as caring family men, and Nero and Domitian as bad emperors. The contents of the will say more about the nature of the emperor and the goodness of the deceased than the expectation for a continued relationship with Rome.[60] More important than this relationship is the hope for the continued safety of the family. In Tacitus's *Annals*, several men condemned to death by Nero are encouraged to name the emperor or his lackeys as heirs, with similar aims. Shortly before committing suicide, Annaeus Mela names Nero's Praetorian Prefect Tigellinus as an heir in the hope that other aspects of his will might stand firm,[61] while Lucius Vetus is advised to name Nero his heir before his own suicide, but he refuses to "pollute a life lived nearly in liberty with final servility" and leaves everything to his slaves.[62] Vetus suggests appointing the emperor an heir is a marker of servility rather than freedom. Given these examples, Prasutagus seems to have endured two forms of servitude, one implicit in a client kingship, the other suffered by all subjects of a tyrant.

Boudica's position as wife of a client king may have earned her Roman citizenship, but it did nothing to ensure that she and her family would have the respect of Rome and her emperor after her husband's death. Nero did not involve himself in the affairs in Britain, and the Romans regarded Prasutagus's kingdom as ripe for conquest. Perhaps if Nero had responded in accordance with the terms of the will, the rebellion might not have occurred.[63] Instead, Boudica became the encapsulation of all that was wrong with a failing client system and mismanagement in the provinces in the time of Nero.

Boudica is omitted from Prasutagus's will, leaving the transmission of Icenian leadership unclear. Numismatic evidence adds further ambiguity concerning the position of Prasutagus and the type of leadership expected after his death. Some evidence suggests the Iceni were experiencing either a split in leadership between allies of Rome and combatants of Roman rule, or a shift from a king to rule by an aristocratic elite. The distribution, circulation, and deposition of coins and changes in metalwork types found in East Anglia have been used to argue both for a uniting of the Iceni and for a possible social upheaval and change in their social organization at the time of Boudica.[64] Silver units of the first half of the first century with the legend ECEN or ECE may name the Iceni, although the presence of a "tribal" marker would be unique among coinage in Britain at this time. Other types bear the names of possible leaders. Proposed names include Prasutagus, Anted, Saenu, and Aesu, leading scholars to suggest the presence of a ruling family.[65] However, the names of rulers may also represent different subgroups of the Iceni, or that the leadership was disputed or divided between Prasutagus and others.[66] Several sites in Icenian territory had mints, perhaps indicating a decentralization of Icenian power.[67]

Other scholars have contested the meaning of coin legends of the Iceni. Recent work has suggested the legends on coins are words of west Germanic or Latin etymology indicating titles rather than personal names: on this reading, "Prasutagus" was the title of the military and political head of state, and "Esuprastus" the chief priest.[68] If this reading is correct, the coins demonstrate the distinct character of Icenian society and their preferences regarding the administration of their people. Unlike the Catuvellauni, for example, they had no *REX* indicated on coinage. Rather, communities in the area came together in the first century when they were under threat. Boudica's husband would have served as the overarching leader who oversaw different administrative districts. His death left the position of "Prasutagus" open. Such conjectures add to the complexity of Boudica's position.

Roman Britain?

Tacitus's account both justifies and questions Boudica's right to rule. Tacitus's refusal to label Boudica a queen distinguishes her from the client regents Cartimandua and Prasutagus. While she was the wife of the client king, Boudica would have presumably benefited from Roman assistance, similar to Cartimandua and Venutius prior to their divorce. She may have been a Roman citizen, but it is unclear how this would have affected her everyday life. Roman citizenship would not have been necessarily antithetical to her local identity; rather, Roman citizenship would have allowed Boudica to integrate Roman social ideas into her native culture, and to advertise different aspects of her identity as she saw fit.[69] Tacitus's Boudica has not accepted a state of servitude. Her power stems from this rejection, and she uses it to amass the largest army of Britons ever assembled.

Boudica was impacted by the Roman invasion, but her homeland did not advertise a cultural shift. Unlike the sites targeted in her revolt, East Anglia had not seen the kind of development visible at Camulodunum. To fully examine the various themes that emerge from Boudica's narrative, it is helpful to have an impression of the location of the Iceni and their targets.

Life in late Iron Age Britain was primarily lived on agricultural settlements, where multiple generations of the same family might inhabit the same thatched timber roundhouse or roundhouses in the same area. Those living in southeastern and eastern Briton built hillforts, as well as other types of settlements, including unenclosed farmsteads and clusters of roundhouses.[70] The largest and most complex Iron Age hillfort was at Maiden Castle in Dorset; figure 2.1 is a reconstruction drawing of this site as it may have appeared at the end of the Iron Age. By contrast, the landscape of the Iceni is flat and, although there are a few defended enclosures, relatively bare of hillforts, earthworks, and other types of fortifications present elsewhere.[71] Prasutagus's compound likely included a group of roundhouses occupied by his extended family.[72] The compound may have been surrounded by a defensive earthen bank and ditch, a deterrent to the chariots used by the Britons in battle. Pastures and fields would have surrounded the compound, as well as the farmsteads of other Iceni.

FIGURE 2.1. The Iron Age hillfort at Maiden Castle, Dorset. Reconstruction drawing by Paul Birkbeck.

Image © English Heritage/Mary Evans/The Image Works.

In the late Iron Age, several settlements or concentrated areas of occupation of this type developed zoning for domestic structures, industry (including metalworking, coin production, and other crafts), farming, ceremonial and burial sites, political centers, as well as defenses. These areas became known as *oppida*, and include Camulodunum and Verulamium, as well as Stanwick in Yorkshire.[73] On the whole, however, late Iron Age society was decentralized, and even territorial *oppida* were not necessarily urban in nature. The design of late Iron Age areas of occupation contributes to literary evidence that emphasizes the practices of the Britons as distinctly non-Roman. Diodorus Siculus, a Greek historian of the first century BC, claims the Britons are simple, shrewd, and modest, free of wealth and luxury and its attendant vices.[74] Diodorus implicitly contrasts the Britons with the Romans by observing the simple lifestyle of the Britons and suggesting that their lack of luxury does not drive them to vice, unlike perhaps the Romans.

Although the Iceni occupied a large area in East Anglia, a central Icenian *oppidum* has not been confirmed.[75] One main site of interest has been at Thetford, a high point in the topography of East Anglia, where a native complex of concentric ditches and ramparts surrounding a central enclosure with three circular wooden buildings covered more than thirty thousand square meters at the time of the revolt.[76] It provided a large space for the community to gather, and may have had a religious, commercial, military, or social purpose. Its location advertised the power of the Iceni to those entering their territory. Sue White's artistic rendering of the site illustrates how it may have appeared during Boudica's lifetime (figure 2.2).

It is unclear whether Thetford was the center of Prasutagus's power and where his family lived in relation to that site. Coins, brooches, and other small finds indicate that this was a site of religious importance and formal ritual deposits rather than a residence. Sealey suggests it may have been the site where the "tribes" met and decided to follow Boudica.[77] The complex was dismantled around the time of Boudica's revolt, suggesting the sacred site was moved.[78] Boudica's family may have lived on or near the site of the later Roman town, Venta Icenorum (modern Caistor St Edmund), at Snettisham, the highest hilltop in the area, or at Saham Toney, where there was a coin mint.[79] Wherever Boudica and her family lived, the entire compound and all of Prasutagus's holdings were appropriated after his death.

FIGURE 2.2. Artist rendering of Fison Way, Thetford, Phase II (AD 40s to 60s).
Illustration by Sue White MAAIS.

As a client king, Prasutagus may have increased his wealth and constructed a palace for his family as a statement of his power. The Flavian
palace at Fishbourne traditionally associated with the client king
Togidubnus gives some indication of the extent of wealth and luxury
possible in southeastern Britain in the second half of the first century.[80]
Within this palace, a large room fronting a colonnaded courtyard featured a mosaic whose central panel was filled with complex geometric
patterns and whose border represented a city wall, with towers in each
corner and gates in the center of each side. A section of this mosaic,
pictured in figure 2.3, demonstrates the complexity of the wall pattern;
the image is unique to Britain but common in mosaics of Rome's west-
ern provinces in the first century.[81] The visual depicts the type of luxury
introduced by the Roman presence, as well as the increased protective
measures and fortifications necessitated by that presence.

Some have proposed that the Iceni rejected this type of luxury and
retained their roundhouses as a traditional marker of identity and a
statement of their opposition to Rome.[82] Shifting the form of one's residence would have implications for the performance of ritual, the cen-
trality of the hearth, and other aspects of daily life that depend upon a
certain type of space. Furthermore, material finds suggest the Iceni were

FIGURE 2.3. Section of city wall mosaic, Fishbourne Palace. Flavian Period.
Image © Lesley Pardoe/Alamy Stock Photo.

slower than the peoples of Southern Anglia to adopt coinage, including coins with Roman designs or named individuals, as well as wheel-made pottery and other elements of the late Iron Age.[83] The major industry of the Iceni was metalworking. Eleven hoards of gold, silver, and electrum jewelry, as well as more than 180 torcs were discovered in the area of Snettisham, Norfolk, dating to the middle of the first century BC.[84] Hoard F from Snettisham (figure 2.4) includes ingots, ends and middle sections of cut-up torcs, and bracelet parts deposited together. Intentional deposits of such items, along with weaponry, horse harnesses, bridles, bits, and chariot fittings, as well as coins, rose significantly in the late Iron Age, denoting the increased wealth of some members of this society. The wealth of the Iceni was increased through coin production; however, a shift between a prioritization of torcs in the late first century BC to chariot pieces in the first century AD suggests an increased warrior element and the need for protection.[85]

Outside of Icenian territory, towns, fortifications, and other markers of urbanization represent the clearest aspect of the Roman impact. Roman life revolved around an urban center and the political, social, and commercial activities of a town. For the Romans, living in an urban settlement differentiated civilization from barbarism. The development

FIGURE 2.4. Hoard F from Snettisham c. 75 BC. From Ken Hill, Snettisham. Ingots, ends, and middle sections of cut-up torcs, bracelet parts.

Image © The Trustees of the British Museum/Art Resource, NY.

of urban areas such as Camulodunum exposed indigenous populations to what the Romans regarded as the correct way to live, including civic and political participation, attendance at religious events and public spectacles, and the celebration of wealth and luxury. Such influence was limited to those living near centers of Roman occupation. Urbanism reflected the power of Rome, but it did not have to be a complete imposition on the local population: while our literary sources present the Roman perspective, archaeological evidence suggests a combination of native and Roman cultural influences.[86] However, to Boudica and her allies, the presence of Roman architecture appeared to be a statement of Roman superiority and the materialization of imperial ideology.[87]

Towns were key to the Roman imperial and military strategy as administration centers; however, their construction and maintenance could exacerbate the burden placed on the inhabitants of a Roman province.[88] Once established, a province owed taxes, natural resources, and often slaves to Rome. For an economy dependent upon subsistence agriculture, such requirements could be overwhelming. Although the Iceni were wealthy, they remained an agricultural economy. Dio suggests

Seneca had loaned 40 million sesterces to kings in Britain, although we do not know to whom. This money could have been used to help fund the building of the Temple of Claudius at Camulodunum, or to support the growth of infrastructure at several *oppida*. The economic burden of Roman rule is one of the grievances voiced by Dio's Boudica and Tacitus' Britons. Dio's Boudica puts the choice to her army: her people have seen how terrible it is to be wealthy slaves to Rome, and surely prefer the poor freedom valued by their ancestors.[89] There is no escape from economic tyranny, and the weight of oppression is getting heavier. This weight is visible in the sites burnt by Boudica.

Boudica targeted three sites whose architecture and cultural significance reflect the Roman impact to varying degrees. Each was significant for the development of Roman administrative and economic interests in southeast Britain. Camulodunum was a *colonia* and the capital of the province, while Londinium was a center of trade. Tacitus labels Verulamium a *municipium*, a town governed by its own laws, whose magistrates may have had the ability to become Roman citizens.[90] Camulodunum, the only established Roman settlement (*colonia*), was the obvious center for attack. This town may have originated as a compound similar to that inhabited by Boudica. After the Claudian invasion, Camulodunum became a legionary fortress of fifty acres. Around AD 49, the fortress was transformed into a provincial capital and veteran colony, the center of Roman administrative rule. Its appearance changed to match its status. Roads extended into the surrounding areas, and the town was organized on a grid.

Within Camulodunum, people were involved in industry, including metalworkers, potters, and tile-makers, and the manner of living changed, as rectangular dwellings with tiled roofs replaced the traditional thatched, circular homes. A few buildings had mosaic floors, and one wall with painted plaster demonstrates the increased luxury and a concern for décor.[91] The contents of the Fenwick treasure, including coins, a bronze *bulla*, and gold and silver jewelry similar to contemporaneous finds from Pompeii, declare the presence of a Roman couple with Italian imports, who buried their riches in the hope of returning after the revolt.[92] Rich burials outside the city confirm the presence of wealthy individuals with leisure time, as well as specialist occupations. Graves at Stanway include warrior equipment, surgical instruments, and even a gaming board, likely for the *ludus latrunculorum*, the "game of little robbers."[93] Public buildings arose, including shops, a central forum and basilica complex, baths, a theater, and the Temple to Claudius.[94]

While other urban centers had defensive walls, Camulodunum depended upon defensive ditches (dykes).[95] Without walls, the city remained vulnerable, especially when Suetonius's legion was away, giving Boudica's army the opportunity to strike. Tacitus criticizes the Romans' neglect: the conquerors took care of their pleasures rather than necessities.[96] A level of burnt, red daub and debris called the Boudican destruction horizon dates to the period of Boudica's attack. Deposits of plaster and glass, pottery and tile, along with other building materials attest to the intensity of the fire that encompassed the entire city.[97] Foodstuffs discovered in abandoned and destroyed buildings include imports from across the Mediterranean, such as figs, olives, and dates, while metalwork findings demonstrate the development of industry. There is little gold and silver, and few skeletons have been discovered; in addition, the excavated homes are relatively empty. This data might indicate that the majority of residents had time to take their belongings and flee before the invasion of the army. At the time of the revolt, Camulodunum had a population of around four thousand.[98] Those who survived soon returned to rebuild the town.

Londinium and Verulamium display different degrees of destruction.[99] There is no evidence for a focused pre-Roman occupation at Londinium, although the site soon provided foreign traders with an entry point to the province.[100] The Roman military may have used the site as a camp during the Claudian invasion. In AD 47/48, the army may have constructed a defensive circuit for the civilian community north of the Thames. The urban site was established at that time under the governorship of Ostorius Scapula.[101] Buildings and roads were situated on a grid, and the commercial center attracted merchants, immigrants, and Britons. A few buildings used for government, industry, or manufacturing, as well as warehouses and the homes of merchants were present at the time of the revolt.[102] New quays (and perhaps a bridge) were constructed near the Thames around AD 52. On the other side of the river, a palace in Southwark may have served as the seat of the provincial governor; the procurator would have had his offices north of the Thames near the core of the Roman town.[103] The procurator Decianus was in Londinium when Boudica revolted, suggesting this had begun to be an administrative center. Rapid building projects in the 50s, including a forum area, industrial buildings, workshops and houses, and possible military enclosures, baths, a palace, and sacred areas, has led Perring to estimate a population of around ten thousand at the time of the revolt.[104] Londinium was unwalled, like Camulodunum, and few buildings survived the conflagration. Excavated buildings are relatively empty, supporting Tacitus's account of the evacuation of the city. A Samian dish and coins of the emperor Claudius discovered at King William Street have burn evidence from the time of the revolt (figure 2.5). Despite its almost total destruction, Londinium was soon rebuilt as the new capital and center of administrative governance.[105]

Verulamium was an Iron Age settlement of the Catuvellauni. At the time of Boudica's revolt, Verulamium was not a major population center, but rather an open landscape with settlements spread over a wide area, defensive dykes, a probable coin mint, elite residences, burial complexes, and other enclosures.[106] Evidence of industry, including weaving, metalworking, and pottery manufacture, suggests the inhabitants were investing in non-agricultural activities.[107] Like Camulodunum, the *oppidum* had zoning for burial, residences, industry, and agriculture.[108] Burial evidence from a cremation cemetery attests to the presence of high-status individuals with imported possessions living at the

FIGURE 2.5. Samian dish and coins of the Emperor Claudius discovered at King William Street, London.

Image © Museum of London.

time of Boudica's revolt. The appearance of a new type of pottery, a large number of imported samian ware, and local coins stamped with VER, VERO, or VERL to designate the site of production suggest the residents used Roman trade networks.[109]

Although it was not founded by the Romans, Verulamium displayed an acceptance of Roman administration. Verulamium may have been the only *municipium* at the time of the revolt, a distinction that gave Roman citizenship rights to local magistrates and councilmen. Tacitus is our only source for this status, and he may be attributing rights to Verulamium that were granted after Boudica, closer to the time of his father-in-law Agricola's governorship. In AD 60/61, the settlement was still developing, and had little or no Roman-styled buildings to destroy. Nevertheless, Verulamium was a high-status settlement with perhaps pro-Roman sympathies, and thus an object of Boudica's ire. In the following decades, the site was built up with a large forum and basilica, a theater, *macellum* (market), and porticoed walkway. It became the *civitas* capital of the region and an important center of Roman control. As Londinium grew and prospered as the new capital, so too did Verulamium, twenty miles away. Grave goods from a burial around AD 85 suggest the extent of one elite man's embrace of a life of luxury: he was buried with a full samian ware dinner service and all other equipment needed for a formal dinner party, suggesting he took Agricola's advice to adopt Roman practices to heart.[110]

Inhabitants of the towns destroyed by Boudica's army would have experienced Roman administrative rule differently. No client regent ruled at these sites at the time of Boudica's revolt. They suggest the types of development the Romans may have had in mind for Prasutagus's kingdom after he died. Each of these places increased in importance after Boudica: Camulodunum was a wealthy city and the center of imperial cult, while Londinium became the capital of the province, and Verulamium became an administrative regional capital. Our ancient authors wrote of the destruction of the towns knowing that they would revive. The Iceni were not as fortunate.

3

Family and Freedom

After Prasutagus died, Boudica's world fell apart. The Romans acted as
if his death granted them control over his home and family, and they
destroyed both with a degree of rapacity so shocking that Boudica was
forced to respond. Rather than focusing her anger against those who
hurt her individually, she fought to resolve the grievances of all Britons
impacted by Rome. The speeches she gives prior to her final battle
crystalize issues facing all Britons under Roman rule. This moment is
the focal point of her narrative in both Tacitus and Dio. Although her
speeches are written in Latin and Greek, respectively, she would have
spoken in her native tongue. Paired speeches given by opposing generals
are a standard feature of prebattle narratives in ancient historiography
and allow the author to envision the words a general would have given
to rouse troops to action on a given occasion. Women rarely deliver
such addresses, and Tacitus and Dio use the opportunity to address
aspects of Roman expansionism that negatively impact women and
families. The next two chapters present Boudica's speeches in Tacitus
and Dio.[1] This chapter discusses Tacitus's Boudica and the connection
she makes between freedom and the disruption of family life caused by
Roman imperial progress.[2] Her people suffer from the economic effects
of Roman control, including land confiscations, taxes, and enslavement,
and they desire freedom, a common refrain in narratives of native resistance. Her Iceni and the neighboring peoples act as a unified community
for which respect for nobility and ancestry are paramount.

Tacitus's Boudica creates a sense of common purpose through dis-
tilling the conflict with Rome into a fight for freedom (*libertas*) from
servitude (*servitium*).[3] The representation of Roman control as a form

of slavery is one of the most broadly used comparisons in ancient texts. With Boudica, the concept becomes literal, as her family falls from the status of clients to that of slaves.[4] Her plight evokes sympathy and rage from the surrounding peoples, inciting them to unify as never before. In Tacitus's *Annals*, Boudica speaks to her troops from a chariot, her violated daughters beside her. The two girls are symbols of the lost freedom of the Iceni at the hands of the lustful Romans. Tacitus focuses on Boudica's position as a mother, fighting for retributive justice on behalf of her daughters and her pride. She personifies the grievances of the Britons, who revolt to preserve their fatherland and to save their wives and children. Boudica's cry for freedom is intimately connected with her motherhood and the theme of sexual chastity (*pudicitia*). Tacitus aligns freedom and chastity by drawing upon historical models, contrasting Boudica's values of chastity, parenthood, and marriage with Roman violence, licentiousness, and greed. This contrast is especially germane to her place within *Annals* book 14. Through the depiction of Boudica, Tacitus builds up his audience's sympathies for the Icenian leader and allows her to reflect larger failures of imperial leadership in Rome.

The Price of Freedom

In his *Agricola*, Tacitus reports that the Britons obeyed the Romans after the conquest of Claudius but were not yet in a position of servitude.[5] He contrasts them with the Gauls, who had already lost both their freedom and their courage (*virtus*).[6] *Virtus*, which included an ethical dimension in addition to martial valor, was closely tied to an individual's morality or moral behavior (*mores*); the Romans considered both concepts integral to the power structures of the empire, and the provincials accuse the Romans of betraying both ideals in their treatment of the conquered.[7] Before Boudica's revolt, the Britons complain about the evils of subjection, and they identify Camulodunum as the seat of servitude.[8] Tacitus reports a meeting of the Britons, who recognize that the hardest step was coming together to deliberate.[9] Their conversation centers on the burden of servitude and the impact of owing tribute to two masters. Nominally, the governor Suetonius led the army and the procurator Catus collected taxes, but the Britons experience their roles differently, claiming the governor ruled over their families, the procurator over their possessions. Discord and concord between the two are equally destructive. The governor has his military, the procurator his slaves, to enforce his will.[10]

The Britons align the loss of their goods through taxation to the harm done to their families through enslavement, conscription into the army, and the taking of hostages. The parallel loss of possessions and kin lies at the core of their grievances against the Romans. The Britons continue by characterizing the Romans as greedy cowards: "Nothing is now exempt from their greed, nothing from their lust."[11] In this reported speech, Tacitus's Britons censure the Romans for their mismanagement of Britain and its effects on family life. The Romans are unable to control even their own desires. They have appropriated land for their veteran colony, dragged away the Britons' children as slaves or hostages, and conscripted men into the Roman army.[12] The Britons have noble motivations for war, fighting for their fatherland, spouses, and families, in contrast to the luxury-driven Romans. Tacitus's Britons claim morality and moderation are on their side, touting almost Roman Republican virtues and contrasting them with the immoderate desires of imperial dynasts.

The generalized complaints of the Britons are echoed by individual rebels, especially Caratacus, son of Cunobelinus. Caratacus and his Catuvellauni had been active in the resistance against Claudius. In his *Annals*, Tacitus suggests their center of power at Camulodunum was appropriated to expedite the suppression of the Catuvellauni and their allies, and to introduce them to Roman laws.[13] Caratacus led the Silures in the revolt against Publius Ostorius in AD 47 and remained strong after the capitulation of the Iceni. As he led them to a final battle in AD 51, Caratacus built up their spirits and spurred them to war through calling upon their desire for freedom, their love for family, and their past success at repressing the Romans. He promised a single battle would either initiate perpetual servitude or allow them to recover their freedom. Using the courage of the ancestors who repelled Caesar, they would free themselves of axes and taxes, and leave the bodies of their wives and children undefiled.[14]

Tacitus's Caratacus uses similar themes as the generalized Britons in the *Agricola* in his exhortation to his troops: freedom from servitude, attention to the ancestors, and anxiety over the treatment of wives and children. In the ensuing conflict, his wife, daughter, and brothers are all captured. Caratacus, rather than committing suicide on the battlefield or fighting to the death, entrusts himself to Cartimandua. Cartimandua betrays him and hands him over to the Romans. He is brought to Rome in chains and paraded in a triumph along with his family, his dependents, and other spoils of war.[15] He cleverly convinces the emperor Claudius it would be better to be remembered for clemency than for putting rebels to death, and achieves pardon for himself and his family.[16] Captivity allows Caratacus to save the lives of his family members but ensures his lasting exile, a position of servitude for the remainder of his life.

In Tacitus's narrative, Caratacus shows a devotion to family and a misguided trust in a fellow Briton. His speech employs the expected tropes of barbarian resistance, suggesting a common set of complaints of subject nations in the Roman Empire; however, he also becomes a moralizing figure of traditional Republican values. His resistance contributes to Tacitus's dichotomous image of the Britons, separating those who became clients of Rome and traded their freedom for the support of the Roman army, like Cartimandua and Prasutagus, and those who refused. The Britons in the *Agricola* and Caratacus in the *Annals* build an image of the type of resistance present in the early years of Roman Britain. Boudica captures the spirit of dissatisfaction and growing resentment and synthesizes the complaints of the Britons into a fight for family, morality, and freedom.

Boudica's Rebellion in Tacitus's Annals

The fates of Caratacus and the Britons emphasize the devastating effects of servitude on the lives of women and children. These effects are made manifest in the persecution of Boudica's family. After reporting the death of Prasutagus and the contents of the will, Tacitus suggests the division of property between his daughters and Nero was intended to safeguard his family from abuse and his land from military expropriation. What happened was the opposite. Boudica does not even have time to grieve before Suetonius's centurions lay waste to his kingdom and Catus's slaves appropriate Prasutagus's household. The treatment of his family is worse: "His wife Boudica was beaten and his daughters violated by lust; every nobleman of the Iceni was deprived of his ancestral goods, as if the Romans had received the entire region as a gift, and the relatives of the king were considered slaves."[17] The independence of the kingdom disappears as the Romans incorporate the Icenian land into the province.

While Tacitus does not necessarily condemn the idea of taking spoils of war, the Iceni were not at war upon the death of Prasutagus. The Romans' actions transcend expectations for a simple annexation of property. Tacitus uses images familiar from the literary motif of the *urbs capta* (captured city), including the assault of respectable women and children and the pillaging of their homes by the conquerors, in order to draw attention to the Romans' breach of trust.[18] The mistreatment of Prasutagus's family and the Icenian elite is a humiliating form of domination that undermines their established power relations with Rome and creates a new hierarchy.[19] Boudica and her daughters are the highest members of the local society and are attacked by slaves and soldiers, many of them Gauls, Germans, or even Britons.[20] Boudica's punishment is humiliating: whipping was reserved for slaves in the Roman world and used on free people only in the case of heinous crimes such as murder.[21] She is treated as a slave by slaves. The fate of her daughters is a further violation.

Tacitus labels the sexual violence against Boudica's daughters an act of *stuprum*. Tacitus chooses a weighted term, for Roman authors use *stuprum* "to describe the offense consisting in the violation of the sexual integrity of freeborn Romans."[22] Tacitus suggests the daughters had Roman citizenship, or at least that they deserve sympathy from his Roman readers. An act of *stuprum* destroys the daughters' *pudicitia*, a term denoting sexual inviolability, also a reference generally applied to free Roman citizens.[23] The choice of pointed Roman terms emphasizes the asymmetry of the violence: slaves punish elite Roman women as if they were slaves. Their sexual disgrace is immoral and suggests an act of tyranny.

Boudica's personal suffering is one in a series of rationales for rebellion, and her story makes manifest the complaints of the council of Britons. Tacitus continues, "Because of this outrage and fearing heavier burdens, having yielded to the condition of a province, they took up arms, rousing the Trinovantes to rebellion along with those others who, not yet broken by servitude, had secretly undertaken to reclaim freedom; their bitterest hatred was against the veterans."[24] The Iceni collaborate with the Trinovantes and attack the veteran *colonia*. The rebel army converges on the Temple of Claudius, which they regard as an "altar to eternal enslavement" (*arx aeternae dominationis*).[25] This architectural backdrop symbolized the power of the Roman emperors. The negative connotations of *dominatio* suggest an alignment between foreign affairs and political tensions in Rome.[26] Throughout his text, Tacitus links *dominatio* to the rule of a tyrant and uses the term to characterize the hereditary principate,[27] the reigns of bad emperors,[28] and the type of power desired by women of the imperial family.[29] Likewise, he uses *servitium* to describe life under the Julio-Claudian emperors.[30] In connecting a site of imperial worship to *dominatio*, and in identifying the core complaint of the Britons as a life of servitude, Tacitus suggests he is using the revolt to elucidate contemporary issues in imperial politics at Rome by creating an equivalency between the native revolt and the lack of senatorial freedom under Nero.[31]

The Temple of Claudius is a metonymy of tyranny for multiple reasons. The temple was likely founded after the death and deification of Claudius in AD 54 and may have been under construction at the time of the revolt. Local Britons were required to fund the temple and to serve as priests of its imperial cult. The enormous monument honored the conqueror of Britain and stood as a statement of Roman rule and Roman architectural style. It was relatively secure, built with solid stone walls, a tile roof, and bronze double doors; an altar would have stood in front of the building. Modern estimates suggest the *cella* could have held over one thousand people.[32] The temple symbolized the relationship between Rome and her subjects, but it seems to have done little to persuade the local inhabitants of Rome's superiority or to encourage an integration of Roman and local systems of belief or ritual. Rather, its funding and upkeep were considered exploitative and prompted the opposite response. The jagged edge on the head of the emperor Claudius (or Nero) that has been separated from the rest of a bronze equestrian statue (figure 3.1) suggests the violence with which rebels may have treated material reminders of the emperor.

In Tacitus's *Annals*, once the rebel army gathered and signs suggested their imminent victory, their attack of the undefended Camulodunum was swift and decisive. The veterans had not evacuated the old men and women so the able-bodied could resist the amassed throng of Britons on their own, and the entire town was burned and pillaged in the onslaught. The soldiers gathered in the Temple of Claudius and were overcome in a two-day siege. The destruction of the provincial capital made a strong statement against Rome and her incursion into Britain by addressing the overall impact of Rome rather than the

FIGURE 3.1. Head of the emperor Claudius (or Nero) from bronze equestrian statue found in River Alde, Suffolk, perhaps from a statue originally placed before the Temple of Claudius at Camulodunum.

targeted annexation of Boudica's land. After departing from the ruins of Camulodunum, Boudica's army marched on, setting fire to Londinium and Verulamium.[33] By attacking symbols of Rome, Boudica's army sent a message that they rejected the Roman impact and a lifestyle that prized wealth, status, and pleasure. Boudica's destruction of urban centers became a symbolic negation of the Roman presence, over and above her personal retribution. Her army avoided forts and garrisons, seeking military stores of grain as their prize and taking no prisoners. Tacitus explains that "they rushed neither to seize or sell (prisoners), nor any other commerce of war, but to slaughter, the gallows, fire, and the cross, as if they were going to pay a penalty, but in the meantime snatched at vengeance."[34] The rebels tortured and killed veterans and allies of Rome, including women, children, and the elderly. They took no prisoners or spoils, as if they knew their victories were short-lived.

Although Boudica began her vengeance with the moral upper hand, Tacitus is critical of her army's unrestrained violence.

Family in the Land of the Iceni

When the Romans seized Prasutagus's property and enslaved his relatives, they disregarded his family's ancestral power and disrupted their family life. Although Tacitus does not provide details of their lifestyle, its disruption is central to Boudica's speech in his *Annals* and deserves clarification. Our earliest literary evidence for family life in Britain is Julius Caesar, who reports that men and women engaged in sexual intercourse with multiple partners, even of the same family.[35] Caesar suggests Britons are not monogamous, but he fails to recognize the possibility of divorce or to consider the circumstances of widowhood. He makes a conventional charge against those he views as barbarians, and readers should be critical of his remark.[36] Tacitus does not make a similar comment: he states Boudica was Prasutagus's wife, although we do not know for how long they were married or if they were each other's first spouses. His account of Cartimandua and Venutius suggests divorce was possible among the Brigantes, but we should not assume similar practices among the Iceni. If a spouse died, a widow may have become the wife of her new guardian or taken into the home of a family member to keep the children within the same family group.[37] If generations of the same family cohabitated in roundhouses on the same settlement, this simple living arrangement may be the source of Caesar's comment.[38]

The practice of living in a kinship group suggests the value of family among the Iceni. Tacitus's Boudica prizes her children above all.[39] Although we do not know their ages when their father died, Boudica's daughters are portrayed as unmarried virgins when the Romans attack. Allason-Jones suggests that girls in Britain married around age twenty, so they need not be considered young children.[40] The Iceni did not distinguish between sexes in their attribution of authority, suggesting power could be held by and transferred to a child of either sex. Scholars have compared Boudica to queen Cartimandua as the two female Britons mentioned by Tacitus, using this as evidence for a possible matrilinear structure among the Iceni.[41] Boudica may have been a member of the Brigantes herself. Evidence of mixed marriages exists from the time of Boudica onward, and Tacitus mistakenly refers to Boudica's revolt as that of the Brigantes later in the *Agricola*.[42] Others have connected the pre-eminence of these women to religious practices in late Iron Age Britain that focused on fertility and the prominence of a mother-goddess.[43] Boudica's daughters may have been political figures, although the power structure of the Iceni remains contentious. If power was transmitted dynastically, Boudica's children ensured that her family's rule would continue. Tacitus's reference to Boudica's multiple children has echoes in the failed Julio-Claudian dynasty in Rome, which was unintentionally matrilinear in nature.[44] Augustus's family ended with the death of Nero, whose only daughter died in infancy. The importance of women among the Iceni is confirmed through Boudica's actions and her ability to claim authority; if the production of children was a marker of successful womanhood, Boudica's two daughters add to her authority.[45]

The Mother Speaks

Boudica is the only individual Briton who speaks in the ancient sources on the revolt, and she embodies the concerns of Tacitus's council of Britons. Boudica becomes the voice of the people, a remarkable unifier who exemplifies the lifestyle and freedom for which she fights. As such, she becomes comparable to a "synecdochic hero" of epic, defined by Hardie as "the individual who stands for the totality of his people present and future, part for whole."[46] Unlike such heroes, Boudica's strength is in her words. She has no *aristeia* or deeds of excellence on the battlefield; rather, Boudica is one woman who represents many. Her speech clarifies what this representation entails.

In Tacitus's *Annals*, Boudica travels among her gathered army and exhorts them to strive for victory before the final battle, uniting them through their common desire for freedom from any master. She denounces the negative impact of the Romans and proclaims the need for the Britons to join together as never before.[47] Boudica capitalizes on the symbolic potential of her body and the bodies of her daughters, utilizing a rhetoric that aligns the loss of chastity with a loss of freedom. The first half of her speech focuses on this rhetoric:[48]

> Boudica, riding in her chariot, her daughters before her,
> approached each tribe, declaring, "It is customary for Britons
> to fight under the leadership of a woman, but at this moment

I am not acting as a woman born of great ancestors, seeking a kingdom and wealth. Instead, I am one woman from the crowd seeking to avenge lost freedom, a body weakened by beating, the violated chastity of my daughters. Roman lusts are so advanced that they leave no bodies, not even old age or maidenhood, undefiled."[49]

In the opening of her speech, Boudica displays both Roman and non-Roman, feminine and masculine traits as she justifies her leadership position. She displays her daughters, visibly demonstrating the immorality of the Romans through a specific example, while emphasizing the universality of the Romans' failures. Adler characterizes her as a "slightly idealized Roman woman" who presents her daughters as a "wronged Roman matron," but she also claims a role as the avenger of her daughters' lost chastity, a role reserved for men.[50] Boudica uses the violation of her daughters as authorization for her uprising.[51]

In focusing on her appearance with her daughters as victims of assault, Tacitus links Boudica's narrative to several historical legends recounted in Livy's history of Rome, building his reader's sympathy. Livy's depiction of Lucretia provides the foremost model of a woman whose loss of sexual chastity indicated an act of tyranny and a loss of freedom. Lucretia, the noble wife of Collatinus, was raped by Sextus Tarquinius, the son of the last king of Rome. Although pure of mind, she regarded her body as impure and committed suicide so that no other woman could use her as an example of immodesty. Before plunging a knife into her body, she demanded that her husband and his friend Brutus avenge her death. In Livy's history, her sacrifice becomes a catalyst for the expulsion of the kings by Brutus and his Roman army.[52] Brutus and Collatinus bring her body into the Forum, where a crowd gathers in wonder at the exceptionally vile crime.[53] Her body is the focus, and Brutus unites the Romans and demands vengeance for a specific act of violence toward a woman. Lucretia's body becomes a symbol of tyrannical servitude and the Romans' fight for freedom from monarchic rule.

For Tacitus, Brutus is the preeminent symbol of freedom. He is heralded in the opening of the *Annals* as the man who brought *libertas* to Rome after the period of the kings.[54] Boudica's actions recall those of Brutus, as he roused the men to arms over Lucretia's dead body. Although Boudica is not the rape victim herself, her daughters' bodies are brought before the public in order to provide the impetus for a similar response.

When Boudica alludes to the Lucretia episode, she becomes the noble Roman, fighting to expel a foreign tyrant. She creates a similar image around which the Britons muster. The bodies of her daughters become silent emblems of tyrannical lust. Tacitus's Boudica reproduces aspects of Livy's image of Lucretia, aiming to achieve a similar political transformation.[55] Her situation and the appearance of her daughters suggest Tacitus intentionally created his episode with Livy's Lucretia and Brutus in mind.

A second scene from Livy strengthens the argument that Tacitus uses past models in order to justify Boudica's cause. While Boudica's appearance with her daughters corresponds to that of Brutus with Lucretia, her words recall Livy's account of Verginia, a maiden killed by her father in order to avoid rape and enslavement to a magistrate. Like Lucretia, Verginia's body is displayed to another incensed crowd and becomes a stimulus for change and the downfall of the decemvirate during the Conflict of the Orders in the middle of the fifth century BC. During the events leading up to Verginia's death, her betrothed, Icilius, speaks in defense of her chastity and laments her lost freedom.[56] Boudica's rhetoric and her role as avenger are reminiscent of Icilius and indicate a transgression of traditional gender boundaries for Roman women.[57] Verginia's father, Verginius, kills his daughter as a way to preserve her freedom and, by extension, her chastity.[58] Boudica's daughters have lost both.

Tacitus's Boudica claims she is not one woman fighting against the violators of her daughters, but that she is one woman in a collective. She brings her daughters onto the field of battle as symbols of violated freedom. The girls do not speak, nor do they follow Lucretia's example and commit suicide. Instead, they become referential props, recalling Lucretia and Verginia in Livy's account of early Rome. Tacitus imagines a similar scene of rising emotion leading to swift action, led by a masculine leader. Boudica is differentiated from her male literary models primarily as a woman who has been subjected to physical harm. She is both a wounded mother pleading for her children, as well as a military general, as she draws a parallel between the theft of chastity and freedom as just causes for revolt.

Tacitus garners sympathy for Boudica through alluding to two episodes of early Roman history. By drawing upon prior models, Tacitus identifies the qualities that define an effective leader and invites an analysis of Boudica as such. Boudica's episode becomes an exploration into the facility of past figures to provide an interpretive framework for a similar situation in a different cultural and historical context. Emblems of courage and chastity from the Roman Republic are pressed into service in order to evaluate the character of a foreign woman on the outskirts of the Empire. Boudica's imitation of Brutus and Icilius forms part of her characterization as an adept leader rousing her troops to action. Boudica's desire for vengeance is derived from personal injury, but it includes freedom for an entire people. Boudica's beaten body becomes a symbol of her commitment to fight, as she places her values of chastity and motherhood in opposition to the violence, licentiousness, and greed of the Romans.

Boudica's Body and Intratextual Narratives

Tacitus's focus on the bodies of Boudica and her daughters is part of a broader rhetoric of the body within his text.[59] Boudica's body is an integral part of her persuasive rhetoric, a locus of her identity and power. Rather than describe her non-Roman appearance, Tacitus emphasizes her motherhood and demonstrates how a woman may use her body to challenge men to match her level of courage. He does this by including Boudica in a literary canon of women who utilize their broken bodies to encourage the men around them to achieve greatness. Lucretia provided one example, but other women in Tacitus's *Annals* help define how Boudica relates to imperial women of her own time.

Boudica holds a central place in *Annals* book 14, and her revolt opens his account of the year AD 60. The significance of Tacitus's placement cannot be underestimated.[60] His narrative of her revolt occurs directly after the Roman general Corbulo's military successes in Armenia, and Suetonius becomes a moral foil to the noble, well-liked Corbulo. Boudica's rise and fall echoes themes of resistance narratives throughout the *Annals*, while her female leadership provides a striking contrast to the actions of Roman imperial women. She encapsulates the various injustices felt by provincial peoples in the single, striking image of a woman with her daughters. This image increases the impact of her brief but powerful exhortation. Her use of her body in this family tableau runs counter to the displays of women of the imperial family in Tacitus's text.

The empresses Messalina, Agrippina the Younger, and Octavia provide negative examples of bodies as emblems of female agency, freedom, and motherhood. Messalina, wife of Claudius, is destroyed by her licentiousness and immorality. At the end of *Annals* book 11, when she realizes her assassins are approaching, she fails to commit a noble suicide, moving a knife ineffectually against her neck. She is struck down by a Roman officer, and her body is given to her mother.[61] Tacitus connects her failed suicide to her immorality: she is unable to achieve nobility even in death. The next empress, Agrippina the Younger, uses her body to gain political ground during the reigns of Claudius and Nero.[62] In the first five years of Nero's reign, Agrippina is able to control her son's excesses, with the help of his tutors, Seneca and Burrus. However, he falls under the persuasive power of his lover, Poppaea Sabina, former wife of the future emperor Otho, and she convinces him to destroy his mother and divorce his wife, Octavia. Once Agrippina loses favor with Nero, some report that she approached him, intent on incest.[63] When assassins come to kill her at the beginning of *Annals* book 14, she orders them to strike at the belly that produced Nero. After her death, some say Nero inspected her body and praised its beauty.[64]

In Tacitus's account, Nero realizes his guilt and debates whether to return to Rome and how to enter the city. He gains confidence after writing to the senate and reporting her death. He accuses her of plotting his own murder and adds a series of complaints, including Agrippina's desire for shared rule (*imperium*).[65] The elites of Rome respond with obsequiousness, decreeing thanksgivings at shrines throughout the city and declaring her birthday among the ill-omened days (*nefasti*), among other acts of sycophancy.[66] Before he enters Rome, Nero's basest followers precede him, ensuring that he and his entourage are well received. When Nero arrives, crowds gather to meet him, including the senate and groups of women and children who observe from bleachers constructed along his route to the Capitol, in the same way they would watch a triumph.[67] Nero's actions match this display: "Arrogant victor of the people's servitude, he proceeded thence to the Capitol, performed thanksgivings and poured himself into every excess that, although poorly restrained, some kind of respect for his mother had delayed."[68] In their actions, the people of Rome appear to celebrate the dissolution of the imperial family with the death of the matriarch, Agrippina the Younger. They rejoice as if Nero had triumphed over a military enemy, and Nero's procession transmits a false image of military victory. Nero is a hubristic victor, exulting in the servitude of the Roman people (*publici seruitii uictor*).

The servitude of the Roman populace, vividly illustrated in Nero's "triumphal" procession, illustrates the basic idea of empire: subjects in an empire owe loyalty to the one who holds power (*imperium*). During the reign of Nero, this concept becomes perverted, as the possession of *imperium* is contested between various members of the imperial household. By the end of *Annals* book 14, Nero has all but transferred the rule of the empire to Poppaea, his wife after Octavia. Octavia is exiled and ordered to die. Because her veins are draining too slowly due to her terror, she is suffocated in a steam room. Adding insult to injury, her head is cut off and brought to Rome to be displayed to Poppaea.[69]

The use of the body to establish or deny exemplary status is vital to Tacitus's narrative of the reign of Nero, and especially concentrated in *Annals* book 14. In the center of this book, framed by female bodies and failed leadership, Boudica proves she is a positive model of fortitude, and encourages the men around her to strive for an equal level of courage. Despite being a woman, Boudica is a successful "Brutus," inspiring her troops to fight for freedom. In the opening of her speech, Tacitus's Boudica aligns the issue of freedom to sexual chastity and the value of family life through literary references and the use of the female body, in order to promote unity and to encourage her Britons to strive for victory. Boudica justifies her place on the battlefield as the symbol of the families they are fighting to protect. She is a bruised mother and noblewoman, seeking vengeance; yet, she also rides a war chariot and appears ready to fight herself. She creates a unified cause through refining the conflict with Rome into the simple dichotomy of freedom versus servitude, and is thereby able to raise an army as no Briton had done before, and as no Roman is able to raise against Nero. She fights against greed and licentiousness, calling upon family, ancestry, and unified strength. Through Boudica, Tacitus aligns issues in the province with freedom in Rome during the reign of a tyrant. In focusing on family and freedom, Boudica becomes a positive model of motherhood, whose individual grievances symbolize the cruelty, greed, and lust of the Romans. Tacitus does not necessarily condemn the Roman presence in Britain or the concept of imperial progress; rather, he draws a parallel between failed leadership styles in Rome and in the provinces, critiquing the immorality with which the Empire is administered.

4

We Learned These Things from the Romans

Tacitus's Boudica garners sympathy through appealing to her motherhood. Dio's Boudica, on the other hand, is an emblem of barbarian strength and fortitude, an Amazonian warrior who criticizes the misplaced values of the Romans. She advertises her foreignness through her appearance, and her fierceness makes her a worthy enemy. In her speech, she draws an explicit contrast between her mode of leadership and that of her Roman contemporaries. She creates an analogy between Britain and Rome in the time of Nero, critiquing the lack of positive imperial models and commenting upon the effect this lack has had on the Romans. While Tacitus's Boudica made general statements about the lack of *libertas*, Dio's Boudica is specific in her citations and emerges as morally superior to members of the ruling family in Rome in her aversions to luxury, immorality, and indolence. Boudica functions as Dio's internal critic of dynastic politics and the gendered aspects of imperial power. She contrasts herself with women who appropriate undue levels of authority as well as women who place their subjects in a position of servitude, and recognizes the threat of imperial women who subvert the power of the emperor and upend the social and political order of Rome. The emperor should be able to control himself and his household: Nero fails at both. In contrasting what she has learned from the Romans with the traditions of her Britons, Dio's Boudica encourages readers to reflect on competing ideologies of gender between Romans and others.

In Dio's text, Boudica's revolt occurs when the emperor is distracted. Nero is infatuated with Poppaea Sabina, who encouraged the murder of his mother, Agrippina; after her death, he indulged in his artistic pursuits and celebrated the newly created festivals of Neronia and Juvenalia, where he performed on the lyre and won. Dio contrasts Nero's lack of political and military leadership in favor of the pursuit of pleasure with Boudica's display of masculinity. In his introduction to the events of AD 60/61, Dio describes the revolt as a foreign disaster during "play-time" in Rome. The fact that the revolt was led by a woman was, according to Dio, "the greatest cause of shame for the Romans."[1] Before any action takes place, Dio introduces Boudica, leaving no doubt about her status as a powerful, worthy adversary: "The one chiefly involved in encouraging them and persuading them to fight against the Romans, the one considered worthy of leading them and who directed the conduct of the entire war, was Boudica, a woman of Britain of royal descent, who had greater intelligence than women often have."[2] Boudica's authoritative leadership stands in direct opposition to Nero's effeminacy. She is the driving force behind the revolt and its clear leader, and she has earned her leadership position through her royal ancestry and by her above-average intelligence.

Before describing the conduct of the war, Dio allows Boudica to speak. She gathers her army, ascends a Roman-styled earthen platform, and presents a visual spectacle not soon forgotten. Boudica is unique in Dio's extant text for her lengthy physical description, and the only woman of Britain described in detail in what remains of our Greek and Roman literary corpus. Dio describes her appearance through a series of superlative adjectives, emphasizing her exceptionality among women and among other warriors:

> She was quite tall in stature, very stern in appearance, her
> gaze most piercing, and her voice was rough. Furthermore
> an abundance of golden hair[3] fell down to her buttocks, and
> she wore a large gold necklace. She wore a multicolored tunic
> and fastened a cloak around her with a brooch. Thus she was
> always dressed.[4]

Dio thus binds Boudica's appearance to her notable intelligence: both her character and her body are more masculine than feminine and justify her status as a powerful foe. She takes up a spear in order to add force to her words and astound those around her, and begins to speak.

Dio's description has no parallel in Tacitus; however, aspects of Boudica's appearance seem to be derived from Diodorus Siculus's descriptions of the Gauls. Such details may not reflect reality, but rather serve as literary *topoi* (purposive stereotypes) used to characterize non-Romans as uncivilized.[5] Written in the late first century BC, Diodorus's universal history describes various peoples of the world. Diodorus assumes all Britons are similar to one another and relates them to the Gauls. The Gauls wear bracelets, rings, corselets, and huge necklaces of solid gold, like the torc worn by Boudica.[6] They wear multicolored clothing and fasten their overcoats on the shoulder with a brooch.[7] Furthermore, they are tall, muscular, and pale,[8] terrifying to behold, and their voices deep and harsh, like that of Boudica.[9] Diodorus adds, "The women of the Gauls are not only equal to the men in their great stature, but also match them in strength."[10] According to Diodorus, the Gauls have no gender differentiation in physical strength or height. This image finds its way into Dio's Boudica in her stature, clothing, and courage.

Archaeological evidence assists in clarifying Dio's and Diodorus's depictions of non-Roman appearances. Recent scholarship has explored material evidence from the late Iron Age and early Roman period in Britain in order to examine how individuals used clothing and ornamentation to create and express their social and cultural identities.[11] Dress had a distinct social role, and shifts in the presentation of the body formed a visible aspect of the transformation of late Iron Age society. Acculturation to Roman practices can suggest an acceptance of the Romans and, perhaps, submission to Roman authority. Both the adoption and hybridization of Roman styles is present in artifacts related to the body, such as hairpins, toilet instruments, and brooches (see figure 4.1).[12] Local artisans explored ways to modify imports into their own versions through using different materials, adapting non-native trends to suit their own purposes and ideas and thereby forming composite Romano-British designs.[13] Sites attacked by Boudica show an increase in evidence of "Roman"-styled artifacts related to the body and grooming in the first century AD.

Boudica's dress has a particular role in identity formation and advertises her continuation of late Iron Age trends. Through her dress and ornamentation, Dio's Boudica structures her identity as

FIGURE 4.1. Roman trumpet brooch (*fibula*) from Britain. Copper alloy with traces of red enamel. AD 99–140. Now in the Museum of London.

Image © HIP/Art Resource, NY.

one of resistance rather than acculturation. Her multicolored tunic or "Gallic coat" is the typical basic item of clothing worn by men and women, which varied in style in order to indicate the wearer's class and age.[14] The coat is a type of tunic with wide sleeves, worn unbelted, which was full-length for women and may have been worn with a shift underneath. A cloak was fastened over the tunic with a brooch (*fibula*). Brooches were both functional and ornamental, worn by men and women, and the type of brooch and how it was worn could assist in an individual's expression of gender, age, class, and ethnicity.[15] This functional use may have been more common to men than women, and it fell out of practice by the late Iron Age.[16] In addition, Dio identifies her mantle as a chlamys, a military cloak whose luxury was suitable for a foreign king and symbolized his power.[17] For a Roman reader, the cloak could indicate Boudica's masculinity: she is dressed for an active role on the battlefield.

The clearest marker of Boudica's wealth, power, status, and tribal affiliation is the gold torc around her neck. Gold torcs, made from twisted strands of metal in a range of styles, have been found at seven different locations in Norfolk and date to the first or second centuries BC. These treasures were buried for safekeeping or intended as votive deposits. The Great Torc from Snettisham (figure 4.2) provides an example. This accessory marks Boudica's local identity and the wealth of her tribe.[18] The torc also communicates her position.[19] Torcs signified military, political, or religious leadership, and were normally worn by men.[20] Discoveries of torc fragments and separate torc terminals within the same hoard have led scholars to suggest that, after the leader's death, the torc was purposefully broken, defunctionalized as a symbol of power (see figure 2.4).[21] By wearing this ornament and the chlamys, Boudica advertises her authority to her Iceni and her allies.

Boudica presents a complex image of Icenian wealth, masculine power, and non-Roman ornamentation of the late Iron Age. Her dress suggests a persistence of local customs and traits, and it may

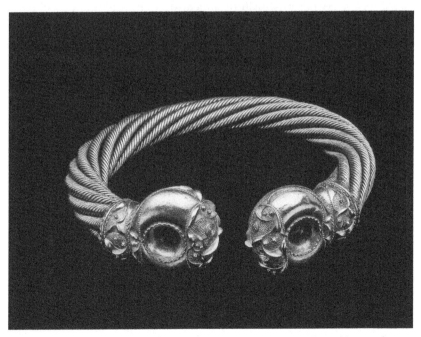

FIGURE 4.2. The Great Torc from Snettisham, c. 75 BC. Eight gold strands, each of eight wires.

Image © The Trustees of the British Museum/Art Resource, NY.

be interpreted as an articulation of her resistance to Roman rule and refusal to adopt Roman norms. The only Roman practice she mimics is her mode of address, as she stands upon a Roman-style platform to deliver her oration. In this detail, Dio indicates that his Boudica acts like a Roman general delivering a call to arms before facing the enemy. Before we explore what she communicates about the cultural impact of Roman rule, we must examine what other images she rejects.

Imag(in)ing the Barbarian

The Romans connected dress and ornamentation to assumptions about character.[22] Our only physical description of Boudica's dress finds a basis in material evidence, but Dio's overarching purpose is to create a foreign queen who epitomizes ideas of the female other. Specifically, she is a fiercely masculine woman inimical to all things Roman. She presents an impression of resilience against subjugation and stands in opposition to other Roman images of Britons, which emphasize the inevitable defeat of the barbarians. Britons appear on honorific monuments and Roman coinage after Claudius's conquest in AD 43, but women are conspicuously absent from these images, as well as from the art of Roman Britain.[23] Rather than faithful representations, these images support Roman assumptions about superiority and the right to rule.[24] For example, abstract images of the defeated "Britannia" provide insight into the Roman representation of barbarian others.[25] Images of women emphasize the otherness of the conquered peoples as both female and barbarian. Through depicting the conquered people as female, the Romans created a visual hierarchy of gender and power: their rule over Britannia became analogous to a man's rule over woman.[26]

Claudius' conquest of Britannia is dramatically represented in a panel on the Sebasteion at Aphrodisias (figure 4.3). This complex was built in the first century AD in honor of the imperial family and dedicated to Aphrodite and the Julio-Claudian emperors.[27] It was decorated with a frieze portraying members of this family in moments of triumph and success. One panel depicts Claudius's conquest of Britannia and is the earliest extant Roman representation of the province. The defeated land is represented as a young female. A heroically nude Claudius towers over Britannia, clutching her hair in his left hand while raising his right, pinning her down with one knee. As she lies on the ground, she

FIGURE 4.3. Claudius and Britannia. Frieze from the Sebasteion, Aphrodisias. First century AD.

Image © Vanni Archive/Art Resource, NY.

raises one hand against Claudius, hair flowing, eyes glancing towards her attacker, her garment ripped, exposing one breast. This personification echoes that of other conquered territories from the Augustan age onward.[28] The bared breast motif and short tunic mark her as non-Roman and uncivilized, and may suggest a wildness and lack of constraint similar to the Amazons, warrior women whose lifestyle threatened Greco-Roman normative expectations of gender.[29] Dio's Boudica proclaims an affinity to this lifestyle, discussed later in this chapter. Amazon women appear primarily in scenes of male domination, such as Achilles defeating the Amazon queen Penthesilea. Such iconography indicates not only the superiority of the male warrior, but also the subordination of the female to a submissive gender role.[30] The Claudius panel, in conjunction with the nearby representation of Nero seizing Armenia, historicizes the mythological theme of the Amazons to represent moments of Roman male violence against barbarian women.[31] The Claudius panel portrays an act of humiliation, as Britannia cowers in the face of potential sexual assault by her conqueror.[32]

In numismatic material, Britannia first appears as a female figure with a spear and shield on copper asses from the reign of Hadrian (AD 117–138). Her posture is unique from those of Roma or Hispania, Gallia or Africa, as she is sitting on a pile of rocks that may represent Hadrian's Wall. The figure wears a full-length garment and a cloak draped over one shoulder. Although we do not see her expression, she rests her cheek in her hand in an image of defeat. Britannia is also found on coins in Roman Britain from the reign of Antoninus Pius (AD 138–161), on which Britannia has a trophy in addition to spear and shield (see figure 4.4); after his reign, they fade from circulation.

In Rome, images of conquered peoples show an increased level of violence during this period. Images of women in warfare are rare throughout the Roman Empire, especially as active participants. However, several appear in the second century, beginning in the reign of Trajan (AD 98–117). A unique image on the frieze of Trajan's column

FIGURE 4.4. Coin from the reign of Antoninus Pius. Britannia with a shield at her side.

in Rome depicts Dacian women torturing Roman prisoners that have been stripped naked and are being prodded with stakes.[33] The column of Marcus Aurelius (emperor from AD 161–180) portrays the sack of a town in disturbing detail, from the beheadings of barbarian men to women dragged by their hair, one breast exposed, or being led into exile as their men are killed before their eyes.[34] Ferris notes a gradual debasement and dehumanization of barbarians on Roman art from the time of Marcus Aurelius onward. The fates of barbarians are graphically depicted, and while this may reflect a more general crisis in Roman society and Roman politics, it also may have desensitized viewers to such violence.[35] This second-century material, visible in Rome during Dio's lifetime, may have provided a background for his depiction of Boudica and the violence of her revolt.

Female barbarians are relatively absent from honorific monuments of Septimius Severus, who was emperor from AD 193–211, when Dio was writing his history.[36] Dio's text echoes the impression given by earlier artistic representations: Boudica, a female barbarian, is in need of Roman control. The image of Boudica that emerges from Dio exudes power and a warrior aesthetic rather than the stereotype of the sexualized female barbarian. Boudica's Amazonian fierceness stands in contrast to images of the defeated Britannia that served as Roman imperial propaganda. Boudica is not a weak, sexualized female, but a masculine leader. Boudica's appearance confirms her non-Roman identity and communicates her authority to her troops and to her Roman enemies.

The Words of Women

Boudica emerges fully formed from the pages of Dio, a warrior queen brandishing a spear, commanding the attention of thousands. In her speech, she justifies her rejection of everything she has learned from the Romans. Her speech is made all the more important by its length and place in Dio's history. In what remains of his text, Dio gives few women the chance to speak; of these women, positive models prove their nobility through emphasizing their motherhood and thereby influencing men to strive for martial honor.[37] Through setting Boudica within the context of female speeches in Dio, we can better understand the content of her speech and Dio's representation of gender and power among her people.

In book 1 of Dio's history, Hersilia, wife of Romulus, leads the Sabine women and their children into the Forum, and they insert themselves between the Roman and Sabine armies. Hersilia and the others demand an immediate peace; otherwise, they demand death for themselves and the children who symbolize the bonds of kinship between the two peoples. They tear their garments to show off their breasts and bellies, reminding the Romans that they are husbands and fathers, the Sabines that they are fathers and grandfathers, and that they, the women, are the mothers of the next generation.[38] The purpose of their action is to arouse pity, and they succeed in their aim.[39] The female bodies are an integral part of their rhetoric of persuasion, symbols of the domestic peace that must exist in order for either group to survive. The display has an immediate impact, and the Romans and Sabines make a treaty.

On another occasion, women are again able to save the state from ruin. Coriolanus, after his great military success against the Volscian city of Corioli, is eventually exiled and joins the Volsci in a siege of Rome. The women of Rome gather together, dress in mourning garb, and approach his camp, with Coriolanus's mother, Veturia, wife, Volumnia, and two children in the lead. Veturia berates her son for reducing her to her lamentable state, and then, like Hersilia, bares her body as the culmination of her persuasive rhetoric.[40] Veturia is successful in her plea: Coriolanus withdraws. Veturia was helpful to the state and used the physical evidence of her motherhood to her rhetorical advantage. Her body is not sexualized, but displayed in an extreme act of mourning.

Dio's record of Hersilia and Veturia is unique among extant historians and biographers: Livy, Dionysius of Halicarnassus, and Plutarch all record these episodes, but without the same use of the female body.[41] Dio suggests that, in Rome, in times of great peril to the state, men must be visually reminded of family and the necessity for peace. These women display the typical female virtues of womanhood without becoming masculine or domineering, and without questioning the masculinity of their men. They suggest an intimate connection between appearance and speech as indicative of character: a woman who speaks with particular reference to motherhood and fertility is able to exemplify and uphold the values of Rome. Women use their loyalty and devotion as wives and mothers as their primary means of persuasion.

Livia, the wife of Augustus, gives one of the two set female speeches in Dio (the other is Boudica) and presents an alternate model.[42] In private conversation with her husband, Livia speaks in defense of

Pompey the Great's grandson, Gnaeus Cornelius Cinna Magnus, who was accused of conspiring against Augustus.[43] Her speech emerges not merely as a successful defense, but as a meditation on the nature of imperial power, the position of the emperor, and her role as his wife. She flatters Augustus's ego, asking if he will refrain from rebuking her because she, "though a woman," would like to propose an idea.[44] After Augustus encourages her to speak, she admits her real interest: as long as Augustus is safe, she has a part in his rule, but if he comes to harm, she too will perish.[45] She advises him to replace severity with clemency, noting that his role is not to punish through resentment, greed, fear, or jealousy, but rather to preserve the state and her citizens.[46] The lives of citizens should be spared, their faults corrected.[47] Livia is persuasive, and Augustus releases the accused. According to Dio, as a result of this display of clemency, no one ever plotted against the life of Augustus or was suspected of doing so.[48] However, Dio is not internally consistent: he adds that Livia herself was blamed for the emperor's death.[49]

Dio's Livia is a pragmatic thinker, a "rhetorician and philosopher of clemency" able to negotiate with the emperor.[50] She is devoted to Augustus,[51] but Dio undermines the nobility of her character and the message of her speech through presenting her as manipulative and overtly self-interested.[52] Dio betrays an anxiety toward women in power through his representation of the negotiation between the emperor and the woman who supports him. Livia assumes her unofficial authority will continue into the reign of her son, Tiberius. Dio's characterization of Livia shifts between the reigns of her husband and son, as she becomes less interested in negotiation and acts more on her own. Livia does not dare enter the senate house, military camps, or assemblies, but endeavors to manage all other affairs as if sole ruler, justifying her actions through claiming she made Tiberius the emperor. She does not want to equal his power, as with Augustus, but to surpass him.[53] For example, she shares in the proceedings where the senate votes for the honors on the death of Augustus, and the senate proposes to honor her as Mother of the Fatherland (*Mater Patriae*), a complementary title to that of emperor, Father of the Fatherland (*Pater Patriae*).[54] Tiberius refuses to allow her this and other titles. After her death, she is voted an honorific arch, which Tiberius ensures is never built. He forbids her deification and limits other honors as well.[55]

Livia gives readers a reference point for the ways in which Dio represents the authority of imperial women. Although she speaks well, her conviction regarding her place in the politics of Rome is unfounded. Livia starts a trend that increases in the following generations, in the reigns of Claudius and Nero and the actions of Messalina and Agrippina the Younger. These two women are the focus of Boudica's critique of Roman politics. Reading Boudica's speech with Livia in mind allows us to clarify some of the issues of gender, status, and power that she is reacting against. In Boudica's view, power depends upon status, morality, and action, and she has earned her place at the top.

Boudica's Speech

Dio's Boudica stands out from imperial women as a woman warrior addressing an audience of warriors. Unlike Tacitus's Boudica or Dio's Hersilia or Veturia, she does not emphasize her position as a wife or mother, but rather speaks directly about the reasons for rebellion and explains why her Britons will win. Her lengthy exhortation seems to respond to Tacitus's concise version in some ways, elaborating upon the differences between freedom and slavery introduced by Tacitus's Boudica, while also introducing and building upon themes that have continued relevance for Dio's third-century audience. In the first part of her speech, she acknowledges that her people have seen how terrible it is to be slaves to Rome, even if it brought them wealth, and argues that they must prefer the poor freedom valued by their ancestors. The Romans are robbers who looted in the aftermath of conquest and now require tribute. Even death is costly, as the Romans require a fee for the burial of the dead.[56] Such economic burdens are immoderate. They are also the Britons' own fault, for they should have cast out the Romans immediately, as they had done with Julius Caesar.[57] Their island is remote and relatively unknown, but still men have trampled it in their unending search for gain. All is not lost, however: for the first time, the Britons have become unified. Boudica exhorts them as her kinsmen, who must look to their future and that of their children:

> However, even if we have not done it before, oh citizens
> and friends and kinsmen, for I consider all of you kinsmen,
> inhabiting a single island and called by a common name, let
> us now do what is fitting, while we still remember freedom, so
> that we may leave both its name and its result to our children.

For if we forget entirely the happiness of our common
upbringing, whatever will they do, brought up in slavery?[58]

Dio's Boudica employs some of the themes identified or implicit in
Tacitus and common to revolt narratives, presenting an image of imperial expansion with the insights of an author of a later era. Dio's extended
discussion of the economic impact of Roman imperial expansion at the
ends of the known world suggests an overburdening of the provinces that
is not due to any emperor in particular, but rather is a common thread
leading to provincial uprisings. Boudica emphasizes the idea of unity and
consolidation in Britain, while criticizing the Romans' inability to distinguish between different "tribes." Significantly, she refers to her army as
citizens, friends, and kinsmen.[59] The Roman flavor of her speech extends
to her identification of freedom: freedom must be acquired both in name
and in deed (ἔργον). Freedom is a type of work, an action, a lifestyle, as
well as the results of that lifestyle. It includes one's property and wealth,
and the produce of the land. By identifying freedom as an action, Dio's
Boudica argues that freedom is a process, and they must fight so that this
idea may extend to the lifetimes of their children.

Boudica thanks her troops for uniting and elaborates upon the
many reasons they should not fear the Romans.[60] The Romans are inferior in numbers and bravery. They need armor for protection and build
walls and trenches to plan for battle. In addition, the Romans are unable
to pursue the enemy or flee. The Britons are superior at sudden attacks,
at capturing prisoners, and at hiding themselves in woods when necessary. They have bravery in excess, needing only tents and shields. The
Romans cannot stand the cold, the heat, nor the harsh terrain, and they
have no understanding of the geography of Britain. Furthermore, they
require bread and olive oil and wine, the type of imports evident in
Camulodunum and other towns. In this part of Boudica's speech, the
Britons emerge as stronger and more adapted to their surroundings.

Boudica's depiction of both armies parallels Dio's narrative of
Britain at the end of the reign of Septimius Severus. The Britons do
not change in Dio's history between AD 60 and his own lifetime, when
Severus journeyed to Britain in AD 208 with his wife Julia Domna, sons
Caracalla and Geta, and about forty thousand additional troops to
complete the conquest of Britain north of the Antonine Wall. He and
Caracalla invaded Caledonia, but the army became separated, caught
in intractable swamps and open to attack. Thousands perished in the

difficult terrain without ever engaging in battle. Severus came to terms with the Caledonians and returned to Eboracum (modern York) in an infirm state. The Caledonians failed to abide by their promises and revolted, leading to a second campaign led by Caracalla. Severus died in Eboracum in AD 211 before succeeding in his aim to subjugate all of Britain. Caracalla made peace with the Britons and ordered his army to withdraw to Hadrian's Wall. The imperial family returned to Rome.

The ongoing revolts in Britain attest to the independent spirit of the Caledonians and Maeatae. In Dio's text, these two hostile groups are even less civilized than Boudica's Iceni. They live as barbarians, without walls, cities, or agriculture, naked and barefoot in their tents, sharing women and raising children in common.[61] Their leaders are chosen from among the boldest. They fight in chariots and on foot, without armor, bearing shields, short spears, and daggers. Furthermore, they can endure any hardship, including cold and hunger, and can live in swamps for days, with only their heads above water. The depiction echoes Boudica's praise of the hardy Britons, with a level of exaggeration beyond credibility. Her speech both monumentalizes her own revolt and increases the significance of Severus's expedition to Britain in Dio's text.[62] Dio explains the difficulty of Severus's attempt to conquer the remainder of Britain while simultaneously suggesting the Romans would gain nothing but further disquietude by the conquest.

Boudica's Role Models

At the end of the first part of her speech, in order to increase their confidence in their impending victory, Boudica employs a type of divination. She releases a hare from the folds of her dress, which runs in an auspicious direction, and the crowd erupts in delight. As she continues, she thanks the goddess of victory, Andraste, and discusses her leadership strategy through citing individuals she has chosen to avoid:

> I give you thanks, Andraste, and I, a woman, call upon you, a woman, not as one ruling over the burden-bearing Egyptians, as Nitocris, nor over Assyrian merchants, as Semiramis (for indeed we have learned these things from the Romans), nor indeed over the Romans themselves, as Messalina before, and then Agrippina, and now Nero (for although he is a man in

name, he is a woman in deed; a sure sign of this, he sings and plays the lyre and beautifies himself).[63]

Boudica first contrasts herself with Semiramis and Nitocris, legendary queens of Babylon. Both women earned praised for making improvements to the walls and sanctuaries of the city.[64] Semiramis, who ruled toward the end of the ninth century BC, set out to build the city and surround it with walls and gates.[65] She was responsible for a network of cities, roads, and other building projects along the Tigris and Euphrates that aided merchants and brought trade and fame to Babylon.[66] She ruled alone after the death of her husband, Ninus, and never married again. Diodorus explains that she feared sharing the rule with a man, a status that may have deprived her of her power. Instead, she had a pleasure garden, where she had sex with the most handsome soldiers among her ranks and then had them killed.[67] Semiramis was also a warrior queen, and Diodorus suggests she disguised herself as a man in order to fight, only revealing herself as a woman after victory.[68] Her campaigns in Baktria were successful. However, she was overly ambitious: she failed in an ill-conceived war against India, losing two-thirds of her force and retreating homeward.[69] Furthermore, she was excessively emotional. Valerius Maximus attests to the extent of her rage: having heard that Babylon had rebelled, she rushed off with her hair undone to sack the city, and she did not rearrange her coiffure until she succeeded.[70]

Nitocris, who ruled five generations after Semiramis, is considered the wiser of the two by Herodotus. She was remembered for her monuments and made progress in Babylon by altering the course of the Euphrates and bridging the river to connect the two sides of the city.[71] She was successful when acting on the defensive, building walls and managing the protection of their city and surrounding areas. However, her character was also flawed. Whereas Semiramis was critiqued for her luxurious lifestyle and licentiousness, Nitocris was known for her beauty and deviousness.

Rather than emphasize obvious character flaws, Boudica focuses on the types of men ruled by each woman and finds fault in that these women did not inspire men to break the bonds of servitude.[72] In Boudica's words, Nitocris ruled "burden-bearing Egyptians," and Semiramis ruled merchants. Boudica distances herself as a successful woman on the offensive and as a leader of a different type of men: she has gained the trust of an army, warriors rather than tradesmen, slaves, and builders.[73] Boudica overlooks other causes for praise or critique of the Babylonian queens, instead drawing attention to leadership style. In Boudica's eyes, Semiramis and Nitocris are antimodels, despite their political and military successes.[74]

In a parenthetical statement, Boudica notes the Britons have learned about these women from the Romans, admitting that her understanding of historical models of leadership derives from her conquerors.[75] Her statement seems unrealistic and may be more of an expression of Dio's own intellect and learning (παιδεία). Nevertheless, Boudica's parenthesis also communicates a rationale for Dio's inclusion of historical predecessors. Dio could have offered a detailed comparison between Boudica and other queens, touting his own historical knowledge, but values her more as a commentator on Rome and the immoral atmosphere clouding the Rome of Nero.[76] Boudica has learned about various models from the Romans and has chosen to be a different type of leader.

Imperial Antimodels

After rejecting the Babylonian queens, Dio turns to recent Roman models of moral ineptitude and weak, feminine leadership. His Boudica presents a tricolon of increasingly condemnable figures, beginning with Messalina, including Agrippina the Younger, and culminating with Nero. Messalina and Agrippina are classified together as rulers of Rome. This characterization reflects a familiar critique of Claudius as an emperor ruled by his wives: through manipulating and deceiving Claudius, these women ostensibly governed Rome.[77] Boudica does not admire the female leaders because they were unofficial corulers rather than queens. Messalina was famous for her licentiousness, and Agrippina for her overwhelming desire for power.[78] Through assessing Agrippina and Messalina as rulers, Dio has Boudica criticize a system of power that allowed these women to act authoritatively. Her evaluation is based on an observable inconsistency, in which the appearance of authority (auctoritas) fails to represent the legitimate possession of power. Boudica's criticism reflects an overwhelmingly negative portrait of the wives of Claudius in texts from the time of Tacitus to Dio that censure the wives of Claudius for immorality, lasciviousness, avarice, and deception.

Messalina was the wife of Claudius in the early part of his reign. She gave him two children, Britannicus and Octavia, but became a known adulteress, famed for her sexual profligacy. Acting in conjunction with Claudius's freedmen, she provides a moral foil to Claudius and his moderation. She brought about the banishment of her niece Julia, who failed to flatter her,[79] and, together with Claudius's freedmen, was responsible for the deaths of many good men.[80] Messalina and the freedmen also sold citizenship and various political offices.[81] Worse than her own licentiousness was her ability to corrupt other women.[82] The populace grew vexed at seeing Claudius as a "slave of his wife and freedmen," and were angered by her public displays of authority.[83] She eventually became obsessed with Gaius Silius, the consul elect, and forced him to divorce his wife. Even Rome's enemies know of Messalina's actions, and the populace pitied Claudius's ignorance.[84] Messalina married Silius while Claudius was in Ostia; the freedman Narcissus, formerly Messalina's partner in crime, informed Claudius. Messalina was killed on the orders of Narcissus. Dio's critique of Messalina's rule focuses on her alliance with freedmen: together, their actions belittle the idea of imperial power altogether.

Claudius swore he would never marry again after the death of Messalina, yet he almost immediately wed his niece Agrippina the Younger.[85] Claudius and Agrippina may have had an incestuous sexual relationship beforehand; whatever the nature of their prior relationship, Claudius had to change the law to allow the marriage to take place.[86] Tacitus suggests Agrippina only utilized her sexual appeal when it would gain her a political advantage.[87] She gained control over Claudius and became a "second Messalina."[88] She was awarded the title of Augusta, implying she was the mother of an emperor,[89] long before her son Nero came into power. Agrippina's power increased as she promoted Nero and diminished Claudius's son Britannicus; Claudius adopted Nero, and Nero married Claudius' daughter, Octavia. The stage was set for Nero's advancement.

Agrippina the Younger exemplifies the danger of the lack of self-restraint or moderation (*impotentia*) of a woman who tests the boundaries of her authority, often in a political context.[90] By acting publicly, she lessened the authority of the men around her. She played the part of a ruler by appearing with Claudius on many occasions.[91] When Caratacus spoke before Claudius and received a pardon, he and his family offered equal thanks and praise to Claudius and Agrippina, seated near the emperor on another platform. The Briton mistook the appearance of corule for actual political equivalency.[92] On another occasion, when Claudius staged a naval battle on the Fucine lake, he and Nero dressed in military garb, while Agrippina wore a golden chlamys to observe the action.[93] The chlamys, the same garment worn by Boudica, made Agrippina appear as a coruler, and even a queen.[94]

After perhaps bringing about the death of her husband, Agrippina ensured Nero's rise to the throne and ruled with him for the first five years of his reign.[95] On coins from the early part of Nero's reign, Agrippina appears with her son, just as she had appeared beside Claudius, implying a symbolic transfer of her own authority.[96] However, when Nero became infatuated with the freedwoman Acte, Agrippina lost her authority. She approached Nero and claimed that she made him emperor and could take his power away.[97] The moment encapsulates the problem with women in unofficial positions: Agrippina's authority is fluid, and though hard won, is easily lost. Nero distanced himself from his mother, replaced Acte with the noblewoman Poppaea Sabina, and allowed Poppaea to have greater influence, so much so that she convinced him to have Agrippina killed.[98]

After Agrippina's death, Nero turns to the games. While he is distracted, Boudica revolts. Her condemnation of Nero concludes her list of antimodels and demonstrates that her success depended upon both her masculine strength and Nero's weak leadership.[99] Messalina and Agrippina the Younger were models of poor leadership for their sexual promiscuity, bribery, alliances with freedmen or others of a lower class, and for the appearance of authority without its actuality. In the case of Nero, the Romans have failed to realize they are serving another woman. As demonstrated through his artistic pursuits, Nero privileges individual pleasure over the good of the collective. Nero is blameworthy for his lack of military prowess and for the impact his character has had on the Romans. Boudica's advice to examine the effects of an effeminate ruler on his people reflects Dio's negative characterization of Nero and his theatrical activities.[100] Like Messalina and his mother, Nero is an antimodel because his name does not match his actions; however, the analogical relationship between these individuals as female rulers differs. Messalina and Agrippina overstepped the boundaries of their authority as women during the reign of Claudius: women are not legitimate rulers. Nero is the emperor but acts womanly through his attention to song, lyre-playing, and beauty, pursuits that win prizes but not wars. Nero undermines his own authority through acting for personal pleasure rather than for the good of the state. Even the Roman army is at fault. Boudica continues her invocation to her patron goddess in this way:

> I pray to you for victory, safety, and freedom from insolent, unjust, insatiable, impious men, if at any rate it is fitting to call these people men, who bathe in warm water, eat prepared dainties, drink unmixed wine, anoint themselves with myrrh, recline on soft couches with young boys and boys past their prime, who are slaves to a lyre-player, and a bad one besides.[101]

Worst of all their faults, the Romans have not revolted against Nero. Instead, they seem to recognize him as a new type of model. Although Nero fails as a positive model of leadership, the Romans emulate him nonetheless. At the end of her speech, Boudica concludes, "Accordingly may Lady Domitia Nero rule no longer over me or you, but rather let her sing and rule over the Romans (for surely they are worthy of serving such a woman, since they have submitted to her for so long), but may you alone, mistress, be our ruler always."[102] Through her characterization of the Romans and the leadership at Rome, Boudica condemns Nero and accuses the Romans of effeminacy by association. Nero's transgressions have tainted Roman *mores*, and the men have grown effeminate due to their enslavement to this leader.[103] Thus Boudica contends that sex should not determine who is allowed to have *imperium*.

Boudica and the Amazons

In the midst of her condemnation of her antimodels, Boudica acknowledges her position of authority as ruler and queen, and she identifies a categorical difference between her culture and that of the Romans. Indeed, Boudica overturns a cultural paradigm by applying a familiar portrait of otherness to the Romans: while Romans denounce barbarians as soft and effeminate, Boudica applies these terms to the Romans. The Romans enjoy excessive luxuries, while the Britons endure every hardship. As she rejects contemporary and ancient models, Boudica aligns herself with the Amazons: she is a warrior woman who believes authority is gained through action and operates independently from considerations of sex. Her comparison both celebrates the fierceness of her warriors and enhances the heroism of the opposing Romans, who are elevated by their eventual victory over such an awesome foe. The alignment allows Boudica to become an inspiring leader, and her speech serves as a statement of her personal excellence and a challenge to her enemies.[104]

Boudica relates her culture to that of the Amazons, praising the character of her Britons, "who do not know how to farm or work, but who are learned precisely in warfare, and who recognize everything as shared in common, even children and wives, and on account of this the women have the same valor as the men."[105] The representation of the Britons as a nonagricultural warrior society does not reflect the reality of the agriculturally dependent allied peoples fighting for her; instead, Boudica represents the structure of her society as similar to that of the Amazons, whose skills lie in warfare and who live by hunting and taking spoils.[106] These warrior women were famed for their courage and skill in battle that made them worthy adversaries for the strongest Greek heroes, from Heracles to Theseus to Achilles. They were nomadic, unlike Boudica, and aligned with the Scythians of the exotic east. Pomponius Mela, writing in the mid-first century AD, characterizes these tribes as free, unconquered, and "so savage that even the women take part in war."[107] Boudica appears as a similarly fearsome warrior, who views her Britons as an equally warlike people. By accentuating their Amazonian qualities, Dio creates a more worthy adversary for the Romans.

Boudica also suggests her people hold wives and children in common, and that because of this the women have the same amount of valor as the men. Amazons controlled their own sexuality, and, more importantly, valued parity with men.[108] Thus the Amazons were seen as dangerous to Roman norms of domestic life. Furthermore, they were honored after death for their actions in war. Women warriors could be buried with similar grave goods as men, including weapons, sacrificed horses, and horse trappings.[109] Through aligning herself with the Amazons, Dio's Boudica reinforces his portrayal of the Britons as the ethnographic opposite of the Romans. Boudica's Britons are a people for whom sex operates independently from gender, and maleness is not a sine qua non of the virtue of manliness.

Boudica's Amazonian qualities reflect overarching cultural similarities in the perception of gender differentiation between the Britons and the mythical woman warriors of the steppe. Her observation on domestic equality has a literary and historical echo outside of Dio, in Hypsicratea, the Amazon wife of Mithridates, the king of Pontus defeated by Pompey in 63 BC.[110] This couple is praised by Valerius Maximus as a model of married love: Hypsicratea is Mithridates's companion, who takes on masculine characteristics, learning to ride horses and use weapons, all in the service of her husband.[111] Plutarch's account differs, saying she was a concubine and served as Mithridates's groom. Nevertheless, she was his peer in courage, and as a term of affection and respect, he called her Hypsicrates, the masculine form of her name.[112] Hypsicratea was not the only woman in Mithridates's ranks; after his defeat, Pompey displayed female warriors in his triumph in Rome in 61 BC.[113] In describing the bodies left on the battlefield, Appian notes, "The women's wounds showed that they had fought as vigorously and courageously as the men."[114] Two years later, Mithridates committed suicide after his son formed an alliance with Pompey. Hypsicratea's fate is unknown.

The literary representation of Boudica draws connections between the warrior woman of Roman Britain and the Amazons, as well as other women operating outside of Roman normative gender boundaries. Beyond literary evidence, the material of Roman Britain suggests similar comparisons can be made. Evidence of specifically Icenian burials has not been found; nevertheless, burial evidence of women identified as warriors suggests their presence on the battlefields of late Iron Age Britain. Women buried with weapons and horse trappings have been identified as warriors; however, grave goods buried with an individual were not necessarily used by that individual. Weapons may be markers of an individual's wealth, status, or importance in the community, but they cannot prove a buried female fought as a warrior. At Wetwang Slack in Yorkshire, a young woman was found buried with weapons and a dismantled chariot. The burial is dated to 300–200 BC, centuries before Boudica, but has been used to suggest that women may have been charioteers. This individual was equipped with everything needed for her next life, including a chariot, food, and an iron mirror. The horse harness of the chariot was covered in pink coral, indicating the woman's wealth.[115] While she may have been a charioteer, the elaborate burial and rich grave goods prioritize her high status and the respect with which she was held by her community.[116] Three similar chariot burials were found nearby.[117] Burials in the area of Camulodunum and Verulamium also have been used as evidence of women warriors and charioteers.[118] While these individual burials may not indicate a widespread practice among the Britons or dating to the revolt of Boudica, the evidence suggests readers need not dismiss the idea of women on the battlefield as lacking historicity.

In the last part of her speech, Boudica is forthright in her evaluation of historical women, as well as her contemporaries in Rome. She critiques the political climate of Rome under Nero and contrasts herself with other leaders, Roman and non-Roman alike. Boudica reflects upon the nature of female leadership and presents herself as superior to other foreign queens, Roman imperial women, and the effeminate Nero. Her words echo Dio's critical representation of Nero and emphasize the dangerous results an effeminate, narcissistic leader may have on an entire populace. Her catalogue begins with a range of failed female leaders whose leadership depended upon deception, sexual profligacy, and the subordination of their people.

Through evaluating women from different cultures with alternate modes of leadership, Dio's Boudica focuses on aspects of each individual that make them models or anti-models for her current situation. She needs an active rather than a passive approach, a recognized rather than implicit authority, and an Amazonian warrior ethic rather than an effeminate aesthetic. She rejects the current Roman emperor for privileging music over the art of war. Her speech reminds readers that appearance should match authority, and authority should not exceed status. Sex may regulate a woman's power in some cultures, but character should outweigh this distinction. Boudica fears for her people and the strength of her warriors, given the Roman presence and the softened, weak model the Romans provide. Her actions suggest the extent to which she lived up to her own ideal.

5

Dux Femina

Boudica earned her place in history as a commander in war. However, ancient texts traditionally recognize war as the realm of men. What happens, then, when a woman leads? Boudica has the character to be a powerful leader: she is from a noble family and possesses wealth, a strong moral character, and a powerful intellect. She is able to unify an army and inspire them to fight. However, in the end, she fails to protect both her daughters and her people.

In order to understand Boudica's complex characterization as both mother and leader in Tacitus's *Annals*, readers must examine the literary and historical backdrop to her actions in war. In this chapter, I first demarcate the roles of Boudica and the other women involved in the revolt, as discussed in Tacitus's *Annals*. Women are central to Tacitus's account as both warriors and observers, and their actions defy Roman assumptions of female weakness. Comparative models from Tacitus's *Germania* present the possibility for women to act courageously in martial situations as nurses and helpmates without becoming warriors themselves. Outside of Tacitus, women warriors in Latin literature of the late Republic and early Empire are memorialized as either positive models who fight to defend their virtue or negative transgressors who enervate the men on the battlefield.

The concept of a *dux femina* (commander woman) is particularly germane to this distinction. Tacitus refers to Boudica as a *dux femina*, activating a host of literary associations while also challenging his reader to contemplate Boudica's place within this distinct literary canon. This literary topos originates with Vergil's Dido but generally functions pejoratively in Roman historiography. The pejorative value of *dux femina* is particularly true in Tacitus's *Annals*, where the term is applied to women of the imperial family. Given this background, Boudica's place in *Annals* book 14 is analyzed as an exploration of the possibility for a unique, non-Roman *dux femina* to lead an army and gain sympathy from her audience.

Women on the Battlefield: Amazons or Observers

Before we explore Boudica as the female leader of an immense army, it is important to note the various roles of women in Tacitus's narrative. Groups of women frame the revolt and play contrasting roles. Women are either involved in the action or are spectators of the theater of war, observing those wielding weapons and reminding them of the families that will be destroyed if they lose. These opposing scenes create gender confusion: are women active or passive? Dependent or autonomous? Comparing the women in these scenes allows us to see how Boudica operates in relation to the expectations of non-Roman women.

Boudica's rebellion follows on the heels of Suetonius Paulinus's destruction of the sacred groves on the island of Mona. Suetonius's attack is unprovoked: rather, it is purely a contest for glory. Gaius Domitius Corbulo, identified by Tacitus as Suetonius's competitor in military accomplishments and popular opinion, achieved great victories in Armenia in AD 59 and 60, and Suetonius desires to match his level of honor.[1] As his men cross the sea, they encounter a terrifying sight: an opposing battle line stands on the shore, including armed men, Druids calling forth dreadful curses, and women running in their midst, who "in black clothing in the manner of the Furies, hair loose, were brandishing torches."[2] Tacitus's depiction of the women in the passage differentiates them from those involved in Boudica's revolt. The women defending the religious center are like Furies, vengeful spirits of the underworld. Together with the Druid priests, they have the power to instill a paralyzing fear in the Romans. The Roman general must shame his army into fighting, as he and his men encourage each other not to pale before a "womanly and fanatic army" (*muliebre et fanaticum agmen*).[3] Tacitus's terms are weighted: *muliebris*, "womanly," is often derogatory in his text and connotes the cowardice and fickleness of women and foreigners.[4] *Fanaticum*, "fanatic," implies the women have been inspired or filled with the spirit of a divinity. Our initial impression of women on a battlefield in Britain is a manic, Fury-like group of worshippers rather than warriors, armed only with torches. They are initially effective but are soon conquered as the Romans forge ahead, striking down the enemy and engulfing them in flames.

Women are similarly frenzied in the imminent attack on Camulodunum. As the forces gather, a number of portents announce impending doom. Among other marvels, "Women, thrown into a state of inspired frenzy, prophesied the end was at hand. Ravings in a foreign tongue were heard in their senate house; their theater resounded with wailing."[5] The prophecies emerge from women driven into a state of *furor*, an uncontrolled frenzy, and by sounds emitted from the senate house and theater, structures indicative of the Roman presence. Indeed, with the presence of a senate house, readers are struck with geographical confusion: is this Rome or Britain? Are these Roman or native women? Readers are soon reminded that this is indeed Britain—in another portent, houses are seen under the water in the river Thames—but the parallel has served its purpose. Boudica is preparing to attack Roman cultural mainstays. The destruction of Camulodunum is an assault on a version of Rome, away from Rome itself. The visions inspire fear among the inhabitants. The veterans fail to send the old men and women to safety, and all are lost. Later, in the attack of Londinium, Suetonius allows all who are able to join his army; those left behind are slaughtered. These include women, identified as the "unwarlike sex" (*imbellis sexus*), and the elderly.[6] Their sex defines the women as helpless members of society, and the army abandons them. Tacitus juxtaposes these women with the religious figures of Mona and the wives and mothers involved in Boudica's last stand.

In the final battle, women provide passive support and active resistance. When the two armies gather, Suetonius's Romans condense in close array, legions surrounded by light-armed troops, with cavalry on the wings. The Britons are less organized. Tacitus records, "The troops of Britons were exulting everywhere in bands and troops, a multitude greater than ever before, and with such fierce spirit that they also brought with them their wives to witness victory, and placed them in wagons they had set up on the edge of the plain."[7] The presence of women betrays the arrogance of the Britons: the warriors have invited the womenfolk to watch their assumed victory. Women frame the battlefield as spectators rather than warriors themselves, observing from wagons rather than chariots. Their vehicles are unfit for war, separating them from the battle and casting them in a supporting role.

Tacitus expounds upon the potential positive role of non-Roman women as observers of war in his ethnographic work, the *Germania*. It is a practice of Germanic tribes to fight with their family members beside them, and to gain encouragement from the shrieks of their women and cries of their infants on the sidelines: "These are to each man the most sacred witnesses, these his greatest admirers."[8] Warriors bring their wounds to their mothers and wives, and these women treat them, providing food and encouragement. They even have the power to renew the strength of their men through exposing the threat of servitude:

> Tradition says certain armies, already wavering and falling back, have been restored by women who, with constant prayers and exposed breasts, have shown the immediacy of captivity, which they fear with extreme intolerance on behalf of their women, so much that other states are bound more efficiently when noblewomen are also demanded among the hostages.[9]

The mothers and wives of the warriors provide constant reminders of the threat of servitude. They expose their bodies, as Hersilia or Veturia, to emphasize what is at stake. If the men lose, the chastity of their women is threatened, and they may become hostages of Rome, exiled from family and fatherland.[10] With the Iceni, the fear of bodily harm was realized in the treatment of Boudica and her daughters. Boudica's women are not cited as nurses or providers of food, nor does Tacitus record that they gave vocal encouragement; however, their appearance on the sidelines is similar, and readers may imagine them spurring on the warriors in like fashion.[11]

The position of the women in Britain as spectators of war reflects a familiar literary trope known as the *teichoskopia*, or "view from the wall," in which women comment upon the fighting from the safety of the city's walls, emphasizing the boundary between participants and observers in war.[12] These women are spatially separated from the battlefield but emotionally invested in the actions of their husbands, sons, and brothers below. The position of the women makes war a spectator sport, separating audience from stage, the site of combat and the exhibition of heroism. Readers see some of the war through their eyes, and one could imagine these women garnering sympathy from any audience. The *teichoskopia* occurs in narratives of war from Homer onward.[13] In Tacitus's *Annals*, the women gathered in their wagons for Boudica's final battle create a similar effect. They do not live in walled towns, and Tacitus revises their vantage point to suit a pitched battle in Britain. The women are ready to observe and praise the defeat of the Romans. With superior numbers, the momentum from the destruction of the towns, and the gods on their side, victory seems inevitable. Although they do not speak, readers are invited to view the battle from their vantage point.

The presence of women on a battlefield is decidedly un-Roman and occurs only in times of great distress, such as the intervention of Hersilia and the Sabine women. Women are rarely active participants in battle, and elsewhere Tacitus denotes the dangers of women becoming involved. While women and children may provide motivations for war, they must remain separate from the fighting. For example, in the civil conflict after the death of Nero, the emperor Vitellius uses his family to support him in his fight against Vespasian. The women look on as he addresses his troops and abdicates power, inviting those assembled to decide whether he should live or die. Vitellius asks the soldiers to show compassion for his brother, wife, and innocent children, holding out his son before him.[14] This elicits pity from the crowd, and they demand he return to the imperial palace. In the ensuing siege of Rome, women join the fight. Verulana Gratilla stands out because she joined the battle, "not attending children or kin, but war."[15] Vitellius's sister-in-law, Triaria, "girded herself with a military sword" and participated in the massacre in Rome between the Vitellians and the Flavians.[16] In Tacitus's estimation, women do not belong in battle without noble motivations, and these women displayed an unwomanly aggression and fascination for war. As supportive family members, women have a positive impact; once they transgress onto the battlefield, they forget their family values.[17]

Women Warriors in Latin Literature

Boudica is separated from the other women by her position on the battlefield among the troops. Tacitus describes Boudica as a female commander (*dux femina*) in both the *Agricola* and in the *Annals*.[18] Her leadership recalls famed women warriors from Herodotus's Artemisia at the battle of Salamis, to the Amazon Penthesilea, who faced Achilles on the battlefield of Troy, to Cleopatra of Egypt, the strongest threat Rome faced from a foreign queen.[19] Her distinction as a *dux femina* connects her specifically to Vergil's Dido, the mythical queen of Carthage and the original *dux femina* of Roman literature. Dido became a leader after her brother Pygmalion killed her husband Sychaeus, and she was forced to flee for her life. In book 1 of the *Aeneid*, the disguised goddess Venus tells her son Aeneas about Dido's escape from Tyre. Dido led her loyal followers to North Africa, where they founded the city of Carthage. Venus closes her narrative of the escape by acknowledging that "a woman was the leader of the deed" (*dux femina facti*).[20] Venus praises the queen for her ability to lead in a time of emotional distress.

Vergil's Camilla, devotee of the goddess Diana and leader of the Volscians, provides a clear example of the power a mythic heroine could exert in war.[21] She is the last warrior described in the catalogue of Latin forces in *Aeneid* book 7, and she draws all the young people and matrons from their homes to watch her as she passes.[22] Camilla is a successful leader of a troop of cavalry,[23] masculine in her fierceness and in her desire for glory.[24] She is identified as a female warrior (*bellatrix*),[25] maiden (*virgo*),[26] woman (*femina*),[27] and queen (*regina*).[28] Camilla proves the fiercest of the Latin warriors, leading a charge and bringing down many of Aeneas's men before she is killed. Her sex sets her apart from other warriors; however, like other heroes, she aims to attain spoils of war. This goal leaves her open to attack.[29] She is struck by the javelin of the Trojan ally Arruns while she rushes toward Chloreus, desirous of his golden armor. After her death, the force of Camilla lives on, and Turnus uses her name as a rallying cry to his troops.[30] In the battle to defend their city, even the mothers assist, fighting in the name of Camilla, who they claim was driven to fight by a true love of country.[31]

Camilla and Dido are initially effective models of leadership in political and military spheres, despite their gender. One further figure shows that a female leader could succeed in setting a positive example. In Livy's history, Cloelia is memorialized for becoming an effective leader and earning new honors during the war with Lars Porsenna in the second and third years of the Republic. Cloelia succeeds because she does not seek to appropriate masculine traits to the detriment of others, but rather reinforces feminine virtues through her actions, utilizing masculine courage in order to protect her female modesty. Cloelia follows the models of Horatius Cocles and Mucius Scaevola, each of whom fought for freedom and won recognition for *virtus*.[32] Cloelia witnessed the honors bestowed upon Scaevola for his bravery and was inspired to seek public honors herself.[33] Her opportunity arose when she was sent as a hostage to Porsenna. After deceiving her guards, she became the commander of a troop of maidens (*dux agminis uirginum*), leading them across the Tiber and back to their families.[34] After her escape, Porsenna demanded Cloelia's return, but his anger transformed into admiration. He praised her masculine bravery as even greater than that of Horatius Cocles or Mucius Scaevola. Porsenna respected Cloelia's courage and allowed her to return to Rome with some of the remaining hostages. She chose the vulnerable young boys and gained further praise for this choice. For her actions, a new type of monument was created: an equestrian statue on the Via Sacra, a tribute to her unique masculine courage and a challenge to young men to emulate her *virtus* for generations to come.[35] Livy's narrative of Cloelia, more *fabula* (fictional tale) than *historia* (history), is designed to demonstrate that a woman could act in a military situation as a positive example of bravery, and, unexpectedly, that she could provide a model for young men.[36]

In imperial Roman historiography that survives, the concept of a *dux femina* generally indicates a threat posed by a female that has taken on the role of a leader with *imperium*. Female commanders invert normative gender roles and have the power to undermine and emasculate the men around them: if women act like men, then men must become weak like women. Authors of the late Republic and early Empire use military metaphors and assign masculine attributes to women who act beyond the bounds of traditional Republican womanhood in order to emphasize the danger of allowing a woman to have influence in traditionally masculine spheres.[37] The military metaphor becomes literal in the actions of Fulvia, the wife of Publius Clodius Pulcher, Gaius Scribonius Curio, and Marcus Antonius (Marc Antony) in turn. As the wife of Antony, Fulvia became known for her overwhelmingly masculine character, and for her participation in the Perusine war of 41 BC, which pitted Antony against Octavian (the future Augustus).[38] Literature of her lifetime and afterward portrays her as confrontational and hypermasculine: to Velleius Paterculus, there was "nothing female about her except for her body," and she was a woman who mixed all kinds of disorder "with military weapons and uproar."[39] To Plutarch, she was a woman "who desired to govern those who governed and to command a commander."[40] In Cicero's *Philippics*, a series of condemnatory speeches against Antony, Fulvia is criticized for making financial as well as military decisions and thereby emasculating her husband.[41] While it is unclear whether Fulvia had an active role as a battlefield commander, our sources suggest she played the role of a woman warrior.

Duces Feminae *in Tacitus's* Annals

As a literary topos, the term *dux femina* (plural, *duces feminae*) signifies a woman who acts as a leader in possession of military authority.[42] While some female leaders seem capable of commanding armies and guiding men to glory, women of the Late Republic and early Empire adapt the idea to new purpose, enervating rather than heightening the glory of their men. Roman historians demonstrate that women who command are in danger of becoming too masculine. Tacitus employs the phrase in reference to women of the imperial household in order to describe women who have usurped an unofficial level of masculine authority.[43] Such women transgress their bounds in military, political, and domestic spheres. In the *Annals*, several women appear in military situations and provide comparative figures for Boudica.[44] Tacitus's interpretation of imperial women hinges on the motivations of each woman's actions and the resulting effect on her husband's reputation.

During the reign of Tiberius, two women are identified as military leaders: Agrippina the Elder, wife of Livia's grandson Germanicus, and Plancina, wife of Gnaeus Calpurnius Piso. These women are variously regarded as helpful or disruptive. Agrippina the Elder is an exemplary wife and mother of six children who survive to adulthood, a model of chastity and female virtue (*pudicitia*); however, she is arrogant and challenges the empress Livia's authority. She accompanies her husband on his campaigns on the Rhine and illustrates her ability to lead on two occasions. First, during a mutiny, she departs from the camp with her young son, Caligula, and does not return until the birth of her next child. Her departure is a spectacle viewed by Germanicus's army, in which she leads a "female and wretched troop" (*muliebre ac miserabile agmen*).[45] The only other instance of an all-female *agmen* in all of Tacitus's oeuvre is in his description of the women of Mona.[46] Tacitus aligns the two groups of women, suggesting that, *mutatis mutandis*, Agrippina's metaphorical female army could have been realized. However, Agrippina is the only strong woman among her group. Agrippina leads the women into exile, and her departure allows Germanicus to reprimand his army and end the mutiny.

On a second occasion, Agrippina asserts herself more forcefully. When Germanicus's army is surrounded, Agrippina prevents the Romans from destroying a bridge in their retreat. Tacitus calls her a "woman great in spirit" (*femina ingens animi*), who took on the duties of a general (*dux*), giving out clothing and bandages and praise to the returning legions.[47] Her actions echo those of the Germanic women cited above, and she is more effective than her husband; however, not everyone views her as praiseworthy. After learning of Agrippina's defense of the bridge, Tacitus's Tiberius launches into an interpretation of Agrippina's actions in the camp: "Nothing is left for commanders when a woman inspects the infantries, approaches the standards, attempts largesse, as though it is not ambitious enough that she leads around the son of the general in the dress of a common soldier and desires him to be called Caesar Caligula."[48] Tacitus gives Tiberius's critique of the influential presence of Agrippina and her son, Caligula. Furthermore, Tiberius considers, "Agrippina is already more powerful among the army than the officers, more powerful than the generals; the mutiny was suppressed by a woman, which not even the name of the emperor was able to check."[49] In Tiberius's view, Agrippina's display of her son, in combination with her militaristic actions, express an excessive level of authority unacceptable for her gender or position.

Tiberius's observations also contain general concerns over the place of women in the public sphere. These concerns are voiced in a senatorial debate between Aulus Caecina Severus and Marcus Valerius Messala Messalinus on Caecina's proposal that wives be forbidden to accompany their husbands appointed to governorships in the provinces.[50] Caecina claims, "A retinue of women presents delays to peace, through luxury, and war, through panic, and transforms a Roman army on the march into the appearance of barbarian processions."[51] Caecina critiques the female sex, assuming an innate weakness as well as a ready ambition, cruelty, and hunger for power, if given license. More to the point, the presence of women among a military procession is a practice of barbarians, not civilized Romans; it is as if Caecina has read Tacitus's *Germania*, recognized the positive public roles of women on the battlefield among the Germanic tribes, and rejected this practice. At the end of the passage, Caecina notes that women have walked among soldiers and presided over cohort drills and maneuvers of the legions.[52] Agrippina the Elder is one of the women implicated in Caecina's critique, and her actions on the Rhine are considered as being in conflict with her domestic virtues. Plancina, the wife of Piso, the couple responsible for the death of Germanicus, is guilty of similar actions.[53] Caecina assumes that women who accompany their husbands to the provinces may become similarly uncontrolled. His overarching anxiety is that power may become divided between husband and wife. He argues that the provincials will have to attend to two leaders, two people's public appearances, with the woman's decisions always the more headstrong and faulty. He echoes the complaint of the Britons concerning their two leaders, the governor and the prefect, who do not necessarily agree.[54]

In closing, Caecina suggests the extent of the problem: "Now, set free from their bonds, they rule our homes, markets, and armies."[55] In his opinion, women should be contained within the domestic sphere, or else they will try to rule all areas of life. Messalinus adequately counters Caecina in his response, but Tiberius's son Drusus ends the debate, noting he would hate leaving his wife in Rome and citing Livia's companionship of Augustus abroad as precedent.[56] Nevertheless, tensions remain, and parity between husbands and wives seems impossible.

Boudica: Dux Femina of Britain

In his descriptions of women in Britain, Tacitus draws upon two main stereotypes of women in war: they are either Amazonian in their fierceness, or they are unwarlike observers. Boudica must be interpreted within the framework of her revolt and Tacitus's consistent focus on women. While Roman women are characterized as negative models of leadership when their actions undermine the men around them, Boudica is able to encourage her army to strive for greater glory and freedom. Tacitus's Boudica is similar to Lucretia, Cloelia, or Dido, for, like these women, Boudica struggles against a situation she views as tyranny.[57] She adopts the role of *dux femina* in both the *Agricola* and in the *Annals*.

In the *Agricola*, Tacitus explains that the Britons rose up in war "with Boudica as their leader, a woman of royal family" (*Boudicca generis regii femina duce*); he adds parenthetically that her position is normative for the Britons, "for they do not consider sex in choosing leaders" (*neque enim sexum in imperiis discernunt*).[58] Tacitus recognizes Boudica's female leadership and defines her form of rule as *imperium*, an official right of command. Boudica's gender is noteworthy but does not detract from the main force of his account of the brief but destructive revolt. Tacitus does not condemn Boudica or the reasons for the rebellion; rather, the unity of the Britons is admirable. Boudica's actions are implied but not elucidated, allowing the overarching theme of *libertas* to remain in the forefront.

In book 14 of the *Annals*, Boudica frames Tacitus's narrative. First, her mistreatment and that of her family at the hands of the Romans provides part of the rationale for the revolt. After this initial recognition of her importance, she disappears. In the destruction of Camulodunum, Londinium, and Verulamium, Tacitus abstracts the rebel army into a multitude of anonymous Britons.[59] The horde is identified collectively as the "victorious Briton" (*victor Britannus*) when they defeat Petillius Cerialis and the Ninth Legion on the way from Camulodunum to Londinium.[60] The army is unified in their rage, and this unity becomes a constant theme.

Boudica emerges to incite the troops to a final battle. Tacitus postpones her introduction as a leader to great dramatic effect. Once the women have been set on the sidelines in their wagons (*plaustra*), Boudica emerges in a war chariot (*currus*) with her daughters. Her light, easily maneuverable vehicle is distinct from the carts of the other women, and her words identify her position as *dux*. As discussed in chapter 3, she approaches each tribe, declaring it was indeed usual for Britons to fight under the leadership of women (*solitum quidem Britannis feminarum ductu bellare testabatur*).[61] Her words differentiate her position from the wives of other warriors and return us to her historical models, both Roman and otherwise. In the same section of the *Germania* where he describes the presence of the witnessing women and children on the battlefield, Tacitus draws a distinction between kings and generals that is echoed in the opening of Boudica's speech. Germanic kings are chosen by birth, but generals are chosen through *virtus*; the generals fight in front, leading by example.[62] Boudica suggests she will provide the type of leadership characteristic of a *dux* rather than a regent.

In her speech, Boudica addresses the themes of her leadership, the reasons for revolt, the inevitability of victory, and the necessity to live free or die trying. The crowd needs an instigator, and Boudica fulfills this role. While the first half of her speech concerns family, the second half stresses the inevitability of their impending victory:

> She declared, "But the gods stand by just vengeance. A legion that dared battle has fallen; the rest are hiding in their camps or considering flight. Neither the uproar nor shouting of so many thousands, nor the attack and combat will be endured. If you [Britons] consider the abundance of troops, the motivations for war, you would realize that our battle line must conquer or fall. This is the intention of a woman: you men may live and serve."[63]

Boudica states her army is sure to win because they have the greater numbers and a more noble motivation. At the end of her speech, she claims the choice between freedom and servitude is gendered, stating her intention to win or die is that of a woman.[64] She challenges the men to equal a woman's level of bravery and dedication to the cause, to reject a life of servitude as an option. Her words imply that both men and women can display *virtus*, and that she will provide the model. Her boldness is a challenge, reminiscent of Cloelia. Boudica's speech is rhetorically effective precisely because she is a woman and can challenge ideas of stereotypical manliness. She harnesses those assumptions and uses them to her advantage.

Boudica's speech serves a rhetorical function, allowing Tacitus to present his reader with a paired set of prebattle speeches. Many of her points are answered by the speech of Suetonius Paulinus that follows. However, Suetonius prioritizes individual glory over unity of action. The stage is set for a rebel victory, but Suetonius is unfazed. He advises his troops to look at the enemy and observe: "There you see more women than young men. Unwarlike, unarmed, they will yield immediately, when they have recognized the sword and courage of their conquerors, who have so often overcome them."[65] Suetonius uses sex as a means of comparison and implies that, under the leadership of a woman, the Britons are womanly themselves. In his estimation, women are unwarlike and unarmed. His observation recalls the women he abandoned at Londinium, but it fails to adequately describe Boudica and her war chariot. His comment is ironic when read in opposition to Boudica, whose sex defines her as one willing to sacrifice her life in hopes of instigating political change. He reinforces the Roman Republican idea that a man may become a role model by striving to gain glory (*gloria*) through martial valor (*virtus*). He does not draw upon specific historical models. Instead, his speech is based on what it means to be Roman. The juxtaposition of the two speeches explicates two different understandings of gender. For Suetonius, women represent unwarlike weaknesses, whereas for Boudica, women may be just as warlike as men.

Boudica defies Roman expectations as a woman in war. She is successful in inciting the army to fight, but the battle does not proceed as anticipated. The Romans act with scientific precision, surrounding the barbarians and destroying them. Boudica depends on superior numbers and does not provide a clear strategy for victory. This is characteristic of Britons, who, from the time of Caesar, excel at guerilla warfare, but not on an open battlefield.[66] While the Romans had a professional military, the Britons were amateurs. War was necessary for territorial defense in Britain but did not involve the same type of strategy and tactical training as for the Romans. In evaluating the Roman success, Tacitus concludes, "Noble praise, equal to ancient victories, was won that day: some record that a little less than eighty thousand Britons fell, with about four hundred Romans killed and not many more wounded."[67] The Romans achieve glory, defined by the comparative numbers of the slain. Even the women on the sidelines are slaughtered, together with their animals.[68]

In her mode of leadership and by her death, Boudica both confirms and overturns aspects of the *dux femina*. In Tacitus's *Annals*, she ends her life with poison, staying true to her sentiment that death is preferable to servitude. Her death is reminiscent of Cleopatra, whose choice to die by the poison of asps was regarded as heroic and saved her from being humiliated and paraded through Rome as part of Octavian's triumph over Egypt. Boudica likewise refuses to allow herself this degradation, denying the Roman general the use of her body in a triumphal procession. For Tacitus, Boudica has served as a foreign commander woman, and her death fulfills the expectations of this literary trope.[69]

By characterizing Boudica as a *dux femina*, Tacitus guides his reader to interpret her speech and actions and the reactions of her army with particular reference to the Vergilian tagline, especially as employed within the *Annals*. Vergil's unexpected juxtaposition is submerged under the weight of the Roman imperial mission, and surrounded by anxieties about women in power. When applied to Roman women by Tacitus, the tag is universally negative, and implies the utilization of authority in the manner of a *dux* but without true *imperium*. Readers then encounter Boudica, a foreign *dux femina* whose battlefield tactics may be questionable, but whose words reflect Roman values of freedom and family. As she challenges traditional notions of masculinity and femininity, she uses her sex as a powerful tool to rouse her troops to fight for vengeance. Both women and men may gain glory through battle, and, in Boudica's case, the women may have even more to lose.

6

I Call Upon You, Andraste

Previous chapters have examined Boudica's place in family, war, and politics. Her final sphere of influence is religion. Religious concerns underlie several aspects of Boudica's revolt, beginning with the portents that warn of the imminent conflict. While Suetonius Paulinus is destroying the center of Druidic worship, his absence allows Boudica time to raise an army, and the Britons claim divine sanction for their actions.[1] Some scholars have drawn inferences from this confluence of events and have derived a religious connection between Boudica and the Druids. Dio does not mention the Druidic associations of Mona.[2] Instead, Dio focuses on Boudica's individual relationship with the divine and her association with a goddess of victory called Andraste and Andate in his text. Dio's Boudica is also involved in ritual and acts as a diviner prior to the final battle. Some have seen Boudica's act as an indication that she was a priestess.[3] Her ritual performance connects her to other diviners in Roman historiography, providing support for her authoritative position in the rebellion. Others have suggested she was revolting against religious oppression, symbolized by the Roman temple at Camulodunum. This argument finds support in the extreme ritual violence enacted upon the bodies of her female captives. Suetonius Paulinus's response in Dio has particular relevance for rituals and the treatment of bodies after death. This chapter traces the importance of women as interpreters of signs in sources outside of Dio, as well as women's role in religion as symbols of fertility and safety, before examining Boudica as one such figure.

In Dio's history, Boudica has a powerful influence as a diviner: after performing a ritual with a hare, her people rejoice in the positive omen. The impact of female diviners illustrated elsewhere in Roman historiography demonstrates why Boudica's act is integral to Dio's representation of the revolt. For female diviners have deep roots within myth and early Roman history. The Etruscan queen Tanaquil illustrates the authority with which they operated, demonstrating the ability of seers to alter the course of monarchy. She is a figure to be respected and feared, for she is in a rare position of power. In Livy's history, Tanaquil is a maker of kings twice over.[4] She is an ambitious woman whose ambition manifested itself in achieving a political position for her husband. A noblewoman of high birth, she married Lucumo, a man of humble origins and thus disdained by the Etruscans. Tanaquil planned their emigration to Rome, where an eagle descended upon them, took Lucumo's cap, and then replaced it. Tanaquil interpreted the augury as foreshadowing her husband's rise to power. Taking the name Lucius Tarquinius Priscus, he eventually became the fifth king of Rome.[5] A second portent appeared when the head of a sleeping child called Servius Tullius appeared to burst into flame, which dissipated once he awoke; Tanaquil read the sign as indicating the child's future greatness and urged her husband to raise Servius from his state of servitude.[6] Servius eventually married his benefactor's daughter and became the next king. Tanaquil's interpretations of both signs and direct instructions prove her authority. Men, even kings, followed Tanaquil's orders.

Other women are not as publicly involved in Roman religion. The Vestal Virgins are the exception, whose sacrosanct bodies symbolized the impenetrability of Rome's borders. The poet Horace acknowledges that his poetic immortality partially depends upon these women and their protection of the eternal city, proclaiming, "As long as the priest ascends the Capitolium with the silent Virgin, I shall be sung."[7] These six women, born of elite families and dedicated to the goddess Vesta for thirty years of their lives, participated in rituals throughout the calendar year, had designated seats in the theater, rode in a particular type of carriage (*carpentum*) during processions, and were publicly visible on numerous occasions. If one of them betrayed her oath of chastity, Rome was considered vulnerable until the Vestal was buried alive in a ritual expiation of the moral stain she had brought upon the city. The idea of female bodies as sacred symbols of the safety of the city runs parallel to the violation of non-Roman female bodies that often accompanied the sacking of a city. Violence toward the female body represented the Roman conquest of an entire town or land. This schema is echoed in the depiction of Britannia on the Sebasteion at Aphrodisias and in the rape of Boudica's daughters. Boudica uses it against the Romans in her treatment of the Roman women captured on her warpath.

While Tanaquil and the Vestals exhibit two ways in which Roman women displayed authority in the religious sphere, non-Roman women were also recognizably involved in religion. Tacitus notes Germanic women were respected as seers and regarded as semidivine in his *Germania*. After telling of the roles of women on the battlefield, Tacitus writes, "They also believe there is a certain sanctity and prescience in women. They do not despise their counsels, or disregard their responses. Under the divine Vespasian we saw Veleda, considered by many for a long time to have the place of a divinity."[8] Tacitus also records the name of Aurinia as one among many women venerated "not through fawning nor as though they had made them into goddesses."[9] In this admission, Tacitus shows he respects the authority Germanic women hold. Moreover, he admires the fact that these women are honored without sycophancy or sham deifications. Veleda's name, which may be a Latinized form of the Celtic *Veleta*, "poet" or "prophetess," indicates her position.[10] She is a central figure in the Batavian revolt of AD 69/70 and is similar to Dio's Boudica in several aspects.

The Batavian revolt grew out of Gaius Julius Civilis's private grievances and ambitions, as well as his people's distress at being conscripted into the Roman army. Civilis was the chieftain of the Batavi and an officer of the Roman army. His three-part name indicates his Roman citizenship. His group of rebels aimed for independence, but Tacitus implies Civilis's true aim was kingship of his own empire.[11] The Batavians could endure the taxes and conscription into the Roman army imposed upon them, but, similar to the Britons in the *Agricola*, the natives reacted against the wrongs committed by the Romans that accompanied their conquest.[12] Specifically, they desired the freedom to continue to practice traditional customs.[13] The revolt began in a sacred grove during a feast of initiates, and Civilis used the ritual occasion to unite the people to his cause.[14] Veleda, a maiden of the Bructeri people, is already an important religious figure and receives a number of gifts. These include a legate called Munius Lupercus, perhaps intended to be her slave, but he dies on the journey. The sending of gifts is a custom among the Germanic peoples that recognizes Veleda's role as a prophet. Tacitus records, "The authority of Veleda then magnified, for she foretold the success of the Germanic tribes and the destruction of the legions."[15]

Veleda was not a warrior but rather served as seer and advocate. Her accurate prediction of Civilis's initial success augmented her status, since, after her prediction, Civilis captured a Roman legionary base. She also helped Civilis arbitrate between the inhabitants of the Colonia Agrippinensis and the Tencteri tribe.[16] However, the rebels were not universally positive concerning her position. As they debate their future, the lower classes decided that, given the choice of masters, they considered it more honorable to be slaves of the Roman emperor than a Germanic woman, suggesting Veleda.[17] Their sentiments echo those of Cartimandua's Brigantes, who align themselves with her ex-husband, refusing to succumb to a woman's rule.[18] No matter a woman's position, whether a prophetess like Veleda or a queen like Cartimandua, power must be earned and the populace continually mollified.

The narrative of Veleda illustrates the high place of female seers among the Germanic peoples and the honors bestowed on them in the form of gifts and deification. Her ability to interpret signs immediately impacted military decisions, although she was not a military leader. In the Batavian revolt, Civilis was eventually defeated by Petillius Cerialis, familiar to readers of Tacitus as the general who lost part of a legion to the wrath of Boudica's army as they marched from the burning Camulodunum toward Londinium. At some point between Boudica and Civilis, Cerialis learned a degree of diplomacy and offered to pardon Civilis and spare his land.[19] Cerialis was relatively lenient to the rebels. He did not require tribute but reconciled them to Roman rule and conscription in the Roman military. Cerialis offered Veleda asylum if she transferred her loyalty to the Roman people.[20] Veleda submitted.

Veleda and Dio's Boudica are similar for meriting respect as diviners. In the middle of her address to her troops, Boudica paused to perform a ritual: she allowed a hare to escape from a fold in her dress, and, when it ran in an auspicious direction, the entire crowd rejoiced.[21] She then called upon Andraste, thanking her for the positive omen of success.[22] Boudica finished her speech and led her army against the Romans. Roman readers would have recognized the reading of signs as a common prebattle procedure; however, there is no clear archaeological evidence for female prophets in late Iron Age Britain. Dio's Boudica assumes the roles of general and diviner in one.

Boudica's patron goddess is significant. Little is known about the religious practices of the Iceni in the late Iron Age, and the goddess Andraste is otherwise unattested. Elsewhere, Dio refers to the same deity as Andate and claims this is their name for Victory.[23] Some have connected this goddess to Epona, a goddess worshipped in Gaul and Britain as a patroness of horses, the cavalry, and travellers on horseback (see figure 6.1).[24] Other known female deities of Britain were associated with fertility, motherhood, healing, and nature.[25] East Anglia is known for deposits of luxury items in water or in pits or shafts in the ground, such as at Snettisham, which suggest that the Iceni made ritual offerings to their gods. Dio's Boudica eschews such deities and practices. In Dio's text, she is neither wife nor mother, but instead a devotee of Victory.

FIGURE 6.1. The goddess Epona, seated between two ponies. Copper alloy. Found in Wiltshire. The British Museum, London, Great Britain (1882, 1214.1).
Image © The Trustees of the British Museum.

She personifies the meaning of her name and calls on the appropriate goddess for her cause.

A Religious War?

For Tacitus, the connection between Boudica and religion is one of timing: Suetonius Paulinus is at Mona, allowing Boudica's revolt to occur elsewhere. The task remains to determine the potential influence of the Druids on gathering allied forces and the possible connection between Boudica and the Druids as religious figures.[26] Our point of departure is the defeat of the priests, women, and allies on Mona. Tacitus explains, "Afterwards a garrison was set over the conquered and their groves, sacred to savage beliefs, were cut down: for they considered it lawful to anoint the altars with captive blood and to consult the gods with the entrails of men."[27] Sacred groves are key sites of native religious practices for the Druids, for Civilis's men, and for other groups on the continent, including Arminius's rebels, discussed in the next chapter. The devastation of the grove is an extreme measure, an uncommon act of Roman aggression.[28] By cutting down a sacred site, Suetonius symbolically negates the importance of local culture. Tacitus suggests his rationale was the ruination of a site that witnessed human sacrifice. Mona also may have provided a sanctuary for fugitives after the revolt of Caratacus. Suetonius thus sought to eliminate remnants of the earlier conflict; however, his search for military glory results in an excessive expression of malice. He eliminates the site and replaces it with a garrison. As he does so, the sudden mutiny is announced.

The conciseness of Tacitus's account has led some to suggest a cause and effect relationship between Suetonius's destruction and Boudica's revolt that extends beyond the convenience of his absence from Camulodunum.[29] Others have argued the priestly class of Druids was losing prominence at the end of the Iron Age as part of the broader social changes occurring at the time and that they would not have been able to influence the Britons to unite.[30] According to Creighton, the demolition of the Druidic center "is the last time we ever hear of Druids in any significant capacity in Britain or Gaul."[31] Late Iron Age social developments, the changing nature of power in southeast Britain, and the impact of the Romans all contributed to the Druids' loss of influence.[32] Despite their waning importance, the Romans threatened this established native religious order.

Tacitus does not claim religious targeting provided a rationale for revolt, nor does he attach too much significance to the role of the Druids in Boudica's actions. Nevertheless, the Romans' disrespect of the Druids may have contributed to the revolt. The Druids were unattached to a specific "tribe" and thus able to communicate across the island and potentially exert influence.[33] Caesar claimed the entire institution of Druidism was devised in Britain and brought thence to Gaul; those most eager to learn about Druidism went to Britain to study.[34] In Gaul, the Druids were philosophers and educators, arbiters and judges.[35] Pliny the Elder, writing a century after Caesar, saw the Druids as magicians and seers.[36] It is unclear whether they had a role in politics in Britain, but Suetonius's response suggests that the Romans thought they possessed a level of authority. Whereas Augustus had forbidden Roman citizens to become Druids, the emperor Claudius attempted to abolish Druidism among the Gauls as a "cruel and inhuman religion."[37] Such religious intolerance is rare for the Romans and centered on the Druids' supposed rituals of human sacrifice.[38]

Human sacrifice is a common denominator of many non-Roman peoples, and it is cited in Roman texts in order to demonstrate the need for Roman expansion and the acculturation of the natives.[39] However, such citations betray a short historical memory: the senate only outlawed the practice of human sacrifice in 97 BC.[40] Despite the senatorial order, Vestal Virgins condemned for breaking their vow of chastity were still buried alive for centuries, and foreign enemies were publicly executed as the climax of triumphal marches, completing the ritual celebration of Rome's success.[41] Not even Augustus was above suspicion. Dio records rumors of human sacrifice after the surrender of Perusia, when his army beseiged the city and the troops supporting Antony under the leadership of Lucius Antonius and Fulvia in the winter of 41–40 BC. Some leaders obtained pardon, but three hundred equestrians and many senators were put to death, sacrificed at an altar dedicated to Julius Caesar.[42] In Dio's lifetime, Septimius Severus, after defeating Clodius Albinus and his legions from Britain, trampled the body of Albinus with his horse, put Albinus's wife and sons to death, and ordered the bodies of the senators that fought for Albinus mutilated. Motivated by a desire for glory and the necessity of raising funds, he executed dissenters and traitors and confiscated or destroyed their property.[43]

Despite such evidence, the Romans condemned those who practiced human sacrifice and bodily mutilation as uncivilized. Julius Caesar records the sacrificial practice of the Gauls known as the "wicker man," a great image of a man whose hollowed limbs were filled with people and then set aflame.[44] Diodorus Siculus notes the Gauls kept their prisoners for five years and then impaled them in honor of the gods, together with the first fruits of the season, as part of a ritual sacrifice.[45] Pliny the Elder supports the idea that the Gauls performed human sacrifice and thanks the Romans for removing such monstrous religious practices from the world.[46] Tacitus suggests the Druids of Mona read human entrails in a perversion of the practice of haruspicy; Dio's Boudica reads the movements of a hare.

Archaeological evidence for human sacrifice from the time of Boudica has been found in Britain and used to support the ancient texts. In 1984, the body of a man was discovered in a bog in the area where the Brigantes lived. Now known as "Lindow Man," he may have been the victim of a sacrificial ritual.[47] He was in his twenties and in good health when he died, some time between AD 20–90.[48] His death came in three stages: he was bludgeoned twice on the back of the skull, then hanged, and then had his throat slit. The first stage would have killed the man. The three-part killing has led many to propose this was a ritual death, and some argue the man was either a Druid priest or a member of the elite ruling class.[49] Lindow Man suggests death could be part of a ritual practice in late Iron Age Britain around the time of Boudica, and the Romans were perhaps right to be concerned. The question remains as to whether Dio intended to associate Boudica with the Druids, or whether his record of her treatment of captive bodies aimed to provide a reflection on the savagery of similar punishments practiced in Rome.

The Captive Women

In times of war, bodies are tortured, punished, or violated by men in an effort to assert power. Boudica and her army engage in violence against the bodies of the Romans, but they refrain from sexual violation. In contrast to other revolt leaders, Boudica takes no captives. Tacitus reports her army's savage treatment of the Romans: they slaughter them using gallows, fire, and the cross.[50] Significantly, the types of torture and death mentioned in Tacitus's *Annals* are all institutionalized forms of punishment used against slaves in Rome, especially cruci-fixion.[51] The violence cannot be construed as uniquely barbarian, as it echoes Roman practices. The punishments exemplify Boudica's desire for justice: her noble family has been treated like slaves by lower-class Romans, and she punishes them as a master would punish slaves. Her vengeance demonstrates an adaptation of Roman punishments that the Romans should understand, and it becomes a statement of her superior status that the Romans tried to take away.

Dio's Boudica builds a ritual association between the experience of victory and the treatment of the body. After Boudica sacks and plun-ders Camulodunum and Londinium, her army wreaks terrible slaugh-ter. Dio describes the "bestial atrocities" performed on the captives, centering on the women: "for they hung up the noblest and most dis-tinguished women naked, and cut off their breasts and attached them to their mouths, so that they seemed to be eating them, and after that they ran sharp stakes lengthwise through the entire body."[52] The muti-lation of the captives is accompanied by other sacrifices, banquets, and "outrageous behaviors" performed in sacred places, especially the grove of Andate. Dio clarifies, "Thus they called Victory, and they revered her most exceptionally."[53]

Boudica's army sacrifices female captives in a ritualistic manner in thanksgiving for their victory. This sacrifice plays into Dio's focus on the female body as the center of Boudica's power. By destroying these bodies, Boudica symbolically destroys the potential for the growth and prosperity of the Romans in Britain. The sacrifice within the sacred grove indicates the bodies are being treated in a ritualistic manner, as part of the celebrations after a successful siege. The noblewomen are selected as worthy tribute to a female goddess. The physical mutilation of their bodies symbolizes cannibalism and specifically eating oneself in the attachment of the breasts to the women's mouths, and sexual penetration through their impalement. The image of the women eating their breasts creates a specific self-destructive cannibalism whereby the parts of the body that symbolize motherhood, sexuality, and reproduc-tion are destroyed.

Dio's horrific account has clear ties to narratives of the treatment of captives and victims elsewhere, including Rome. Boudica's treatment of the noblewomen becomes more significant if readers consider Dio's use of the female body elsewhere in his text. Boudica's army attacks the body parts celebrated in Dio's history as symbols of the productivity and continuity of Rome. In his narrative of early Rome, women like Hersilia and the mother of Coriolanus bared their breasts in order to remind the Romans of their motherhood, fertility, and the future of Rome. These women succeeded and provided positive examples of women acting in public for the good of the state, using their bodies as proof of their feminine virtues. With Boudica, Dio excises all references to motherhood that were so central to Tacitus's interpretation. Boudica's devotion to a female goddess of Victory rather than fertility, chastity, or motherhood is reflected in her masculine appearance, in her condemnation of the effeminate bodies of the Roman men, and in her treatment of the female captives. These women attest to the increasing Roman presence in Britain. They are the wives of the veterans, traders, and merchants, as well as native women that allied themselves with their conquerors.[54] The destruction of their bodies is impious and vengeful by Roman standards, but the lesson is clear: besides halting the Roman army's incursion into Britain, Boudica's revolt aimed to erase the Roman presence, as well as their ability to remain. The destruction of the towns suggests this erasure is possible; the mutilation of the bodies strikes at the heart of Roman values and Roman desires for imperialist expansion and productivity.

The Roman Response

Suetonius Paulinus interprets the violence of the Britons' rituals as comparable to tyranny. After hearing of Boudica's attack on Camulodunum, Suetonius Paulinus rushes from Mona, advises everyone to abandon Londinium, chooses a battlefield, and prepares for battle. In Dio's history, his prebattle speech draws an implicit connection to the Rome of Nero, aligning Boudica's treatment of bodies in war to that of the citizen body during the reign of a tyrant. Unlike Tacitus's *Annals*, which transmits the two speeches one after the other, Dio delays Suetonius's exhortation from that of Boudica and separates his speech into three separate addresses, presented to three divisions of troops. To the first group of soldiers, he emphasizes the superior military training of his men, urging them not to fear the overwhelming number of Britons: the rebels were able to destroy two cities merely because Camulodunum was betrayed and Londinium abandoned.[55] To the second division, Suetonius urges courage, and he promises one battle can recover what they lost. They should rule without fear and become examples for posterity. Since they have it in their power to do so, they should choose "to be free, to rule, to be wealthy, and to be prosperous."[56] To the third division, Suetonius suggests his men will suffer the kinds of outrage and torture the other captives suffered if they lose, adding, "it is better that we fall fighting courageously than be captured and impaled, to see our own entrails cut out, to be skewered on red-hot stakes, to die by being melted in boiling water, to suffer as if thrown to wild, lawless, impious beasts."[57]

Suetonius defines the treatment of the captives as torture and overlooks the significance of the violence as integral to a ritual of victory. The forms of torture he mentions would be familiar to a Roman audience that had witnessed the rage of a tyrant—the emperors Nero or Domitian of the first century, or Commodus or Caracalla during Dio's lifetime. Suetonius's threats are particularly reminiscent of the actions of Nero, known for his temper and his savage treatment of suspected or confirmed traitors. Nero's tutor, Seneca, listed the numerous fears a public official faced with the emperor's suspicion or displeasure, which included death by fire, the sword, chains, wild beasts, crucifixion, the rack, the hook, impaling stakes, chariots that tore victims apart, and clothing smeared with pitch and set ablaze.[58] Such torments illustrate the exceptional cruelty of a man led by emotion rather than morality, and they were utilized with especial force after the great fire of Rome in AD 64. According to Tacitus, in order to stop the rumor that Nero had started the fire, the emperor blamed the Christians. As punishment, Christians were crucified, torn apart by wild animals, and set on fire. The religious group was already infamous for what Tacitus calls "abominations" (*per flagitia*) and a "destructive superstition" (*exitiabilis superstitio*) that did not fade after the death of Jesus, but rather spread from Judaea to Rome.[59] A multitude was convicted, not really for setting the fire, but rather for their "hatred of the human race" (*odio humani generis*).[60] Their fates are emblematic of the type of cruelty to which Nero descended in the latter part of his reign, and the populace eventually pitied the Christians who were being punished "not for the public good, but out of the savagery of one man."[61]

The punishment of the Christians illustrates the tortures the emperor was capable of employing against a perceived threat. The Christians were blamed less for the fire than for the introduction of new religious beliefs. Religious intolerance, rare in the history of the Roman

Empire, reared its ugly head in the time of Nero, and both the Druids of Mona and the Christians in Rome fell victim to his wrath. Whereas Boudica's army destroyed the bodies of the noblewomen as part of a grotesque ritual, Nero condemned the Christians to become part of a perverse spectacle of entertainment, and even his audience of Romans recognized the excess of his actions.

Death and Dispersal

In his speech to the Roman army, Suetonius draws a comparison with the actions of a Roman tyrant, characterizing the enemy as slaves, as well as wild beasts. Through dehumanizing the enemy, Suetonius echoes stereotypes of the Britons present in earlier sources. He argues that the gods, experience, and prestige are all on the Romans' side. They must conquer or die, making Britain a noble monument, with the bodies of the fallen forever possessing the land.[62] The final battle that follows juxtaposes the chaos of the Britons against the precision of the Romans. Boudica is not mentioned. When the Britons retreat, they are hemmed in by the women, watching from the sidelines. As if in reparation for the deaths of their women, Suetonius's army slaughters them all. After their loss, the Britons regroup, but Boudica gets sick and dies in the meantime. Her death effectively ends the revolt, proving her symbolic value as the figurehead of the resistance. The Britons give her a lavish burial and disperse, regarding themselves as defeated.[63] Although Dio does not record the rituals that accompanied her burial, he suggests Boudica was sent to her next life in splendor.[64]

7

The Wolf and the Hare

Although Boudica's revolt occurred on the outskirts of the known world, ancient accounts still conform to certain expectations of conflict narratives. Tacitus and Dio draw upon similar tropes in order to evoke pathos for the victims, while at the same time promoting the inevitability of Roman imperial expansion. Literary allusions connect Boudica to other resistance movements in the early Roman Empire. Boudica gains thematic import as an integral part of both Tacitus's and Dio's reflections on the nature of Roman provincial governance and the Roman presence on the edges of the empire. While she may seem a temporary roadblock on the highway of Roman imperial progress, authors allude to other revolts in order to emphasize the political and cultural ramifications of her actions. Comparing her revolt to other native revolts demonstrates both the sameness of provincial uprisings as well as the uniqueness of Boudica as an individual. Boudica stands out for her characterization as a positive model of both *virtus* and Roman Republican motherhood, setting her apart from her male predecessors. By placing Boudica within the context of native revolts, the function of her character in a broader literary discourse emerges, as well as the significance of her actions, despite the lack of long-term results.

Boudica and the History of Native Resistance

Revolts are relatively rare in the early Roman Empire and stem from ubiquitous problems with the negotiation of power between Rome and her provinces. The early stages of Roman military and administrative control are fraught with difficulties resulting from the negotiation of power and leadership between Rome and her subjects. Roman administration altered the lives of the elites and those originally in power, and it oppressed the common people through taxes and other forms of tribute. Roman building projects and other lifestyle markers threatened the cultural identity of the conquered. In his comparison of five revolts, Dyson emphasizes that resistance arises after the native populations have been conquered and are experiencing the impact of the Romans.[1] Numerous factors combine to allow for an individual, charismatic leader to rise from the ranks and inspire a people to revolt. Boudica is unique as a female leader, and this influences the way in which her revolt is discussed.

Three general issues lie at the core of many rebellions and emerge with special force in the narrative of Boudica. One rationale is a perceived Roman avarice that exceeds expectations and is therefore intolerable. The Frisians, for example, revolted in AD 28 because they regarded the tribute required of them as proof of overwhelming greed. The Romans took possession of their herds, then their fields, then enslaved their wives and children. When rage and protest failed, the Frisians went to war.[2] The second reason for rebellion arises from the transmission of power among ruling families. The royal families of Armenia and Parthia, whose power struggles are transmitted in book 12 of Tacitus's *Annals*, are used to comment upon the failures of the very idea of dynastic power.[3] Through reporting on the provinces, Tacitus offers a comparable, subtle critique of the imperial family and the continuation of the Julio-Claudian dynasty in Rome.[4] Tacitus creates conversations between Roman and non-Roman leaders in order to reflect upon the nature of leadership itself. In the midst of the conflict between Armenia and Parthia, the client king Meherdates seeks guidance from the emperor Claudius. Claudius advises Meherdates to take the position of a guide toward his citizens rather than a master toward his slaves, and to strive for clemency and justice. He explains, "These are unknown to barbarians and therefore all the more welcoming."[5] Claudius's comment is ironic, given his own subjective administration of justice and susceptibility to the desires of his wives and freedmen.[6] He assumes non-Romans are fickle and liable to betrayal, and advocates pardon and peace as the best way forward.[7] His attitude illustrates the third main reason for rebellion: the desire for freedom from servitude to any master.

Boudica's revolt incorporates the various rationales for rebellion, and Boudica herself provides a rallying point for those disgusted and disenchanted with the Roman governance of Britain. In Tacitus's historical overview of the Romans in Britain, Boudica's revolt follows that of Caratacus and continues his cause. She responds to the overarching complaints of the Britons and provides leadership and unity. In Dio's history, Boudica places herself within the context of the Romans in Britain, and she argues that the servitude she and her forces face is their own fault: they should have expelled the Romans as soon as they arrived, as their ancestors had done to Julius Caesar.[8] The isolation of Britain should have kept it safe from attack; however, the Romans' insatiable greed overcame even their aversion to crossing the Ocean.

The theme of Roman avarice at the cost of native freedom runs throughout Boudica's narrative, aligning her closely with two revolts that rocked the Roman Empire at the beginning of the first century: the revolt of Bato in Illyricum in AD 6–9 and the rebellion of Arminius in Germania in AD 9. Dio and Tacitus subtly refer to these revolts, placing Boudica on par with the earlier conflicts. Boudica echoes the earlier leaders' views on freedom and their harsh critiques of Roman imperialism as an exercise in unwarranted cruelty and the willful rejection of native cultures. Like Arminius or Bato, Boudica had the potential to stem the advance of the Romans and to destroy cultural and architectural inroads already made. Boudica brought attention to failures in provincial governorship and had the potential to have a disastrous impact on Roman expansion and control.

Boudica and Bato

The biographer Suetonius regarded the *Bellum Batonianum* of AD 6–9 (known as the Illyrian, Dalmatian, or Dalmatian-Pannonian rebellion) as the gravest foreign conflict the Romans faced, after the Punic Wars.[9] The geographical area had been contested from the time of Caesar onward. As in Britain, the inhabitants were familiar with some aspects of Roman culture, including the Latin language, but were uneasy with the requirements of their subjugation.[10] The uprising began when the Daesitiates, led by Bato, refused to join Tiberius in his war against the Germanic tribes. The Daesitiates were joined by the Breuci, led by a different Bato, as well as the Dalmatians, Pannonians, and others.[11] As with Boudica's united army, this was a rare occasion in which various peoples came together against a common enemy. The future emperor Tiberius faced the rebels after sending Marcus Valerius Messalla Messallinus, governor of Dalmatia and Pannonia, ahead of him. Tiberius eventually brought his entire forces from Germany, and Augustus sent his grandson Germanicus (Tiberius's nephew) with an army of conscripted freedmen to join him. The Roman army grew to fifteen legions and auxiliaries, totaling around one hundred thousand men and including the majority of Rome's forces. The revolt involved few pitched battles: the rebels, like the Britons, were adept at using guerrilla tactics, concealing themselves in the woodlands and hills and raiding the Romans. Nevertheless, the Romans wore them down. Bato the Breucian was defeated in AD 8 and put to death; Bato of the Daesitiates held out for another year.

After both sides suffered heavy losses, Tiberius and his army eventually besieged Bato's stronghold at Andetrium (near modern Gornji Múc, Croatia), routing the army. According to Dio, the army fled to the mountainsides, and the Romans hunted them down "like wild animals."[12] The retreat of the rebel army did not demand mass destruction, but the dehumanizing of the enemy into wild animals may have facilitated the actions of the Romans. By creating an uncivilized, wild enemy, a massacre seemed less morally contentious. Germanicus pursued the deserters to Arduba (perhaps modern Vranduk, Bosnia and Herzegovina), the final site of resistance. A dispute arose between those seeking sanctuary and the inhabitants as to whether they should continue the resistance. According to Dio, the women "desired freedom, contrary to the opinion of the men, and were prepared to endure anything other than servitude."[13] In the ensuing battle, the women grabbed their children and either threw themselves into the flames of the burning city or cast themselves into the river. Germanicus took the city, and the surrounding areas made peace with Rome. Bato surrendered. He sent his son to Tiberius as a pledge of peace, and he then arrived and spoke in defense of his people, seeking clemency for his men but nothing for himself. Dio records, "In the end, when asked by Tiberius, 'Why did it seem best to you to revolt and wage war against us for such a long time?' He replied, 'You are the cause of this. For you send as guardians of your flocks neither dogs nor shepherds, but wolves.'"[14]

Several similarities present themselves between the burning of Arduba, the speech of Bato, and the revolts in Britain. While both Bato and Boudica emphasize the necessity for freedom, Bato's idea of *libertas* is gendered. For him, servitude is conscription into the Roman army and the heavy burden of taxation. In his defense, Bato rationalizes his revolt through condemning Rome's wretched treatment of the native populations in the provinces. After creating a province, Rome sent poor administrators, characterized by Bato as aggressive wild beasts rather than protective shepherds. Bato's metaphor gains significance when compared to Boudica's speech in Dio. At the end of her speech, Boudica denounces the weaknesses of the Roman army in comparison to the strength of her people, and ends her exhortation by proclaiming, "Let us show them they are hares and foxes trying to rule over dogs and wolves!"[15] She commands her warriors to view themselves as the antagonists, fierce protectors of their territory and defenders of their pack. The metaphor is that of hunter versus the hunted, and it reverses Dio's characterization of the Romans as hunters of the wild rebels in the Illyrian rebellion. Boudica substitutes the Iceni and their allies for the Romans as the aggressors against foreign insurgents. By setting herself up as the alpha female, Boudica re-emphasizes the difference between her methods and those of the other leaders she alludes to in her speech, from the defensive policies of the Babylonian queens to Cartimandua's client queenship.

Set next to each other, Boudica and Bato react against analogous abuses in provincial administration. Bato and his men revolt against extreme taxation, conscription into the Roman army, and food short-ages. Boudica likewise resists servitude caused by crippling taxation and the recall of loans. Both reject the cruelty of the Romans and their imperialist strategy, which sought to gain lands and peoples indiscrim-inately, without a consistent or clear plan of integration or acceptance. The lack of integration is perhaps best demonstrated by the reactions of the women. For the women at Arduba, it seems any form of Roman rule would constitute servitude. The women express their devotion to free-dom and prefer death to servitude.[16] Tacitus's Boudica gives a similar statement, and, unlike Bato, chooses death before surrender.

Boudica and the Varian Disaster

The end of Bato's revolt becomes increasingly significant as a Roman victory when juxtaposed with the Varian defeat of the same year. When Tiberius left Germania to address the revolt of Bato, the vast redeploy-ment of the Roman military left the area around the Rhine vulnerable.

In AD 9, Rome suffered a devastating military defeat known as the *clades Variana* (Varian disaster).[17] When Tiberius returned to Rome a hero, he found the city in mourning and postponed his triumph out of respect. The defeat of Bato gained prestige as the Romans considered the alternate outcome: had he not been defeated, Bato would have surely joined Arminius, the general responsible for this disaster, and attacked Rome.[18] Together, these two men and their vast armies might have had a chance at dismantling the empire.[19] Tacitus characterizes Boudica's revolt as a *clades* at multiple points in his narrative, suggesting a similar potential; an overview of the Varian disaster allows readers greater insight into Tacitus's representation of Boudica and the impact of her rebellion.

The revolt in Germany arose in part due to the unwanted influence of the Romans. The area inhabited by Arminius and his allies was experiencing swift cultural change with the presence of the Romans. Dio records,

> The barbarians were adapting themselves to Roman customs and becoming used to markets and making peaceful assemblies. They had not yet forgotten the ways of their ancestors and native habits and life of independence and the power from having arms. As long as they were unlearning these things slowly and in some ways under watch, they were not disturbed by the change in lifestyle and were changing themselves unknowingly.[20]

According to Dio, the natives fail to realize the impact of the Romans and are unfazed as long as they still have the right to arms and a sense of independence. However, the corrupt governor, Publius Quinctilius Varus, forces the Germanic peoples to conform to Roman customs with an unwarranted rapidity. Varus gives orders as if addressing slaves and exacts money as if from a subject nation.[21] These actions instigate a feeling of resentment and the Germanic peoples' sense of their own servitude.

The rebellion is spearheaded by Arminius, a Roman citizen of Germanic origin, who had been sent as a tribute and educated in Rome after the campaigns of Livia's son Drusus in 11–9 BC. He was well regarded by the Romans and eventually became a commander of Varus's auxiliary forces. Tacitus calls him a "true friend."[22] However, Arminius sought freedom—to him, even service in the Roman army was just another form of slavery.[23] Behind Varus's back, he organized an alliance of several Germanic peoples, including the Cherusci and the Chatti. His understanding of the Roman military allowed him to capitalize on the Romans' inability to withstand guerrilla tactics, and to arrange his own army in a Roman military fashion.[24] The mass of Roman troops on the Rhine prevented him from revolting openly, so he invited Varus to the land of the Cherusci, who acted so submissively they succeeded in convincing Varus they would remain peaceful without the presence of soldiers.[25] Various portents warned of the danger to come, including a statue of Victory in the province of Germany that turned from facing enemy territory to facing Italy.[26] The meaning of the portent is similar to that of the fallen Victory statue in Camulodunum: the gods had turned their back on the Romans.[27] Portents notwithstanding, Varus was taken completely unawares. Arminius tricked Varus into advancing on an unfamiliar path to put down a feigned uprising and removed himself on the pretense of needing to assemble his allied forces. His army attacked the Romans as they marched through the swampy Teutoburg forest. Over the next few days three whole legions perished, between fifteen thousand and twenty thousand men, and their bodies were left to rot. Survivors were ransomed or enslaved.[28] Officers took their own lives, while others were sacrificed in a religious ceremony, their bones cooked and used in rituals.[29] Varus committed suicide. Rome went into mourning.

The Varian disaster was memorialized as the worst defeat of the reign of Augustus. Augustus regarded the loss as a disgrace, and it allowed his detractors to critique his peaceful reign as "stained with blood."[30] Furthermore, Arminius's annihilation of the Roman army effectively ended the Roman advancement north of the Rhine. The Teutoburg forest became a grotesque site of human sacrifice and a military graveyard. Vengeance came a year after Augustus died.[31] In AD 15, after quelling a mutiny of his troops on the Rhine, Germanicus marched on the Chatti, taking them by surprise. He encouraged widespread slaughter of even women and the elderly, in an attempt to transform his men's guilt over their own recent mutiny into glory.[32] Arminius's father-in-law, Segestes, submitted with a band of kinsmen and dependents, including his daughter Thusnelda.[33] Segestes and his kin were provided a home, and Thusnelda gave birth to a son in Ravenna.[34] Strabo records that Thusnelda and her son, Thumelicus, were paraded through Rome in

Germanicus's triumphal procession, while Segestes observed as a guest of honor.[35] Arminius was enraged that his wife and child had become hostages, and he went to war.[36]

In the most poignant flashback of his corpus, Tacitus recounts Germanicus's visit to the Teutoburg forest, where evidence of the Varian disaster remained untouched.[37] The ground was strewn with weapons and unburied bones, severed heads were nailed to trees, and, in the nearby groves, altars stood where the tribunes and centurions of first rank had been immolated.[38] The ritualistic sacrifice of the leading members of the Roman army is reminiscent of Boudica's treatment of the female bodies and the violence with which captives might be dispatched. Prior to engaging in battle, Germanicus and his army bury the bodies and pay homage to the dead.[39]

At the time of Germanicus's march through the Teutoberg forest, Arminius had been in power for twelve years.[40] He was defeated in the following year, and two of the three standards of the legions lost in AD 9 were recovered.[41] An arch was built near the Temple of Saturn in Rome in recognition of Germanicus's recovery of one of these standards.[42] Under Claudius, Publius Gabinius recovered the last remaining legionary eagle from the defeat from the hands of the enemy.[43] The Rhine continued to form a geographical border for the north of the Roman Empire. Client kings controlled areas east of the Rhine and north of the Danube.

Arminius's campaigns contrast the absolute success and brutality of the Varian disaster with the betrayal of his father-in-law, Segestes, and the capture of his pregnant wife, a noblewoman who displayed "the spirit of her husband rather than that of her father."[44] The loss of Thusnelda meant that Arminius's son would be raised by the Romans as a hostage, as he had been. The second half of Arminius's tale focuses on the negative impact of the Romans on Arminius's family. His fears are realized years later, when the Cherusci ask Rome for a client king and are presented with Italicus, Arminius's nephew. Italicus is distrusted because he was raised in Rome. The Cherusci complain that even Arminius's son would not have been trusted, as he would have been corrupted "by the bread of dependence, by slavery, by luxury, by all foreign habits."[45] Their statement implies Arminius's son died before he could rule, but their anxieties are clear: once a child is taken hostage, he is a foreigner to his own people, an instrument of imperial control.

Tacitus's repeated references to the *clades Variana* establish this disaster as the event to which all other revolts are compared.[46] It was the conflict that effectively ended the Roman expansion to the north and established Arminius as the "liberator of Germany."[47] This loss led Augustus to advise Tiberius to confine the empire within its current limits, and Tiberius followed his advice.[48] The slaughter might have been prevented had Tiberius been able to remain in Germany instead of leaving for Illyria, or if Varus had been less arrogant and autocratic.[49]

Tacitus draws upon the memory of Varus in elucidating the complaints of the Britons in the *Agricola*. Observing their numbers, they proclaim, "Thus the Germanic tribes had shaken free from the yoke, defended by only a river, not the Ocean!"[50] Their observation highlights the geographical isolation of Britain, as well as their superior numbers of warriors. By placing reminders of Varus within the mouths of Britons, Tacitus suggests this defeat was (or should be) universally known and remembered. The Britons call to mind the success of the unified Germanic peoples in order to place their actions on a similar plane.

Tacitus builds on his reference in his *Annals*, where he introduces Boudica's rebellion as another *gravis clades* (grievous disaster).[51] This term creates an immediate linguistic affinity with the former revolt, suggesting Boudica could have stemmed the Roman expansion, as Arminius had done. Tacitus repeats the term *clades* to describe the devastating attack on Petillius Cerialis and his Ninth Legion after the burning of Camulodunum, as well as the destruction of Verulamium.[52] The repetition acknowledges the impact of Boudica's rebellion and her use of surprise attacks to great success. In his account of the life of Nero, the biographer Suetonius likewise refers to the rebellion as a *clades*, and Dio uses a Greek equivalent, labeling the revolt a πάθος δεινόν (emotionally shattering disaster).[53]

Tacitus aligns the two revolts as well as their leaders, indicating the powerful potential of Boudica's revolt to stem the Roman imperial progress, while suggesting readers sympathize with both leaders as individuals whose families have been adversely impacted by the Romans. Both Boudica and Arminius destroyed legions and sacrificed Roman captives; both revolts depended upon a charismatic leader, and both leaders initially took the foreign enemy by surprise. Furthermore, both leaders are disgusted and dismayed at the treatment of their family members at the hands of the Romans, adding personal injury to political reasons for revolt. Both fear for their children, Boudica for the chastity of her daughters, Arminius for the future of his son: the loss of chastity for a girl and the upbringing of a son in Rome compromise each child's potential to continue a dynasty and rule in his or her native land. For these leaders, the presence of the Romans has proven destructive to family, loyalty, and the values of their people, leaving no choice but revolt.

The End of the Iceni: Suetonius's Revenge

The true test of Boudica's impact is in the reception of her revolt. Boudica dies and is buried splendidly, even though her rebellion fails. Boudica's death and the defeat of her army result in the immediate dispersal of the survivors, mass famine, and Roman vengeance. After this conclusion to the affairs in Britain, Dio's narrative returns to Rome, to the exile and death of the empress Octavia and to Nero's marriage to the domineering, immoral beauty, Poppaea Sabina. Boudica's reflections on gender, power, and the effect of Nero's effeminacy on the Roman populace provide a subtle foreshadowing of events to come in Rome. Boudica recognized the characteristics of poor leadership and presented an alternative model. However, her ultimate loss on the battlefield undermines the power of her words, and her revolt results in increased Roman activity in Britain rather than the empowerment of the Britons.

Tacitus records that the rebellion continued until the replacement of Suetonius Paulinus, even though it had lost its superior numbers and strength. Tacitus acknowledges the memory of Boudica remained powerful and influenced events in Britain. Upon hearing of the barbarian defeat, Poenius Postumus, the camp prefect who refused to bring his legion to assist Suetonius, threw himself on his sword. His suicide results from shame, as Postumus refused to allow his soldiers to seek glory.[54] His death is juxtaposed with the admirable model provided by Boudica. Poenius is dishonored in death, while Boudica's suicide proves her *virtus*. After her death, reinforcements are sent from Germany to assist in the completion of the war. Fire, the sword, and famine combine to defeat the barbarian forces.[55] Suetonius treats the rebellion as a personal injury, and his cruelty is hubristic rather than triumphant, vengeful and open to criticism.[56] Although he successfully returned the Britons to a state of servitude, his actions are morally flawed.

Julius Classicianus, who may have been a Gaul by birth, soon replaced Catus as procurator.[57] His enmity with Suetonius caused him to send notice to Rome that the fighting would never cease as long as

Suetonius remained. Accordingly, Nero sent the freedman Polyclitus to establish a concord between Suetonius and Classicianus, and to resolve the rebellion.[58] Polyclitus was a terror to the Roman army in Britain but a source of laughter for the natives, who could not believe a freedman had such power over a general and his army, and could reduce them to a state of servitude.[59] Tacitus uses the same language as at the opening of the revolt, when the noblemen of the Iceni were reduced to servitude by the slaves of one of their two Roman masters. The conflict is framed by the same issue: men of higher status are forced to obey those of lower status. The barbarians are discomfited by the negation of social order in the exertion of authority, and their reaction points toward the indignity of Suetonius's dismissal from his governorship. Petronius Turpilianus replaces Suetonius, and lazy inaction replaces rebellion, although they call it "peace."[60] Thus concludes Tacitus's account.

Within his narrative, Tacitus invites readers to interpret Suetonius's governorship in contrast to the leadership shown by Gnaeus Domitius Corbulo. Tacitus's detailed narrative of Boudica in the *Annals* falls between his accounts of Corbulo's actions in the east between AD 58–63. Together, the military activities in Parthia and Armenia and the revolt in Britain form the core of Nero's foreign measures. Nero manages foreign affairs through his magistrates, Corbulo in the east and Suetonius in Britain, and the two men employ opposing forms of diplomacy toward those living in the provinces. Corbulo had been successful as a general in Lower Germany during the reign of Claudius, earning fame for his strictness and for his management of rebellions of the Chauci and Cherusci.[61] When Vologaeses and his Parthians ousted Radamistus from his throne in Armenia and replaced him with Tiridates in AD 54, the seventeen-year-old Nero took an initial interest in foreign affairs and was praised for appointing Corbulo as the general responsible for securing Armenia.[62] Allied kings readily obeyed the noble Corbulo,[63] and in AD 58 he was able to conquer Tiridates and destroy Artaxata, earning Nero a triumph.[64] Corbulo showed clemency to those who surrendered, killed those who resisted, and captured the city of Legerda before being replaced by Tigranes, a Cappadocian brought up in Rome as a hostage.[65] Corbulo was sent to Syria, and Tacitus's narrative moves from the east to the far west, to the revolt of Boudica. He returns to the affairs in Parthia and Armenia in the opening of book 15. Lucius Caesennius Paetus, governor of Cappadocia, fails to bring Armenia under Roman control, and his loss is so complete that it lessens Corbulo's glory. Corbulo secures

Syria, regains command from Paetus, and comes to an understanding with Vologaeses to evacuate Armenia and reinstate Tiridates.[66] This truce is interpreted as a triumph, and victory monuments over the Parthians are set up in Rome.[67] The treaty fails and Corbulo threatens war; a new treaty is established with Tiridates and Vologaeses. Tiridates trusts in Corbulo and places his diadem before a statue of Nero, with the expectation that he will receive it back from Nero if he journeys to Rome as a suppliant.[68] According to Dio, the Romans thought Corbulo would attempt a political coup and become the next emperor. However, he never made a move toward a political takeover, and Tiridates mockingly called him Nero's slave.[69] Eventually, Nero became suspicious and ordered his death in AD 67. Corbulo chose suicide instead.[70]

Tacitus's narrative of Corbulo focuses on the difference between truth and speciousness.[71] The victory monuments over the Parthians and Tiridates's symbolic placement of his diadem before the statue are all empty signs that project a false image of the power of the Roman emperor. Tacitus centers on the theme of appearance versus truth to indict Nero's foreign policy. Nevertheless, he praises Corbulo's method of dealing with the Parthians: he treats them like his own troops, severely punishing the intransigent, while acting kindly toward those who obey.[72] When the city of Tigranocerta welcomes Corbulo with a golden circlet, Corbulo leaves them untouched, "so that they would retain more readily their complaisance."[73] After the annihilation of Artaxata, Corbulo's clemency secures him a reputation for justice. Those he has conquered are compliant and trust his advice. Thus, while deception and false appearances underlie the narrative, Corbulo's glory is founded on true military victories and diplomacy. Corbulo emerges as a strong general and respected leader, whose only fault was to keep faith with Nero.

Perhaps surprisingly, Corbulo does not have a set speech in the *Annals*. His strict management of his army and negotiations with Vologaeses and Tiridates are more central to his characterization than a prebattle exhortation. Instead, in the midst of affairs in Parthia, Tacitus presents his readers with the narrative of Boudica and her concise declaration against Roman greed, in contrast to Suetonius's untiring search for glory. Despite his overall success in defeating the rebellion, Suetonius did not return to Rome in triumph. No observable commemoration of Suetonius's victory over Boudica exists in Rome—no sizeable monuments or account of a triumphal procession—which seems adverse to the spirit of Neronian Rome and the emperor's love of spectacle.[74] Nero may have distributed a donative in Suetonius's name, as indicated by lead tesserae with NERO CAESAR on the obverse and PAULLINI on the reverse.[75] The absence of a triumph may have been intended to promote the swift reintegration of Britain into the Empire, rather than to make Britain into an example of defeat.[76] The reintegration included an increased presence of the Roman military, the rebuilding of Camulodunum and Verulamium, and the development of Londinium into a provincial capital. Native resistance continued to simmer, boiling over during the governorship of Agricola twenty years after Boudica's defeat.

Calgacus's Reception of Boudica

The reception of Boudica begins at the moment of her death. Boudica's revolt is mentioned once more in Tacitus's works as an example of the Britons' ability to unite against the Roman incursion into their native lands. After rebuilding the sites destroyed by Boudica, the Romans expanded further into Britain during the Flavian era when Agricola was governor. They met with resistance from Venutius of the Brigantes and Calgacus, leader of the Caledonians. Boudica's revolt introduced many issues that resurface during the governorship of Agricola, inviting readers to see Agricola as a positive model where Suetonius failed, and to see Calgacus as a new Caratacus or Boudica, facing similar concerns. Agricola attempted to expand the power of Rome into the land of the Caledonians in the far northwest.[77] In the *Agricola*, the grievances of Boudica's Britons are repeated in the speech of Calgacus, suggesting that not much changed in the years following the revolt.[78]

Scholars have interpreted Calgacus as a representative of traditional Roman values of the Republic, even though he is a fierce Briton. He becomes a symbol of courage in his fight against Roman imperialism and displays the *virtus* of a good man operating under a tyrant, like Agricola with Domitian. Before the final confrontation with Agricola and his army at Mons Graupius in AD 83, Calgacus harangues his troops, emphasizing the need for freedom over slavery and condemning the Romans for striving to conquer the very edges of the world.[79] He denounces the Romans as the "robbers of the world" (*raptores orbis*) who lust for total dominion.[80] He states, "To robbery, slaughter, plunder, they attach the false name of empire [*imperium*]; they make a desert and call it peace."[81] Calgacus, like Boudica, is concerned with the impact of the Romans on family life, especially women and children. He continues, "Nature has willed it that each man's children and his kin be dearest; these are stolen through conscriptions to serve elsewhere; our wives and sisters, even if they escape enemy lust, are defiled under the name of friendship and hospitality."[82] For Calgacus, living under Roman rule has caused a rupture in language, in which words have lost their true meaning. Robbery and slaughter are forms of *imperium*; a desert or wilderness is peace; the destruction of family life is another form of hospitality. All are cast into various forms of servitude, whether conscripted into the army or sent as hostages to Rome. Those left behind must pay taxes and work the land, and are dissuaded from displays of courage.

Calgacus calls upon his troops to live again as an unconquered people, citing the revolt of Boudica as evidence of the Britons' ability to rise up against Rome. He proclaims, "The Brigantes, with a woman as their commander, were able to burn a colony, take a camp by assault, and, if success had not turned to carelessness [*in socordiam*], to cast off the yoke."[83] Tacitus mistakes the Iceni for the Brigantes, but his reference is clear.[84] Boudica is once more identified as a commander woman (*femina duce*). However, Calgacus accuses her army of celebrating too soon: their good fortune bred carelessness, laziness, or stupidity (all implications are present in the phrase, *in socordiam*), and Calgacus blames them for not throwing off the yoke of servitude completely. He contrasts her army with his unconquered men, the select heroes of Caledonia. Tacitus's Calgacus relies on Roman stereotypes about women in power, who are either too stupid to lead or too careless to finish what they started. Additionally, he discounts the bravery of the Romans and their allies, and he suggests the Gauls, Germans, and Britons fighting with the Romans will come to his side once their fear turns to hate. He cites wives, parents, and country as the main incentives to fight,[85] and, in closing, asks his troops to remember their ancestors and descendants as they march into battle.[86]

Calgacus's speech is received favorably, with the shouts, songs, and discordant cries typical of barbarians.[87] Yet, Calgacus also loses to the Romans, and his army falls apart. Despite their enthusiasm and the powerful omnipresence of Calgacus on the battlefield, Agricola wins.[88] The problem with Calgacus is the same as that with Boudica. The issue is not based on gender, but the failures of Britons to plan pitched battles. The aftermath causes readers to reconsider Calgacus's devotion to family. As men and women wail indiscriminately, rage continues to drive their actions: "sometimes they were broken to pieces by the sight of their loved ones, more often agitated, and most writers agree that certain men took out their rage against their wives and children, as though they pitied them."[89] After defeat, family becomes the biggest loser; the mercy killings are not unique in Latin historiography, but are especially poignant when compared with the prebattle narrative.[90] Calgacus's speech dramatizes the connection between family and freedom and the pitiable results when his army loses both at the same time.

Caledonian Wit

After the battle of Mons Graupius, Agricola was recalled to Rome by Domitian. Five years later, Domitian headed for the Rhine and the Danube, but not Britain. Tacitus treats this oversight as a failure. According to the opening of Tacitus's *Histories*, Britain was "conquered, and quickly abandoned," implying a withdrawal of forces from much of the land Agricola had gained.[91] In the opening of his *Agricola*, Tacitus suggests the principate was characterized by servitude from its foundations through the rule of Domitian. The brief reign of Nerva was the first time in which the principate and *libertas* coexisted.[92] For those living on the edges of empire prior to Nerva, the choices were few: submit or resist, win or die trying. Rebel leaders rarely consider the alternatives— going to Rome in exile, sending children as hostages, becoming client regents—as viable options. These are just alternate forms of servitude. As in so many resistance narratives, Boudica's fight combined political and economic issues with moral ones. Her values were threatened by the Romans, by the luxurious lifestyles of the men, and the immorality of the imperial women.

After the period covered by Tacitus's texts, the Romans were driven back by the Caledonian tribes in the north in AD 117, and Hadrian built his wall, slicing Britain in two. Antoninus Pius built his own fortification further north. As conflict continued to plague the island, one final episode recorded by Dio suggests Boudica's values retained their efficacy long after her lifetime. After reporting the death of the emperor Septimius Severus, Dio discusses his lasting policies and impact, including laws on adultery that were rarely implemented. He elaborates with a moment from the life of Julia Domna, the wife of Severus, during their time in Britain at the end of Severus's life. Julia Domna is joking with the wife of Argentocoxus, a Caledonian, about the unrestrained practice of intercourse among women and men in Britain. The woman replies, "We fulfill the necessities of nature much better than you Roman women, for we consort openly with the best men, while you are debauched in secret by the worst."[93] The Caledonian suggests that Roman women, including perhaps the empress and other members of the elite, break the laws against adultery with the worst kind of men, whereas women of Britain have sex with the best men and are thus morally superior. She echoes the Britons in the *Agricola* and Boudica in the *Annals*, who condemned the insatiable Roman lust and greed. Her remark is just as applicable to the situation of AD 60 as it is to her contemporary situation a century and a half later. While the Britons confirm the value of morality and status in choosing partners, the Romans fail at every turn.

The strength of Boudica's portraits in Tacitus and Dio provides the impetus for her lasting fame. Tacitus presents early reception pieces on the impact of Boudica and her memory, as interpreted by his father-in-law Agricola and the rebel Calgacus. Dio's Britain remains untamed, a place where women may speak their minds and interact with men on an equal plane. Through these authors, readers come to see the influence of Boudica on the Roman perception of Britain and the ways in which ancient authors interpreted her place in the history of imperial expansion. Boudica becomes a symbol of strength in the face of servitude, even though stereotypes surrounding the portrayal of women in leadership positions remain unchanged.

Epilogue

Warrior Woman

In her extensive afterlife, Boudica has been celebrated as a nationalist icon, champion of feminism, and emblem of freedom, whose main contribution was to help formulate a sense of national identity in Britain.[1] Despite her failure to stem the Roman incursion into Britain, she proved the Britons were able to unite against a foreign enemy. She is memorialized in texts spanning from Tacitus, in the generation after her death, to films, novels, and other artistic responses in production today. The range of adaptations proves the malleability of Boudica's story. Seen from different perspectives, she encompasses the ideals of queen, rebel, mother, and warrior woman.

Boudica is memorialized as a symbol of freedom, nationalism, and womanhood. She provides an image of the oppressed provincial and is the female embodiment of insurgency. To the sixth-century British monk, Gildas, Boudica was a "treacherous lioness," a murderer of rulers.[2] After Gildas, there is scant evidence of Boudica until the rediscovery of an eleventh-century manuscript of books 11–16 of Tacitus's *Annals*, stored in a monastery at Monte Cassino, brought her story back to light. In the fifteenth and sixteenth centuries, Tacitus became common reading material in Britain, and Boudica earned her place in histories and in poetry.[3] During the reign of Elizabeth I, Boudica received a positive reception as a warrior woman and orator.[4] The Elizabethan era also brought the gender tension in Boudica's narrative to the fore. Under James I, several playwrights and historians re-envisioned her as dependent upon the warrior Caratacus, the true leader of the rebellion, or increased her barbarian, fearsome womanly nature.[5]

In the eighteenth century, Boudica became a focus for celebrating British nationalist interests and the idea of British nationhood.[6] Parallels were drawn between the Roman and British Empires, and Boudica became part of an imperial narrative. There is a certain irony in such representations, as Boudica is portrayed as vehemently anti-Empire in our ancient texts. William Cowper's "Boadicea: An Ode" (1782) has had a lasting impact on Boudica's representation as an imperial icon. In this ode, the Druids prophesy the fall of Rome and the ultimate rise of the Britons from a world destroyed by Roman invaders; their prophecy spurs Boudica to fight and die, and the final stanza predicts the glorious future of Britain:

> Ruffians, pitiless as proud,
> Heaven awards the vengeance due;
> Empire is on us bestow'd,
> Shame and ruin wait for you![7]

For Cowper, Boudica's vengeance manifests itself in nothing less than the destruction of Rome and the rise of Britain, the next great world empire. His poem prompted others to embrace her as a figurehead of British imperialism in the following century.[8]

During the reign of Queen Victoria, Boudica was celebrated as an early figure of "Victory."[9] Henry Selous found her a worthy figure for commemoration and won a prize at the Westminster Hall Exhibition of 1843 for his cartoon, "Boadicea Haranguing the Iceni."[10] The poet laureate, Alfred, Lord Tennyson, connected Boudica firmly to the Druids and emphasized her love of liberty, but at the expense of her maternal side.[11] In his "Boädicéa," written in 1859 and published in 1864, she is a powerful, savage, uncontrolled barbarian. Following Cowper's lead, Tennyson's Boudica predicts the fall of Rome and the rise of the British Empire. The last lines of the sixth and final stanza conclude Tennyson's image of imperial destruction:

> Out of evil evil flourishes, out of tyranny tyranny buds.
> Ran the land with Roman slaughter, multitudinous agonies.
> Perish'd many a maid and matron, many a vainglorious legionary.
> Fell the colony, city, and citadel, London, Verulam, Cámulodúne.[12]

Boudica's royal image persists through the end of the nineteenth century, and she is among those featured in a window in Colchester's City Hall that commemorates queens connected to the history of the city. Queen Victoria appears at the center, and under her portrait is the

FIGURE E.1. Boadicea Stained Glass Window, detail from the Ladies
Window, Moot Hall, Colchester Town Hall. 1902.

Photograph Caitlin C. Gillespie.

dedication: the window was presented by Ladies of the Borough and
their committee president, Emily F. Sanders, Mayoress of Colchester
from 1898 to 1899. Boudica gazes out from the lower right corner of the
window, clasping her spear, her portrait dominated by a gold diadem
and gold necklace (figure E.1). A corresponding window of kings connected to Colchester features Edward the Elder (AD 922) at the center;
Caratacus, the Roman emperor Claudius, and Cassivellaunus are among
those commemorated on the border.[13]

The canonical image of Victorian Boudica is that of Thomas
Thornycroft (1816–1885). In 1851, Thornycroft sculpted an equestrian
statue of Victoria for the Great Exhibition, which was so popular he was
encouraged by Victoria and Albert to create a bronze group, "Boadicea
and Her Daughters."[14] Thornycroft died before casting his sculpture in
bronze, and it took years before the necessary funds were acquired to
finish the project. In 1902, a year after Victoria died, the statue group

was dedicated by Thornycroft's son and placed on a great stone plinth where the Westminster Bridge joins the Victoria Embankment, facing the Houses of Parliament. As seen in figure E.2, the statue celebrates the warrior woman: she grasps a spear in her right hand, raising the other in defiance. Mantle billowing out behind her, she is the image of Britain's power. She is fearless and does not need to hold the reins of her rearing horses. Her daughters gaze forward in determined support. Their flowing garments expose their breasts, but they are not the fearful, defeated victims of Roman lust. The inscription on the east side of the pediment quotes Cowper: "Regions Caesar never knew / thy posterity shall sway."[15] On the front pediment, we read,

FIGURE E.2. "Boadicea and Her Daughters," Thomas Thornycroft (1815–1885). Erected 1902, Thames Embankment, London. Bronze.

Photograph Caitlin C. Gillespie.

BOADICEA
(BOUDICCA)
QUEEN OF THE ICENI
WHO DIED IN AD 61
AFTER LEADING HER PEOPLE
AGAINST THE ROMAN INVADER

The inscription identifies her dual identity as queen and military leader. The imperious warrior glares defiantly from her chariot, scythes protruding outward from its wheel axles. It is a monumental affair, a vehicle Thornycroft wrote to a friend that Prince Albert wanted to appear as "the throne upon wheels."[16]

Boudica's chariot is emblematic of her modern persona. In our ancient accounts, Julius Caesar details the Britons' mode of fighting with chariots: this unique and effective method initially dismayed and confounded the Romans and became a marker of the Britons' ability and achievements in warfare.[17] The addition of the scythe may be adapted from the first-century AD geographer Pomponius Mela's description of chariots in Britain, which he compares to those of the Gauls that have scythes attached to the wheels.[18] Despite Mela's claim, scythed chariots have no archaeological basis. Nevertheless, this type of chariot is a staple of Boudica's image, replacing her light, maneuverable wooden vehicle, as well as Dio's Roman platform, as a symbol of her authority. The scythed chariot image may originate with Francis Heyman's frontispiece for Tobias Smollett's *Complete History of England* (1757) and thence became canonical.[19]

Thornycroft's confident rebel, commander of her throne-chariot, became the standard image of Boudica's modern self. The statue on the Thames was a gathering place for suffragists in 1906. In 1908, Mary Lowndes's gold silk banner for the National Union of Women's Suffrage Societies reduced her image to the symbol of the scythed chariot wheel, surrounded by spear points and mistletoe on a background of blue and green.[20] She has been adopted in campaigns and slogans as a figure for female suffrage ever since.[21]

In the World War I era, a more sympathetic image appeared. James Havard Thomas's statue of Boudica in the marble hall in Cardiff City Hall shows Boudica as a protective mother, a figure of comfort for her two children (figure E.3). She strides forward with her arms around her young daughters, unwarlike and unarmed. Her gaze focuses firmly

FIGURE E.3. "Buddug/Boadicea," J. Havard Thomas (1854–1921). Sculpted 1913–1915 for Cardiff City Hall. Marble.

Photograph Caitlin C. Gillespie.

ahead as she leads her family onward. One daughter glances down, clutching her shawl around her, as the other looks up at her mother for guidance. Thomas's statue rejects the Victorian image and instead presents a sympathetic image of a woman experiencing the emotional duress of war. Thornycroft's powerful, diademed barbarian warrior appears instead as a war-weary, dignified mother.

Thomas's statue was unveiled in 1916 as part of the series of statues commemorating heroes of Wales, and it is the only female among them. The simple inscription gives her Welsh name (BUDDUG) as well as Boadicea, and the year of her death, AD 61. Although she was not Welsh, Boudica earned her place in the marble hall because she forced Suetonius to leave his campaign against the Druids on Mona in northwest Wales. Juxtaposing the two statues allows us to see how twentieth- and twenty-first-century Boudica began to wear all of her guises, depending on the context. Her image was further influenced by the development in archaeological interest in Roman Britain over the course of the twentieth century.[22]

Boudica's chariot represents a willingness to act decisively and to strive ever forward. This allows her to symbolize imperialist expansion in the nineteenth century and feminist interests in the twentieth century. She is a member of Cecily Hamilton's 1909 work, "A Pageant of Great Women," along with Elizabeth I, Queen Victoria, Joan of Arc, Florence Nightingale, and others, and has a place setting in Judy Chicago's feminist art installation of the 1970s entitled "The Dinner Party," now in the Brooklyn Museum. Her scythed chariot appears in the 1967 film, *The Viking Queen*, and in the 2003 film *Boudica*, starring Alex Kingston. A 1987 cartoon portrays a toga-clad Margaret Thatcher driving a scythed chariot, Roman laurels of victory in her hair.[23] Modern museums, including the Norwich Castle Museum, have recreated versions of Boudica's chariot. A close approximation to her ancient vehicle is the chariot discovered buried at Wetwang Slack, now in the British Museum. The iconic scythes have been removed, and the chariot resembles a simple wooden platform on wheels.

Boudica's statue on the Thames remains a site for protest and an invitation to consider the meaning of her image. In 2005, a century after the suffragettes gathered around her, Banksy put a yellow clamp on the wheel of her chariot, demanding renewed attention for the monument and the politics behind monumental art. In 2016, this same statue was interpreted by Tom Holland in an op-ed for *The New York Times* as a marker of "euroskepticism" that captured the "spirit of Brexit," the shorthand for the referendum for the withdrawal of the United Kingdom from the European Union.[24] Holland's piece invites inquiry into Boudica's relevance for current discourses surrounding the relationship between Britain and continental Europe. Such modern citations of Thornycroft's statue illustrate how different audiences have manipulated this figure as relevant for the history of Britain and British identity. Boudica provides a ready reference point for discussions of exclusion and integration, whether based in politics or gender.

The question of Boudica's impact and relevance for modern rhetoric of this type is inherent in the representation of Boudica's role in the history of Roman Britain in museum displays from London to Norfolk. Museums that address the Romans in Britain tend to overlook underlying issues in Boudica's tale in order to tell a straightforward narrative.[25] The Verulamium Museum at St Albans, as well as the archaeological park of this town on the river Ver, dwells momentarily on Boudica's destruction and burn evidence before turning to the development of the Roman town. Verulamium advertises itself as "the Museum of everyday life in Roman Britain," and displays remain true to that focus. The Museum of London, by contrast, includes elements of everyday life as integral to the representation of the grand history of the city. The Roman Gallery follows the prehistory of the settlement on the Thames. Boudica's revolt is the cause of the destruction of the first London: the corner case, "Chariots of fire?" includes burnt coins, a samian dish, and other debris that provide evidence of the destruction. The narrative celebrates Suetonius Paulinus as the governor who came "to the rescue" of London's inhabitants. Turn the corner for a parallel case concerning a fire in Londinium in AD 120–125: the narrative explains that even after Boudica burned the city, inhabitants continued to use wooden frameworks that left their homes vulnerable to fire. In this gallery, Boudica is a digression from the linear narrative of London's progress.

The Norwich Museum and Art Gallery in Norwich Castle reclaims Boudica as a local heroine. The exhibition, "Boudica and the Revolt against Rome," attempts to tell her story as seen and experienced by the Iceni, although most of the revolt narrative presented throughout the gallery is adapted from Tacitus. Display cases feature Iron Age material from the surrounding area, introducing visitors to life in the land of the Iceni and the importance of regional identity. Gold torcs, horse-related material, coins, and a reconstructed chariot are among the elements that invite the viewer to envision the revolt from the perspective of Boudica and her people. Before the revolt, the Iceni are proud and independent, but after Boudica, they slowly adopt Roman customs and cultural expectations.

The Norwich Museum stands in contrast to the pro-Roman displays at Colchester, where Boudica is presented as an indisputable outsider. The Castle Museum at Colchester traces the development of late Iron Age and Roman Colchester from the origins of the *oppidum* onward. Both the Romans' maltreatment of the local inhabitants and the horror of the rebellion are illustrated through objects and text. Boudica is arguably a villain or a heroine. As material evidence demonstrates, the Boudican destruction horizon has yielded numerous finds that contribute to our understanding of the development of the city, but at great cost. Viewers are reminded by a reconstruction of the Temple of Claudius that Boudica's main contribution to Colchester's development was the burning of the temple and the thousands who died in the conflagration. There is even a poll that allows visitors to vote on whether Boudica was right or wrong to destroy Colchester. Moving beyond the destruction, examples of modern interpretations recognize Boudica's wide-ranging legacy, from Thornycroft's statue to Mary Lowndes's suffragette banner, from band names and fashion design tags to brand names for beer, soap, and other products.

Modern museums thus incorporate Boudica into overarching historical narratives, while recognizing that her name is evocative of destruction and progress, resistance and resilience. Her name has marketing value for promoting tourism in East Anglia, and for advertising products that might embody a similar strength of character or independent spirit. The name of Boudica is a hybrid of multiple interpretations, from ancient texts through modern media, and leaves room for further adaptations. Novels, films, and other artistic productions waver between representing Boudica as a powerful queen or as a victim, often of passion, which has no ancient parallel. Her story has been found relevant even to the practice of psychoanalysis: in 2015, she was used as the primary example of the powerful mother for a psychoanalyst exploring the impact of her empowering image on the female psyche, questioning whether Boudica, the mighty mother, can empower us all.[26] Boudica's story demands that audiences think critically about how to evaluate the ancient evidence, how modern representations inform current impressions, and how Boudica remains relevant today. Boudica's modern reception continues to demonstrate what her contemporaries already knew: Boudica was a proud mother and fierce warrior, masculine leader and feminine moralist, non-Roman freedom fighter and harsh avenger. No matter where her image appears, she continues to demand attention.

Notes

Introduction

1. See Webster (1978, 15) on the meaning of Boudica. See de la Bédoyère (2003, 48) on *Boud*—and *Bod*—as known components meaning something like victory.

2. Jackson (1979). See Woodman (2014, 172 at *Agr.* 16.1) on the various spellings in manuscripts of the *Annals*. Tacitus's Boudicca, due to orthographical mistakes in the Middle Ages, became Boadicea.

3. The ancient sources are Tacitus, *Agricola* 14.3–16.2; *Annals* 14.29–39; and Dio 62.1–12. See Ireland (1986) for a compilation of primary sources on Roman Britain.

4. On women and power, see Benoist (2015) for a summary, and Mattingly (2013, 94–124) on power, sex, and empire. Cf. Hälikkä (2002) on power and the body.

5. Modern biographies and historical accounts include Dudley and Webster (1962); Andrews (1972); Webster (1978); Sealey (1997); Hunt (2003); Trow and Trow (2003); Hingley and Unwin (2005); Aldhouse-Green (2006); Collingridge (2006); and Johnson (2012).

6. E.g., Braund (1996); Adler (2008); and Johnson (2012).

7. E.g., Aldhouse-Green (2006); Rogers (2015).

8. Allason-Jones (2005); de la Bédoyère (2015).

9. On the histories of Cluvius Rufus, see Wiseman (2013, 109–14).

10. See Black (2001, 415–21 and 426–27) for the argument that Dio's account was based on that of Cluvius Rufus, and Tacitus on Fabius Rusticus or Pliny the Elder. Adler (2011b, 142n8) argues Dio used Pliny as his main source, as well as Cluvius Rufus. On Paulinus's memoirs, see Plin. *HN* 5.1.14. Cf. Syme (1958, 297 and 765) Orsi (1973, 532) thinks Tacitus used Paulinus as a source; Reed (1974, 926–33) believes both authors are based on Paulinus, and that Tacitus also used Fabius Rusticus, who drew on Paulinus, while Dio may have used Pliny as an intermediary.

11. Cipriano (1979) argues Dio only had a fragmentary knowledge of Tacitus. Roddaz (1983) argues Tacitus cannot be considered a source for Dio, contra Freyburger-Galland (1992).

12. Tac. *Hist.* 1.1.3.

13. Tac. *Agr.* 9.6.

14. The endings of the *Histories* and the *Annals* are fragmentary, but these are the generally accepted chronological extents of each work. Tacitus is the main source for his own biography.

15. On the genre of the *Agricola*, see Ogilvie and Richmond (1967, 11–20); Marincola (1999, 318–20); Whitmarsh (2006); Woodman (2014, 1–11).

16. As noted by Braund (1996, 155). See Tac. *Agr.* 5.3.

17. On the *Agricola* as a statement of Roman imperial ideology, see Shumate (2006); R. Evans (2003); and Rutledge (2000), contra Lavan (2011).

18. Tac. *Agr.* 37.6, 40.1. Mattingly (2006, 118) locates this battle near the Moray Firth, near Inverness, although the exact site remains debated.

19. Dio 66.20.3.

20. Suetonius claims he is attempting to rival Corbulo in *virtus* and *gloria* (Tac. *Ann.* 14.29.2).

21. Dio is the source for all of his own biographical information. Swan (2004, 1–38) provides an introduction to Dio's life and the Augustan books of his history. See Millar (1964) for a survey of Dio's work.

22. Dio 72.4.2–3.

23. Dio 73.12.2.

24. Dio 80.5.2. See Swan (2004, 1–3) for a fuller chronology.

25. Millar (1964, 2) notes the seemingly arbitrary nature of Xiphilinus's epitomization. On Xiphilinus, see Brunt (1980, 488–94); Gowing (1997, 2561–63).

26. See Luce (1991, 2904–05).

27. E.g., Tac. *Hist.* 1.2–3; *Ann.* 16.35.1; as observed by Luce (1991, 2905). On exemplarity in Roman historiography, see Hölkeskamp (1996); M. Roller (2004) and (2009). Cf. Chaplin (2000) on *exempla* in Livy's history, and Gillespie (2014) on Agrippina the Younger in Tacitus's *Annals*.

28. Tac. *Ann.* 3.65.1. On this principal obligation of histories, see Luce (1991).

29. Luce (1991, 2914–16).

30. Tac. *Agr.* 3.1.

31. On the deployment of *exempla* in imperial Greek historiography, see Gowing (2009).

32. On Dio's treatment of Augustus, see Swan (2004); Manuwald (1978); Gowing (1992).

33. Tac. *Ann.* 4.32.1–2.

34. On Tacitean style as a means to communicate his views of the political situation in Rome and on character types, see Henderson (1989); Sinclair (1995); Devillers (1994); Plass (1988); on portraits of women and power, see Späth (1994); Hälikkä (2002); L'Hoir (1994). On women in Tacitus, see (among others) Baldwin (1972); Bastomsky (1992); Fischler (1994); Kaplan (1979); Marshall (1984); Rutland (1978).

35. Dio 72.18.3.

36. Adler (2011a, 144n34) summarizes the bibliography on Dio's relationship with Thucydides; the stylistic relationship is well attested, while the influence of Thucydides on Dio's intellectual viewpoints is under debate.

37. Recent discussions include Webster (1994), Rutledge (2000), Clarke (2001), and Isaac (2004, 304–23) on the link between Roman stereotyping of foreigners and Roman imperial expansion.

38. Studies on "otherness" in the ancient world find traction in postcolonial theory and the work of E. Said (1978) especially. See Mattern (1999); Raaflaub and Talbert (2010); Romm (1992).

39. Hartog (1988) is the seminal study for the idea of mirroring in Herodotus's *Histories*. See Vout (2007) and Mattingly (2013) on Tacitus's separation of Romans and others.

40. See Adler (2011b) on such speeches in Roman historiography that valorize foreigners and criticize Roman society and the failures of Roman imperialism; on Boudica's speeches, see pages 119–38 on Tacitus and 141–61 on Dio. See Levene (1999) on morality as a significant feature in deliberative speech.

41. Tacitus places numerous speeches in the mouths of Rome's enemies: e.g., Calgacus (*Agr.* 30–32), Civilis (*Hist.* 4.14.2–4, 17.2–6), Arminius (*Ann.* 1.59), Boiocalus (*Ann.* 13.55–56), in addition to Boudica. Set speeches are prominent in Dio's history at historical turning points and elsewhere, although Swan (2004, 27) describes Dio's speeches as "[s]howy productions, aimed equally at self-presentation . . . and at energizing history." See Fomin (2016) on speeches in Dio as primarily rhetorical exercises with few or no ties to historical truth.

42. See Dickinson and Hartley (1995) for an example of how Tacitus has been used to clarify the archaeology of Roman Britain.

43. For a background to the archaeology of Roman Britain, see Haverfield (1923); Richmond (1955); Frere (1999); Millett (1995); Mattingly (2006); Rogers (2015). Davies (2009) discusses the archaeology of the land of Boudica. Hingley and Unwin (2005, 63–110) summarize the archaeological evidence for Boudica's revolt.

44. Cf. Liebeschuetz (1966); Dickinson and Hartley (1995).

45. Mommsen (1886) developed the term "Romanization" to suggest the civilizing process of the Romans, including language, material culture, art, urbanization, and religion. Haverfield (1923) built on Mommsen. Millett (1990a, 1990b) built on his predecessors but emphasized the willingness of the Britons to adopt Roman cultural mores rather than the imposition of Roman ways on indigenous populations. Tacitus (*Agr.* 21) provided a focus text for the definition of Romanization. See Freeman (1997) on the origins of the term. See Revell (2009, 5–10) on the history of the term. See Hingley (2000) on the influence of British imperialism on Haverfield's formation.

46. Syme (1988, 64) calls the term "vulgar and ugly, worse than that, anachronistic and misleading." Cf. Mattingly (2013, 38–41). The Theoretical Roman Archaeology Conference meetings of the 1990s focused on the meaning of Romanization. Freeman (1997) deconstructed the term as denoting too much of an acculturative model. Cf. Hingley (2000) for the rejection of the term, and Revell (2010) for a feminist critique.

47. See Hingley (1997).

48. See Revell (2009, 5–10); and Millett (1990a, 1990b) on elite-driven change, although Millett acknowledges the idea of nonelites as modeling themselves after elites as problematic. Mattingly (2006, 15–16) takes issue with this "trickle-down" model of emulation.

49. Forcey (1997).

50. Mattingly (2006, 84) continues, "This was not an uncritical adoption of Roman material culture and social practices, but rather the careful selection of certain prestigious elements of Roman culture to be used to accentuate social differentiation in Iron Age society and to construct new forms of elite identity."

51. Webster (2001, 2003) suggests "creolization," a linguistic term indicating the merging of two languages into a dialect that blends the two. On pidginization, see Carr (2003). On bricolage, see Terrenato (1998). On discrepant experience, see Mattingly (2006 and 2013, esp. 203–45). On additional postcolonial perspectives, see Webster and Cooper (1996).

52. Rogers (2015).

53. Revell (2016). See Hill (2001b) for a summary of approaches to the study of identity. See Mattingly (2013, 217) for a list of factors contributing to identity.

54. Cf. Forcey (1997); Häussler (1999); Laurence (2001).

55. See Moore (2011) on the term "tribe."

56. Noted by Moore (2011, 339).

57. Haselgrove (2016, 476). Cf. James (1999) and Rogers (2015) on this oversimplified view.

58. Moore (2011, 344).

59. Cf. Mattingly (2006) for the use of quotes around "tribe" and page 59 for the justification.

60. Dio 62.6.2–3.

Chapter 1

1. On the geography of Britain, see Caes. *BGall.* 5.12, 5.14; Strabo 4.5.2; Tac. *Agr.* 10.2.6; Dio 77[76].12.1–5; Hdn. 3.14.6–8. Caesar describes the island as triangular in form (Caes. *BGall.* 5.13; cf. Diod. Sic. 5.21.3–4; Strabo 4.5.1). Tacitus has been criticized for describing the island as "wedge-shaped"; Woodman (2014 133–34) suggests this phrase indicates a shield with a figure-eight shape. Agricola was the first to circumnavigate the island, and Septimius Severus accomplished the feat again a century later (Dio 39.50.3–4).

2. On the history of Roman Britain, see Mattingly (2006). For introductions, cf. Richmond (1955); Frere (1999); and Shotter (1998). For the Roman conquest, see Collingwood (1932); Salway (1982); Webster (1980); Birley (2005); and Creighton (2006).

3. Strabo (3.5.11) notes Crassus was the first commander to set foot in Britain while seeking a route to the Tin Islands, but he did not stay long.

4. Tacitus (*Ann.* 2.24.4) cites the marvels reported by survivors of Germanicus's fleet who reached the shores of Britain: "Forceful whirlwinds and unheard-of birds, sea monsters, bodies—uncertain whether man or beast—were seen and believed because of fear."

5. See Mann (1985, 1) on Britain as an idea, "a kind of ideological and cultural reference point—a focus for self-expression or self-promotion and for the negotiation of power."

6. Pliny the Elder mentions a Greek tradesman, Midacritus, who imported tin from the islands as early as 600 BC (Plin. *HN* 7.197); Herodotus doubts Britain's existence (Hdt. *Hist.* 3.115, 4.152); Diod. Sic. (5.21.1–2) records no foreign army visited or campaigned against the island. Potter and Johns (1992, 13) cite cargo wrecks on the seabed that indicate the trade of tin and scrap metal across the English Channel by the Middle Bronze Age (c. 1200–1100 BC).

7. Cf. Romm (1992, 140–49) on the island as representing the symbolic limit of the possibilities for Roman rule.

8. On the idea of Caesar and newness, see Plut. *Caes.* 23.2–4; Dio 39.50. Cf. Braund (1996, 42). Caesar's British campaign of 55 BC is mentioned at Caes. *BGall.* 2.4, 3.8, 2.14, 3.9, 4.20–38; Strabo 4.4.1; Dio 39.51–53. Caesar's campaign of 54 BC is mentioned at Caes. *BGall.* 5.1–24; Dio 40.1–4; Cic. *Fam.* 7.6, 7.7, 7.8, 7.10, 7.17; *QFr.* 2.13, 2,15, 3.1; *Att.* 4.15, 4.17, 4.18. On Caesar in Britain, see Tac. *Agr.* 13; Suet. *Iul.* 25, 47; Plut. *Caes.* 16.5, 23.2; Vell. Pat. 2.46–47; App. *BCiv.* 2.150; Livy *Per.* 105.5.

9. Dio 40.1.2.

10. Mattingly (2006, 65) suggests the area around Deal in Kent.

11. Dio 39.53.2.

12. Caes. *BGall.* 5.20–22.

13. Tac. *Agr.* 13.1.

14. Greek and Roman writers attribute common features to the Celtic tribes of Germany, Gaul, and Britain, assuming people of these regions share cultural practices as well as similar languages. On the ethnographic tradition and preconceptions about northerners, see Syme (1958, 126); Woodman (2014, 12); Dauge (1981); Isaac (1990, 2004); Woolf (2011).

15. *AWP* 23.

16. Caes. *BGall.* 5.14.

17. Caes. *BGall.* 6.13, 6.14. Cf. Pompon. 3.19.

18. Caes. *BGall.* 6.14.

19. Caes. *BGall.* 5.14.

20. On Etruscan women, see Theopompus, quoted by Athenaeus (517d–518a).

21. On chariots, see Cic. *Fam.* 7.6.2, 7.7.1. On the lack of silver and gold, see Cic. *Att.* 4.16.7; *Att.* 4.15.10; *QFr.* 3.1.10; *Att.* 4.18.5.

22. On the lack of a threat, see Strabo 4.5.3, 2.5.8; Diod. Sic. 5.22.1.

23. See Cunliffe (2004) on networks of interaction between Britain and the continent and Haselgrove (1984) on Gaul as a precedent.

24. On the products of Britain, see Tac. *Agr.* 12.5–6; Caes. *BGall.* 5.12; Diod. Sic. 5.22–23; Strabo 4.5.2.

25. See Bryant and Niblett (1997, 276) on Braughing as a center of importation before AD 10, when this center transferred to Camulodunum.

26. Haselgrove (1982); Cunliffe (1988, 1991), contra Hill (2007). Haselgrove (2016, 494) clarifies concerning *oppida*, "whilst some of them were indeed population centres engaged in the kind of political, religious and economic activities we associate with urban settlements, including occupational specialisation, craft activity and long-distance exchange, others show little or no sign of this, or represent only short-lived episodes of nucleation as part of complex regional settlement trajectories."

27. Webster (1978, 31) notes that coins as early as Gallo-Belgic A and B were minted in Gaul c. 150–50 BC; the second coin wave appears with Diviciacus of the Suessiones (Gallo-Belgic C) and is the first to be copied by the Britons. For introductions and catalogues on coins, see Allen (1970); Van Arsdell (1989); Haselgrove (1987); Nash (1987); de Jersey (1996); and Cottam et al. (2010).

28. Creighton (2000, 22–54).

29. See Creighton (2000, 146–73) on Latin on coinage; cf. Allen (1980, 185–87), with bibliography.

30. See Brunt (1990) on Latin and the elites; cf. J. Williams (2007) on the importance of Latin on coins of the late first century BC.

31. Creighton (2000, 31).

32. See Ogilvie and Richmond (1967, 46) on Tacitus's representation of the conquest in the *Agricola*.

33. On Augustus's planned mission in 34 BC, see Dio 49.38.2; on 27 BC, see Dio 53.22.5; cf. Hor. *Carm.* 1.35.29–30. Cf. Braund (1996, 78–80).

34. Mann (1985, 6).

35. Prop. 2.27.5–6; Hor. *Carm.* 3.5.1–4, 1.35.29–32; 1.21.13–16, 4.14.47–48.

36. Cf. Tac. *Agr.* 10.6.

37. Augustus names Dubnobellaunus and Tincommius as the two kings that sought him as suppliants (Aug. *RGDA* 32). See Rose (1991) on the Ara Pacis.

38. P. Crummy (1997, 23); Potter and Johns (1992, 34).

39. See Tac. *Ann.* 2.24; Suet. *Calig.* 44, 46; Dio 59.25.1–3. Tacitus (*Agr.* 13) summarizes the Romans in Britain and planned campaigns through Claudius.

40. Suet. *Calig.* 44.2.

41. The Atrebates had been friendly to Rome since the time of Caesar, and the Catuvellauni may have threatened them, although Dio suggests there was an internal uprising (Dio 60.19.1). Claudius was persuaded by Verica to send forces to Britain (Dio 60.17.1). The Britons may have threatened vengeance because the senate refused to return certain deserters (Suet. *Claud.* 17.1). Verica then disappears from the sources.

42. The Second Legion was commanded by the future emperor Vespasian (Suet. *Vesp.* 4.1). Plautius waited for Claudius to arrive before attacking (Dio 21.1–2).

43. Suet. *Claud.* 17, 24; Dio 60.19–23. The account of the Claudian invasion from Tacitus's *Annals* has not survived. On issues in Dio's account, see Hind (2007).

44. Dio 60.22.1.

45. *CIL* 920.8–9, as transcribed and translated in Barrett (1991, 12). See Barrett (1991) on the arch in Rome. Dudley and Webster (1965, 186) suggest the tribal leaders and tribes included Togidubnus, Prasutagus (or another king of the Iceni), the ruler of the Brigantes (maybe Cartimandua), maybe kings of the Coritani and Dobunni, rulers of the Catuvellauni and Trinovantes, and the Cornuvii and Parisii.

46. See Mann (1985, 7–8).

47. See Tac. *Ann.* 12.31–40; Suet. *Ner.* 18; Tac. *Ann.* 14.29–37; *Agr.* 15; Dio 62.1–12.

48. See Mattingly (2013, 6); Braund (1996, 28–29); Woodman (2014, 15–18). Recent studies on how the Roman ruling elite conceptualized their imperial project include Richardson (2008) and Lavan (2013).

49. Cic. *Rep.* 3.

50. Dion. Hal. 1.5.2–3.

51. Verg. *Aen.* 6.851–53.

52. Braund (1996, 29).

53. Tac. *Agr.* 11–12. Cf. Caes. *BGall.* 5.12.

54. Woodman (2014, 150) notes the unique hendiadys and translation of *factionibus et studiis*.

55. Tac. *Agr.* 12.1–2.

56. Tac. *Agr.* 20.2. As noted by Woodman (2014, 17).

57. Tac. *Agr.* 21.1–2.

58. See Woodman (2014, 204). Straub (1977) suggests Tacitus sees citizenship as a new form of freedom.

59. Cf. Pliny (*HN* 3.39) on the imperial mission to "give civilization to men" (*humanitatem homini daret*); cf. Mart. (11.53) for the praise of Claudia Rufina, a woman of British descent, for her Romanness. See Dauge (1981) on Romans and barbarians and *humanitas* versus uncivilized as part of this ideological system.

60. Tac. *Agr.* 21.2.

61. Revell (2016, 28) clarifies, "[*Humanitas*] incorporated the aspect of a shared humanity in terms of treatment of other people, and proper respect towards the structures of society as a whole, but it also brought with it overtones of culture and civilisation." Cf. Veyne (1993) on the concept of *humanitas*.

62. Woolf (1998, 55). Cf. Creighton (2006, 85) on *humanitas* as "a shared ideological sense of 'self.'"

63. Plin. *HN* 3.39: *humanitatem homini daret.*

64. On the years between Caesar and Claudius (55 BC–AD 43) see Stevens (1951); Potter and Johns (1992); Manley (2002); Birley (2008). Creighton (2000, 220) describes Claudius's invasion as essentially an "annexation" of the land of Cunobelinus.

65. Tac. *Agr.* 13.1.

66. Caesar claims the Britons called an area in the woods that they had fortified with an entrenchment and rampart, where they gathered in order to avoid enemy attacks, an *oppidum* (Caes. *BGall.* 5.21.3). On the term *oppidum*, see Drinkwater (1975, 56–57). See Mattingly (2006, 109) for the clarification that few settlements were worthy of the name "town" in AD 60.

67. Tac. *Ann.* 12.32.2.

68. Todd (2004), 44.

69. Hill (1997).

70. On the history of the Iceni and East Anglia, see Davies and Williamson (1999); and Davies (1999, 2009, 2011).

71. Potter and Johns (1992, 43), as mentioned by Tac. *Ann.* 12.13; Caes. *BGall.* 5.21.

72. On the ancient wealth of Norfolk, see Davies (2009, 80–84). Cottam et al. (2010, 78) estimate 97 percent of Icenian coin types show horses.

73. See Talbot and Liens (2010).

74. E.g., Van Arsdell (1989, 74), type 80.

75. Cf. Aldhouse-Green (2003, 102, fig. 15) for a warrior horsewoman or female charioteer.

76. It is unclear whether the colony was renamed before or after Boudica's revolt. See P. Crummy (1997, 53–54).

77. See Rivet (1983), Waite (2007, 53–57), Frere (1999, 70–74) on the first revolt.

78. Tac. *Ann.* 12.31.1. Rivet (1983) suggests the Iceni involved were not the whole "tribe."

79. Dio 60.9.1–5. Pliny (*HN* 5.1) acknowledges Suetonius as his source for the ethnography of the area beyond the Atlas Mountains.

80. Hill (2007, 37).

81. Cottam et al. (2010, 90) suggest that this coin is modeled on a silver unit of Cunobelinus (*ABC* 2873).

82. Mossop and Allen (1979) suggests the obverse should read SUB RI(CON) PRASTO (under king Prasutagus), and the reverse, ESICO FECIT, "Esico made [this]."

83. J. Williams (2000). See J. Williams (2007) on the new reading as the first full Latin sentence on a coin in Britain (SVB ESVPRASTO ESICO FECIT: "Under Esuprasto Esico made [it])."

84. For the earlier date, see Griffin (1976–77); Bulst (1961); Syme (1958, 2:765–68); Frere (1999, 87); Ogilvie and Richmond (1967, 194); and Birley (2005, 43–52). For a later date, see Overbeck (1969, 143–44); and Carroll (1979).

85. See Tomlin (2016, 58) on the significance of this collection of 405 stylus tablets, the largest assemblage found in London to date. See Tomlin (2016, 55–56 and 156–59) on tablet <WT45>, a contract dated 21 October AD 62 between Gaius Valerius Proculus and Marcus Rennius Venustus for the transport of provisions from Verulamium to Londinium by 13 November, with payment details.

86. Dio 62.2.1. On Seneca's role, see Sánchez (2004).

87. E.g., Tac. *Ann.* 13.42.4.

88. See Drinkwater (1975) and de Filippis (1979) on the role of the Trinovantes.

89. Tac. *Ann.* 14.32.1. Cf. Dio 62.1.2. See Nice (1993) on superstition in the accounts of Boudica.

90. Tac. *Agr.* 16.1.

91. Dio 62.2.2.

92. Waite (2007, 84).

93. See Waite (2007, 81–93) on this legion.

94. De la Bédoyère (2003, 66) and Waite (2007, 101) note burn evidence of this time at Chelmsford to suggest this settlement was also destroyed by the rebels.

95. On the movements of Suetonius and his army, see Benario (1986).

96. Tac. *Agr.* 16.2.

97. Sealey (1997, 38) estimates his numbers around ten thousand men.

98. Tac. *Agr.* 16.1–2. Cf. Tac. *Ann.* 14.33.2.

99. Dio 62.1.2–3. Webster (1978, 95) notes this goddess may be related to Andarta in Gaul, and the word seems to mean "the unconquerable."

100. On the status of Verulamium as a *municipium*, see Revell (2009, 67–73); M. Jones (2004, 166); Black (2001), 421–23. On the history of Verulamium, see Niblett (2001).

101. Tac. (*Ann.* 14.33.2) is the only classical reference to Verulamium by name. Suetonius (*Ner.* 39.1) mentions two towns, not three.

102. Cf. Hingley and Unwin (2005, 89) on the selective destruction of Verulamium.

103. Tac. *Ann.* 14.33.2. Mattingly (2006, 111–12) suggests perhaps ten thousand died in Colchester, and the casualties in the three sites totaled between thirty thousand and forty thousand Romans and provincials, including at least seven thousand soldiers, taking into account evidence that most of the inhabitants of Londinium and Verulamium had fled before the rebels arrived, and Tacitus's attestation that the army was replaced with seven thousand additional troops (Tac. *Ann.* 14.38.1).

104. Dio 62.8.1; Tac. 14.34.2.

105. Webster (1978, 111).

106. Webster (1978, 111–12) suggests Mancetter. Gould (2004) suggests Godmanchester. Waite (2007, 167–97) re-evaluates the evidence and suggests Venonis (modern High Cross).

107. Dio 62.8.3.

108. Dio 62.12.1–6.

109. Tac. *Ann.* 14.37.2. Mattingly (2006, 93) suggests that this number may include the total deaths of the Britons in the revolt and in the vengeful actions of the Romans that followed; furthermore, he suggests 100,000—250,000 Britons perished in the conquest period from AD 43–83, considering the total population of Britain was about 2 million.

110. Dio 62.12.6.

111. See Waite (2007, 144–54) on Postumus.

112. Tac. *Ann.* 14.38.1; Suet. *Tit.* 4.1. See Webster (1978, 101).

113. Classicianus was a provincial, not an Italian. He is commemorated on a tombstone now in London (*RIB* 12), which gives his full Roman name, suggesting he gained citizenship.

114. Tac. *Ann.* 14.39.3.

115. See Tac. *Agr.* 16–17; *Hist.* 2.66, 1.9, 1.59–60, 2.57, 2.65, 2.11, 2.86, 2.97, 3.22, 3.44, 3.45, 4.68; Stat. *Silv.* 5.2.142–49 on Caledonia.

116. Fulford (2008) reviews Nero's building program and imperial policies in Britain after the revolt.

117. For example, the inscription from the Forum at Verulamium dates its dedication to AD 79, during the reign of Titus when Agricola was governor (*RIB* 3123).

Chapter 2

1. Cf. Haselgrove and Moore (2007). See Hill (2007) for these shifts as long-running internal developments rather than reactions to the Roman conquest; contra Haselgrove (1982); Cunliffe (1988, 1991).

2. See Davies (1999, 14) on shifting tribal relationships.

3. Haselgrove (2004). On Iron Age communities in Britain, Cunliffe (1991) remains fundamental; see Haselgrove (1989) on the later Iron Age in southern Britain.

4. Willis (1997).

5. The Crownthorpe hoard, comprised of a drinking set of a wealthy Icenian, is unique in East Anglia for its combined Roman and local aesthetic. See Davies (2009, 137–41).

6. See Allason-Jones (2005, 7–8) on Boudica's age.

7. Livy 1.46.8.

8. Livy 1.48.7: *foedum inhumanumque.*

9. Livy 1.48.8–9.

10. See Braund (1996, 25–27) on stereotypes of foreign rulers.

11. Strabo 17.54.1.

12. Prop. 3.11.

13. Cf. Prop. 3.11.39–46.

14. D. Roller (2010, 139).

15. On the defeat of Antony and Cleopatra, cf. Prop. 4.6.

16. Hor. *Carm.* 1.37.21–32.

17. Dio (51.12.1–13.3) perpetuates this portrait.

18. On Cleopatra as "other," see Wyke (1992). Cf. J. Luce (1963) on Cleopatra as the *fatale monstrum.*

19. She is often compared to Vergil's Dido. See J. Benario (1970).

20. On Cleopatra's death, see Baldwin (1964); D. Roller (2010, 148). On the honor of her death, see Hor. *Carm.* 1.37; Dio 51.11–14.

21. D. Roller (2010, 149–50).

22. Kehne (2001).

23. Elsewhere in Tacitus, few queens emerge, and none last. Berenice of Cilicia, a client queen ruling Judaea in the AD 40s, is the only other woman Tacitus refers to as a *regina* (Tac. *Hist.* 2.81; cf. Suet. *Tit.* 7; Dio 66.15.3–4). The Armenians briefly tried out a woman ruler, Erato, but she was quickly expelled (Tac. *Ann.* 2.4.2).

24. On Cartimandua, see Howarth (2008); Casson (1945); Richmond (1954); Mitchell (1978); de Filippis (1978); Braund (1984a).

25. Birley (1979, 27).

26. De Filippis (1978). Cf. Braund (1996, 118–46).

27. Brigantes means the "upland people" and may refer to all those in the north, rather than a unified sociopolitical entity (Moore 2011, 347). Seneca divides those in Britain between the Britons and the Brigantes, suggesting this geographical separation (Sen. *Apocol.* 12).

28. The site of Cartimandua's capital has been contested. See Hanson and Campbell (1986, 76–77) for the suggestions of Stanwick, Almondbury, Barwish, and others. Cf. Turnbull and Fitts (1988) for Stanwick but not Almondbury. Howarth (2008, 41–44) suggests Stanwick was Venutius's capital. Haselgrove's (2016) edited volume on fieldwork in the area of Stanwick from 1981 to 2011 convincingly argues for Stanwick as the most qualified site for the seat of power for a ruler who had a client relationship with Rome (see pages 466–81 for a comparison of the archaeology of Stanwick with literary sources on Cartimandua and the synthesis on pages 482–88 especially).

29. Cf. Howarth (2008, 36–38) on the triple goddess Brigantia as a warrior and mother, a goddess of protection, fertility, and prosperity.

30. Richmond (1954, 47); Braund (1996, 197n4); Turnbull and Fitts (1988, 383).

31. Tac. *Ann.* 12.32.1–2.

32. See Webster (1993) on the war with Caratacus.

33. Tac. *Ann.* 12.36.1.

34. Tac. *Ann.* 12.40.3.

35. Tac. *Ann.* 12.40.2–4.

36. Tac. *Hist.* 3.45.3.

37. Howarth (2008, 41) argues for two conflicts, the first between AD 51–57 and the second in AD 69. Richmond (1954, 50) proposes Cartimandua and Venutius may have reconciled between the two conflicts. Mitchell (1978) argues for one conflict, in AD 69. Braund (1984a) argues for two conflicts, and that the second resulted from the promotion of Vellocatus.

38. Tac. *Hist.* 3.45.4.

39. Braund (1984b, 182–87).

40. See Braund (1984b, 39–53) on the question of citizenship, common of client kings in the East. The evidence of citizenship extended to a client king in Britain includes the epitaph of Togidubnus (formerly spelled Cogidubnus), the king of the Regni tribe in the southeast. The epitaph records the name Tiberius Claudius Togidubnus, suggesting that he had Roman citizenship and was entitled to the *tria nomina*. On Togidubnus, see Barrett (1979); Bogaers (1979). On the spelling as Togidubnus, see Woodman (2015, 164). For his epitaph (*RIB* 91), see Collingwood and Wright (1965, 25–26).

41. E.g., Tac. *Ann.* 11.16.1–3.

42. Braund (1984b, 189).

43. Braund (1984b, 182–84).

44. Braund (1984b, 184).

45. Tac. *Agr.* 14.2: *ut haberet instrumenta servitutis et reges.* Cf. Tac. *Hist.* 2.81.1, *inservientes reges.* Gowing (1990), 316) argues that Tacitus's client kings "reflect and lend unity to a consistent concern of the historian: the indictment of Julio-Claudian foreign policy," and that Nero is the worst offender.

46. Allason-Jones (2005), 17.

47. Damon (2012, 227n3) notes the debate about these rivers, identified as the Trent, Tern, or Avon, and Severn.

48. Tac. *Ann.* 12.31.3.

49. Tac. *Ann.* 12.32.1.

50. Cf. Braund (1984b, 63). Togidubnus was the last of the client kings in Britain.

51. See Barrett (1990) for this argument based on the evidence of Claudius's establishment of client relationships after the death of Gaius.

52. Although not discussed by Tacitus, king Herod of Judaea provides an exception: Herod was allowed to arrange for his succession in his will (Braund 1984b, 139). He also left Augustus a fortune (Joseph. *AJ* 17.188–91).

53. Cf. Braund (1984b, 139–43) on wills of client kings during the principate. Cf. Woodman (2014, 307) on Prasutagus's will.

54. Tac. *Ann.* 14.31.1.

55. See Braund (1984b, 26) on the idea of succession.

56. See Braund (1984b, 144). See Champlin (1991, 112–26) on wives and daughters inheriting.

57. Tac. *Agr.* 43.4.

58. Ibid.

59. See Champlin (1991, 150–53) on the emperor as a coheir.

60. Cf. Classen (1988) on *moderatio* in the *Agricola* as a reflection on the principate.

61. Tac. *Ann.* 16.17.5.

62. Tac. *Ann.* 16.11.1.

63. Gowing (1990, 327).

64. Hutcheson (2007, 369) suggests social upheaval, contra Davies (1999, 41).

65. See Van Arsdell (1989, 211–12, type 770, 775, 780).

66. Johns and Potter (1992, 43). Webster (1978, 48) notes the names ECENI, AESV, and SAEMV as perhaps indicative of a division of the different peoples.

67. Davies (2009, 119) cites mints at Saham Toney, Needham, and Thetford.

68. See Nash Briggs (2011, esp. 92–97). Nash Briggs (2011, 97) derives Prasutagus from the Latin *praeses* ("governor") and *-tagus* (Gaulish for "magistrate").

69. See Revell (2016, 55) on integration rather than assimilation or segregation as the mode mostly adopted in Roman Britain, which included "participation in shared institutions, but the maintenance of the group identity and some degree of cultural distinctiveness."

70. Mattingly (2006, 58).

71. Davies (2009, 95–100).

72. See J. Smith (1978) on roundhouses as occupied by extended families.

73. P. Crummy (1997, 11–28); Niblett (2001, 46–47); Mattingly (2006, 58–59).

74. Diod. Sic. 5.21.6.

75. The area of occupation is attested through finds of over fifteen thousand silver Iron Age coins from c. 65 BC to the time of the Roman invasion (Hingley and Unwin 2005, 27).

76. Cf. Gregory (1991).

77. Sealey (1997, 12).

78. Gregory (1991, 90).

79. Hingley and Unwin (2005, 33).

80. On the Roman palace at Fishbourne, see Cunliffe (1998). See Creighton (2006, 54–61) for a reconsideration of the early site.

81. See Cunliffe (1998, 66 and 69) on the room and the mosaic, and page 71, figure 33 for a drawing of the reconstructed mosaic.

82. E.g., Rogers (2015, 69–70). Cf. Hingley (1997, 95).

83. Hill (2007, 34–37). Cf. Davies (1996, 1999); J. Williams (2001).

84. See Davies (2009, 100–106) on Snettisham.

85. Hill (2007, 34). Cf. Hill (2004).

86. Revell (2009, 76–77).

87. Häussler (1999, 2) suggests, "Rather than merely *reflecting* or *reproducing* ideologies, imperial architecture is intended to *communicate*—more, it wants to *persuade*" (original italics).

88. Revell (2009, 49) and Braund (1996, 83–84) on Strabo 4.5.1.

89. Dio 62.3.1–5.

90. Tac. *Ann.* 14.33.2.

91. P. Crummy (1999, 93).

92. See N. Crummy (2013–14) on this treasure.

93. P. Crummy (1997, 66–70).

94. See P. Crummy (1997, 51–72) on the development of Camulodunum.

95. Allason-Jones (2005, 72).

96. Tac. *Ann.* 14.31.4.

97. See P. Crummy (1997, 79–84) on the destruction layer.

98. P. Crummy (1997, 64).

99. Tomlin (2016, 37) argues there is no clear evidence of the revolt at Londinium.

100. Perring (2015, 21).

101. Perring (2015, 23).

102. On the development of Londinium, see Milne (1995, esp. 42–45); Creighton (2006, 93–107).

103. Perring (2015, 25).

104. See Perring (2015, 23–26) on the first town, prior to Boudica.

105. See Perring (2015, 26–27) on the rebuilding after Boudica, including a fort built over the destruction debris in the southeast part of the town, shops, waterworks, baths, and other structures. Londinium experienced a major urban development in the 70s, including a forum and basilica, and amphitheater dated to AD 74.

106. Hill (2007, 32–33). On Verulamium, see Niblett (2001); Bryant and Niblett (1997); and Haselgrove and Millett (1997).

107. See Bryant and Niblett (1997).

108. On town planning, see Bryant and Niblett (1997, 279).

109. Niblett (2001, 52).

110. Niblett (2001, 86–87).

Chapter 3

1. A version of the arguments presented in these two chapters first appeared in Gillespie (2015). Copyright © The Classical Association of the Atlantic States.

2. See Levene (2009) for a background to the function of speeches in historiography and on speeches in Tacitus's *Histories* as integral to his analysis of imperial power; cf. Devillers (1994, 195–261) on speeches in the *Annals*.

3. On *libertas* in general, see Wirszubski (1950). On *libertas* and Tacitus, see Hammond (1963); Ducos (1977); Shotter (1978); Morford (1991); and Strunk (2016). See Halfmann (2002) and Liebeschuetz (1966) on *libertas* in the *Agricola*. See Kotula (2001) on revolts in the first century arising from the local population's refusal to accept injustice.

4. See Lavan (2013, 124–55) on Tacitus's use of the metaphor.

5. Tac. *Agr.* 13.1.

6. Tac. *Agr.* 11.4. See Griffin (2000, 143–63) and Champlin (2003, 210–34) on Nero's promotion of *honos* and *virtus* as including music and other artistic performances.

7. See McDonnell (2006) on *virtus* as essentially martial valor during the Republic; *virtus* took on an ethical dimension in the Empire. See Edwards (1993, 1–33) on *mos* and *virtus* as forms of "symbolic capital" connected to power structures of Rome.

8. Tac. *Agr.* 15.1: *mala servitutis* (the evils of servitude); *Agr.* 16.1: *ut sedem servitutis* (the seat of servitude).

9. Tac. *Agr.* 15.5.

10. Tac. *Agr.* 15.1–2.

11. Tac. *Agr.* 15.3: *nihil iam cupiditati, nihil libidini exceptum.*

12. Tac. *Agr.* 15.4. Woodman (2014, 168) notes this complaint is found in the speeches of other foreigners, citing Caes. *BGall.* 3.2.5, 7.14.10; and Livy 38.43.4.

13. Tac. *Ann.* 12.32.2.

14. Tac. *Ann.* 12.34.1.

15. Tac. *Ann.* 12.35.3–36.3.

16. Tac. *Ann.* 12.37.1–4. See Braund (1996, 112–16) on Caratacus as a moralizing figure.

17. Tac. *Ann.* 14.31.1.

18. See Paul (1982) on the *urbs capta* motif and Ash (1999, 66–67) on typical features of the sack of a city. For literary examples, see Sall. *Cat.* 51.9; Livy 29.17.15.

19. Mattingly (2013, 118).

20. Cf. Tac. *Agr.* 32.1.

21. Lavan (2013, 149).

22. C. A. Williams (2000, 103). Lavan (2013, 149n60) notes Tacitus could have used the less weighted terms *raptus* or *vis.*

23. C. A. Williams (2000, 106). See Val. Max. (6.1.pr), where Valerius invokes *Pudicitia* and identifies her as a province of the free.

24. Tac. *Ann.* 14.31.2.

25. Tac. *Ann.* 14.31.4.

26. Tacitus uses foreign affairs to comment upon the political situation in Rome and Roman morality elsewhere in his corpus. See O'Gorman (1993) and Krebs (2011) on the *Germania*. See Keitel (1978) on Parthia and Armenia as a commentary on dynastic politics, whether Roman or foreign; cf. Gilmartin (1973) on Corbulo's campaigns in the east. See Roberts (1988, 127) on *dominatio* and *servitio* in the principate; cf. Percival (1980); and Wirszubski (1950, 160–67).

27. On *dominatio* as designating despotic and illegitimate power, see Buongiovanni (2003). Augustus's rule is first labeled a *dominatio* in Tacitus's discussion of potential successors (Tac. *Ann.* 1.3.1), and he is criticized for giving largess to veterans in his desire for *dominatio* (Tac. *Ann.* 1.10.1).

28. After Livia's death, Tiberius's reign becomes an unmitigated *dominatio* (Tac. *Ann.* 5.3.1); Nero uses *dominatio* to order the death of Vestinus (Tac. *Ann.* 15.69.1), and he blames all of the crimes perpetrated under Claudius's *dominatio* on his mother (Tac. *Ann.* 14.11.2).

29. Livia reminds Tiberius that she gave him *dominatio* as a gift (Tac. *Ann.* 4.57.3); Sejanus accuses Agrippina the Elder of desiring *dominatio* (Tac. *Ann.* 4.12.3; cf. *Ann.* 6.25.2); Agrippina the Younger is chaste after her marriage to Claudius, unless it aided in her *dominatio* (Tac. *Ann.* 12.7.3), and she desires Seneca as a tutor for Nero so that the mother and son team can take advantage of his advice in their desire for *dominatio*

(Tac. *Ann.* 12.8.2); after the death of Claudius, Agrippina burns with desire of *dominatio* (Tac. *Ann.* 13.2.2; cf. *Ann.* 14.2.2).

30. E.g., Tac. *Ann.* 1.2.1, 1.7.1, 1.81.2, 3.65.3, 6.32.4, 6.48.2.

31. Roberts (1988) demonstrates how the language of freedom and servitude aligns senatorial and provincial freedom in Tacitus's *Agricola*; cf. Oakley (2009) on freedom and the senate. See Lavan (2013, 139–42) on this lack of freedom in the reign of Domitian.

32. P. Crummy (1997, 75) estimates the number and notes the *cella* was 285 sq. m. in area.

33. Tac. *Ann.* 14.33.2.

34. Tac. *Ann.* 14.33.2.

35. Caes. *BGall.* 5.12; cf. Dio 62.6.3, 77.16.5.

36. On charges of incest leveled against non-Romans, cf. Tac. *Ann.* 12.6.3.

37. Allason-Jones (2004, 278).

38. See Allason-Jones (2004, 273–87) on extended families cohabitating in the same roundhouse or group of roundhouses.

39. Allason-Jones (2005) is fundamental to the study of women in Roman Britain. Cf. Watts (2005) on women and status, daily life, religion, and death in Roman Britain.

40. Allason-Jones (2004, 280).

41. See Allason-Jones (2004, 279) for evidence of women as heads of households in Roman Britain, including Veloriga, who describes herself as such on a curse tablet from Bath (*Tabulae Sulis* 53).

42. Allason-Jones (2005, 275).

43. Potter and Johns (1992, 160).

44. Cf. Corbier (1995).

45. Allason-Jones (2005, 278) argues that a family with two children was most common in Roman Britain.

46. Hardie (1993, 4); on the "synecdochic hero," see Hardie (1993, 3–11).

47. On the inability to unify, see Tac. *Agr.* 12.2.

48. The second half of her speech is discussed in chapter 5.

49. Tac. *Ann.* 14.35.1.

50. Adler (2008, 181–82); cf. L'Hoir (2006, 141).

51. The sexual misconduct of the Romans toward barbarian children is repeated in the speeches of Calgacus (Tac. *Agr.* 31.1) and Civilis, leader of the Batavian revolt in AD 69 (Tac. *Hist.* 4.14.1).

52. See Livy 1.58–60; for Lucretia's speech, cf. Dio 2.11.18–19. See Joshel (1992) on Livy's use of Lucretia and Verginia as catalysts in the development of the Roman state.

53. Livy 1.59.3.

54. Cf. Tac. *Ann.* 1.1.1. Brutus's descendant, Brutus the murderer of Caesar, is likewise heralded as a freedom fighter (cf. Tac. *Ann.* 3.76.2, 4.35.5).

55. Adler (2008, 181): "this historical connection serves both to 'Romanize' Boudica and to present a justification for the rebellion somewhat akin to Rome's expulsion of a 'foreign' monarchy."

56. See Joshel (1992) on Livy 3.44–49; for Icilius's speech, see Livy 3.45.6–11.

57. L'Hoir (2006, 140–41).

58. Livy 3.48.5.

59. Hälikkä (2002, 87) defines this rhetoric as including "any discourse concerning the human body, its actual and symbolic functions and meanings, applied either by the author, persons on themselves or other persons in the narrative."

60. In Tacitus's *Annals*, external affairs provide a foil to domestic affairs and the politics of the principate in particular. See Ginsburg (1981, 53–79) on the arrangement of external and internal affairs in the *Annals*.

61. Tac. *Ann.* 11.38.1.

62. Tac. *Ann.* 12.7.3.

63. Tac. *Ann.* 14.2.1.

64. Tac. *Ann.* 14.9.1.

65. Tac. *Ann.* 14.11.1.

66. Tac. *Ann.* 14.12.1.

67. Tac. *Ann.* 14.13.2.

68. Tac. *Ann.* 14.13.2.

69. Tac. *Ann.* 14.64.2.

Chapter 4

1. Dio 62.1.1.

2. Dio 62.2.2.

3. The Greek word Dio uses, ξανθοτάτην, implies blonde or golden, as in the color of a lion's coat; however, many Celts had red hair, and this color is implicated as well.

4. Dio 62.2.3–4.

5. See Stewart (1995) and Woolf (2011) on ancient ideas of ethnography and the creation of mythologies through imperial conquest.

6. Diod. Sic. 5.27.3.

7. Diod. Sic. 5.30.1.

8. Diod. Sic. 5.28.1.

9. Diod. Sic. 5.31.1.

10. Diod. Sic. 5.32.2.

11. See Revell (2016, 106–10) on the archaeology of dress and the presentation of the body as connected to identity and socialization.

12. Cf. Carr (2001); Hill (1997); Jundi and Hill (1998). See R. Jackson (1985) on cosmetic sets.

13. Carr (2001, 119).

14. See Allason-Jones (2005, 109–41) on fashion and clothing, and especially 109–18 on the basic tunic and cloak; cf. Wild (1968). See further Rothe (2013) on gendered dress as indicative of cultural roles and expressions of local identity.

15. See Jundi and Hill (1998) on brooches and identity. Davies (2009, 142) discusses the rear-hook brooch used by the Iceni.

16. Cf. Wild (1985, 393–99).

17. Vergil's Dido wears such a garment (Verg. *Aen.* 4.137), as does Tacitus's Agrippina the Younger (Tac. *Ann.* 12.56.3). Kaplan (1979, 413) notes that this garment is "generally equated with the *paludamentum,* or military cloak, and as such it is a garment rarely worn by women."

18. Hutcheson (2007, 359–60).

19. See Jundi and Hill (1998) on evidence that brooches, along with mirrors, rings, earrings, bracelets, and necklaces became increasingly common in the first c. AD, along with items for the care of the body, such as tweezers and ear scoops. See Johns (1996) on the history of jewelry in Roman Britain. See Revell (2016, 45–48) on ear

scoops as a marker of a fusion of Roman and local identities (as opposed to resistance or rejection).

20. Allason-Jones (2005, 122).

21. Cf. Davies (2009, 100–106) on the Snettisham torcs.

22. See E. Evans (1935) for an early study.

23. Ferris (1994, 26). See Henig (1995) and Toynbee (1962, 1964) on art in Roman Britain.

24. For example, on the road to Londinium outside of Camulodunum stood the tombstone of Longinus Sdapeze, a member of the first Thracian cavalry involved in the Claudian invasion, who died around AD 55. The victorious Longinus appears astride his horse, which stands over a cowering Briton. The tombstone is now in the Colchester Castle Museum; the inscription is *RIB* 201.

25. On Boudica's association with Britannia, see Collingridge (2006, 337, 346, 370–71).

26. Kampen (1996, 18): "Barbarian is to Roman as woman is to man . . . province is to Rome as woman is to man." See Rodgers (2003, 82) on the double otherness of the female barbarian. See Ferris (2000, 38) on male barbarians in Augustan art as usually in the act of surrender, seeking clemency, or as bound captives.

27. R. Smith (1987, 88).

28. E.g., Ferris (2000, 40–41) discusses the man and woman on the Alpine trophy of Augustus; the man is clothed, while the woman has one breast exposed. Ferris (2000, 43, image 19) portrays conquered Spain as a woman with one breast exposed. Ferris (2000, 48–50) mentions the barbarians on the Grand Camée de France, including a mother and child in a position of defeat. See Levi (1952) for an overview of images of barbarians on Roman coins and sculpture.

29. See Warner (1985, 280–81). Cf. Rodgers (2003, 84) on the bared breast motif. See Ferris (2000, 55–58) on the Sebasteion panels. See Kampen (1996, 20) on the Amazon as other. See Erim (1982) on Britannia as an Amazon, contra R. Smith (1987). On the myth of the Amazons, see Blok (1995).

30. On Amazons in art, see Von Bothmer (1957).

31. Ferris (1994, 26).

32. Ferris (2000, 58) suggests the group is modeled after a Hellenistic group of Achilles and Penthesileia.

33. Trajan's Column Scene XLV, 117. The numbering of scenes follows Chicorius; see the modern edition of Lepper and Frere (1988). See Ferris (2000, 66–67). R. Smith (2002, 79–81) argues the men are Dacian, not Roman soldiers. Mattingly (2013, 117) aligns the scene with the following image of the subjugation of the Dacians, the execution of men, and the seizure of women (Scene XXIX, 72).

34. Aurelian Column Scene XX. See Ferris (2000, 86–98).

35. Ferris (2000, 118).

36. Ferris (2000, 123–24, 165).

37. Women who speak in Dio include Hersilia (Dio 1.5.5–6; cf. Livy 1.13), Lucretia (Dio 2.11.18–19; cf. Livy 1.58), Coriolanus's mother (Dio 5.18.9–12), Portia (Dio 44.13.1–14.1), Sophonisba (Dio 17.57.51), and Cleopatra (Dio 51.12.1–7). Livia (Dio 55.14–22) and Boudica have the longest speeches of women in the extant Dio; for a comparison, see Adler (2011a).

38. Dio 1.5.7.

39. Cf. Dion. Hal. 2.45.1–46.1.

40. Dio 5.18.10.

41. For Veturia, see Livy 2.40; Plut. *Cor.* 33–36; Dion. Hal. 8.39–54.

42. On Dio's representation of Augustus, see Reinhold and Swan (1990).

43. Dio 55.14–22. Cf. Sen. *Clem.* 1.9. Seneca dates the speech to 23–13 BC, while Dio dates the speech to AD 4, when Cinna was *consul designatus*. On Dio's version, see Swan (2004, 147–55), and esp. 148 on the larger role given to Livia than in Seneca's version, "possibly reflecting the influence of the imperial women under the Severan dynasty." On this speech as a way to characterize Livia, see Adler (2011a).

44. Dio 55.16.1.

45. Dio 55.16.2.

46. Dio 55.18.5.

47. Dio 55.20.2.

48. Dio 55.22.1. Cf. Sen. *Clem.* 1.9.8–12.

49. Dio 55.22.2. This accusation is not explicit in Tacitus (*Ann.* 1.10) or Suetonius (*Aug.* 19.1–2).

50. Adler (2011a, 139).

51. Dio (56.42.4) notes her loyalty to Augustus even after his death.

52. Adler (2011a).

53. Dio 57.12.3–4.

54. Dio 56.47.1. Cf. Tac. *Ann.* 1.14.1.

55. Dio 58.2.1–3, 58.2.6. Cf. Tac. *Ann.* 5.2.1.

56. Dio 62.3.1–5.

57. Dio 62.4.1.

58. Dio 62.4.3.

59. Dio 62.4.3: ὦ πολῖται καὶ φίλοι καὶ συγγενεῖς.

60. Dio 62.5.1–6.

61. Dio 77[76].12.1–5.

62. See Swan (2004, 26–28) on the historical function of speeches in Dio's history.

63. Dio 62.6.2–3.

64. Cf. Hdt. 1.84–87, 3.155.5; Prop. 3.11.21–26.

65. Mayor (2014, 193) notes her rule lasted from 810–805 BC.

66. On Semiramis, see Diod. Sic. 2.4–20.

67. Diod. Sic. 2.13.4.

68. Diod. Sic. 2.6.6. Cf. Mayor (2014, 187).

69. Diod. Sic. 2.16–19.

70. Val. Max. 9.3 ext. 4.

71. Hdt. 1.85–86.

72. Collingridge (2006, 239).

73. Livy's Brutus (Livy 1.59.9) gives a similar contrast between military men and artisans in calling the Romans to arms against the Tarquins.

74. By contrast, Dio's Julia Domna sees them as positive models and wishes to make herself the equal of Semiramis and Nitocris (Dio 79.23.1–4). Swan (2004, 6) argues Dio reproaches Julia for this view.

75. Dio 62.6.2

76. Adler (2011b, 151) calls the citation of the Romans as the source of information "clunky" and "unrealistic." Cf. Braund (1996, 143).

77. Cf. Suet. *Claud.* 25.5.

78. Cf. Tac. *Ann.* 12.7.3. On sex as a way to discuss *imperium*, see Vout (2007, 1–51).

79. Dio 60.8.4–5.

80. E.g., Gaius Appius Silanus is accused of a treasonous plot after refusing to have sex with Messalina (Dio 60.14.1–4). When an actual plot is discovered, Messalina and Narcissus and other freedmen seize the opportunity to wreak vengeance (Dio 60.15.5); they save the lives of those who bribe them (Dio 60.16.2) and allow others to suffer. She has Vinicius and Asiaticus killed for not committing adultery with her (Dio 60.27.4, 60.29.6).

81. Dio 60.17.5, 17.8.

82. Dio 60.18.1–4.

83. E.g., she saved Sabinus, a former prefect of the German bodyguard, in a gladiatorial fight (Dio 60.28.2–4).

84. Dio 60.28.4.

85. Suet. *Claud.* 26.2.

86. Dio 60.31.6; Tac. *Ann.* 12.7.2.

87. Tac. *Ann.* 12.7.3.

88. Dio (60.33.2) labels Agrippina as "another Messalina" for her use of the *carpentum*. Dio repeats his mantra that Claudius was a slave to his wives, this time so much so that he killed both of his sons-in-law on their account (Dio 60.31.8).

89. Cf. Flory (1988) and Kolb (2010, 14–22) on the definition and role of the Augusta.

90. On *impotentia*, cf. Tac. *Ann.* 12.57.2, 1.4.5, 3.33.3. Rutland (1978, 16) translates *impotentia* as a "lack of self-control and unwillingness to recognize and function within the bounds of limitations." Cf. L'Hoir (1994, 6). Agrippina is also *atrox* (bold, severe), like her mother, Agrippina the Elder (cf. *Ann.* 13.13.3, 4.52.3). See Kaplan (1979).

91. Dio 60.33.1, 60.33.7. E.g., she practiced the daily *salutatio* along with Claudius. Cf. Barrett (2002, 167).

92. Tac. *Ann.* 12.36–37, esp. 12.37.4.

93. Dio 60.33.3; Tac. *Ann.* 12.56.3.

94. The observations made in this paragraph appeared formerly in Gillespie (2014, 284–87).

95. Dio 61.3.2.

96. Cf. Ginsburg (2006, 72 and 78–79).

97. Dio 61.7.3.

98. Dio 61.12.3.

99. Gowing (1997, 2581): "Dio subtly suggests that the woman to whom the Romans owed their defeat was not Boudicca [*sic*], but Nero."

100. On Nero and the theater, see Edwards (1994); and Morford (1985). Gowing (1997, 2558–90) explores Nero's theatricality in Dio and suggests Dio links Nero's attraction to the theater to his increasing effeminacy and unsuitability as emperor. Dio betrays his antipathy to Neronian spectacle elsewhere (Dio 74.14.1, 78.137, 80.14.3).

101. Dio 62.6.3–4.

102. Dio 62.6.5.

103. Cf. Tac. (*Ann.* 13.24.1) on the danger of men becoming decadent, promiscuous, or corrupted through viewing theatrical performances.

104. See Mayor (2014) on Amazons and women warriors across space and time. Cf. Hardwick (1990, 34) for Amazons as "emblems of heroic achievement" that promote the excellence of their opponents.

105. Dio 62.6.3.

106. See Hdt. (4.110–17) on the Amazons.

107. Pompon. 3.34–35.

108. Mayor (2014, 21–25 and 138–41). Cf. Hdt. 4.110.

109. Mayor (2014, 63–83).

110. See Mayor (2014, 339–53).

111. Val. Max. 4.6.2.

112. Plut. *Pomp.* 32.8.

113. Plut. *Pomp.* 45.4; App. *BCiv.* 12.17.117.

114. App. *BCiv.* 12.15.103. Cf. Plut. *Pomp.* 35.3.

115. Hill (2001a, 2).

116. Noted by Aldhouse-Green (2006, 97–98).

117. Dent (1985, 85–92); Green (1995, 18–19).

118. On burials, see Niblett (1999, 2000, 2004); Philpott (1991).

Chapter 5

1. Tac. *Ann.* 14.29.2. On Corbulo, see Tac. *Ann.* 13.5–9, 13.34.2–41, 14.23–26, 15.1–17, 15.24–31. Cf. Gilmartin (1973). Tacitus notes that Corbulo does not tolerate rivals (Tac. *Ann.* 15.6.4).

2. Tac. *Ann.* 14.30.1.

3. Tac. *Ann.* 14.30.2.

4. L'Hoir (1992, 88–89). Cf. Rutland (1978, 15–16).

5. Tac. *Ann.* 14.32.1. Cf. Dio 62.1.1–2.

6. Tac. *Ann.* 14.33.1. On women as unwarlike (*imbellis*) and weak (*inermis*), see L'Hoir (1992, 86).

7. Tac. *Ann.* 14.34.2.

8. Tac. *Germ.* 7.4. The type of womanly shrieking (*ululatus, Germ.* 7.3) is reminiscent of Amazonian women warriors; in the *Aeneid*, Camilla and her female companions shout like the Amazon Penthesilea and her troops (*magnoque ululante tumultu*, Verg. *Aen.* 11.662). Livy notes Alexander the Great said that the Germans fought with women (*cum feminis*, Livy 9.19.10).

9. Tac. *Germ.* 8.1.

10. On the chastity of Germanic women, cf. Tac. *Germ.* 19.1.

11. On the moral superiority of the Germanic peoples in the *Germania*, see O'Gorman (1993). On women in the *Germania* as positive role models for the Romans, see L'Hoir (1992, 127). In Tacitus (*Hist.* 4.18), Julius Civilis marshals his female relatives to rally their men to victory.

12. See Fuhrer (2015) for the argument that the women observers are emotionally involved although spatially separate in a *teichoskopia*.

13. E.g., Helen names the heroes for Priam in Homer's *Iliad* (3.171–242).

14. Tac. *Hist.* 3.68.

15. Tac. *Hist.* 3.69.

16. Tac. *Hist.* 3.77.6–7. Cf. Benoist (2015, 274).

17. For the positive example of women who accompany sons and husbands into exile, cf. Tac. *Hist.* 1.3.1.

18. Tac. *Agr.* 16.1; *Ann.* 14.35.1.

19. On Artemisia, see Hdt. 7.99. On Penthesilea, see Verg. *Aen.* 1.490–93; and Prop. 3.11.13–16. Cf. Cuchet (2015) on women warriors between the Classical and Hellenistic eras, including Artemisia II against the Rhodians, Ada I at Halicarnassus, and Artemisia I at Salamis.

20. Verg. *Aen.* 1.364.

21. See Sharrock (2015, 159–68) on Camilla as a positive model of the woman warrior in Roman epic.

22. The full catalogue is *Aeneid* 7.647–817; Camilla is described in lines 803–17.

23. Verg. *Aen.* 7.804.

24. E.g., *furens* (raging), Verg. *Aen.* 11.709.

25. She is referred to as *virgo* (Verg. *Aen.* 11.507, 508); she preserves a love for arms and her chastity (Verg. *Aen.* 11.584–85).

26. Verg. *Aen.* 7.805. She is compared to an Amazon (Verg. *Aen.* 11.648), and her female companions are compared to Amazons (Verg. *Aen.* 11.659–63). Penthesilea is the only other woman in the *Aeneid* called *bellatrix* (Verg. *Aen.* 1.493). Camilla is not called a *dux femina*; that label is reserved for Dido.

27. E.g., Verg. *Aen.* 11.734.

28. E.g., Verg. *Aen.* 11.499.

29. Verg. *Aen.* 11.782. The desire for spoil is not necessarily womanly; however, Servius glosses *femineo* as *inpatienti* (not steadfast) and *irrationabili* (irrational).

30. Verg. *Aen.* 11.432.

31. Verg. *Aen.* 11.892.

32. Livy 2.13.6–11. Cf. Val. Max. 3.2.2. On Cloelia as an *exemplum virtutis*, see M. Roller (2004).

33. Livy 2.12–13.5.

34. Livy 2.13.6. On Lucretia as the *dux Romanae pudicitiae* (master of Roman sexual chastity), cf. Val. Max. 6.1.1.

35. Livy 2.11. Cf. Val. Max. 3.2.2.

36. Her character seems paradoxical: M. Roller (2004) has identified her as a "manly maiden," a *dux femina* with *virtus* that becomes a model for men. Other ancient authors confirm her role as an *exemplum virtutis* (cf. Sen. *Dial.* 6.16.1–2).

37. E.g., Livy's Tanaquil harangues her husband Servius like a general before a battle (Livy 1.41.2). Cicero berates Clodia as the female general (*imperatrix*) of a womanly troop (*mulieraria manus*) (Cic. *Cael.* 66).

38. On Fulvia as a *dux femina*, see Hallett (2015).

39. Vell. Pat. 2.74.

40. Plut. *Ant.* 10.3; for her role in the Perusine war, cf. *Ant.* 10.28–30.

41. Cic. *Phil.* 5.11, 6.4.

42. The *dux femina* tag is utilized by Tacitus's near contemporaries. For example, in Seneca's *Phaedra*, Hippolytus condemns woman as "the leader of evils" (*dux malorum femina*, Sen. *Phaed.* 559).

43. L'Hoir (1994, 6).

44. Cf. Ginsburg (2006, 112–16) on the *dux femina* trope in Tacitus's characterization of Agrippina the Elder, Agrippina the Younger, and Plancina.

45. Tac. *Ann.* 1.40.4.

46. Tac. *Ann.* 1.40.4: *muliebre et miserabile agmen*; cf. Tac. *Ann.* 14.30.2: *muliebre et fanaticum agmen*.

47. Tac. *Ann.* 1.69.1–3.

48. Tac. *Ann.* 1.69.4.

49. Tac. *Ann.* 1.69.4–5.

50. On the comparison between this debate and that of Cato and Lucius Valerius on the Lex Oppia in book 34 of Livy, cf., inter alios, Ginsburg (1993, 89–96); Milnor (2005, 180–85); L'Hoir (1994, 11–17).

51. Tac. *Ann.* 3.33.2.

52. Tac. *Ann.* 3.33.3.

53. Tac. *Ann.* 2.55.6. Plancina and Piso are regarded as responsible for Germanicus's death by poison (Tac. *Ann.* 2.71.1–2).

54. Tac. *Ann.* 3.33.4; for the Britons, cf. Tac. *Agr.* 15.2.

55. Tac. *Ann.* 3.33.4.

56. Tac. *Ann.* 3.34.6.

57. Benoist (2015, 270): "The intervention of women in these contexts is always a 'normative' one, strictly delimited by the legitimate struggle against tyrants: in Lucretia's case, the Etruscan tyrant Tarquin; in Cloelia's, the Etruscan people and their illegitimate domination of Rome; in Dido's, her wicked brother, the tyrannical Pygmalion; and in Boudicca's [*sic*], the effeminate Roman tyrant Nero."

58. Tac. *Agr.* 16.1.

59. Cf. Tac. *Ann.* 14.31.2 (*rapiunt arma*); 14.32.2 (*multitudine barbarorum*);14.33.2 (*barbari*); 14.34.2 (*Britannorum copia*).

60. Tac. *Ann.* 14.32.3.

61. Tac. *Ann.* 14.35.1.

62. Tac. *Germ.* 7.1.

63. Tac. *Ann.* 14.35.2.

64. Tac. *Ann.* 14.35.2.

65. Tac. *Ann.* 14.36.1.

66. Adler (2011a, 136) cites disorderliness as a feminine trait. Cf. Braund (1996, 138): "She shows great bravery, but it is a bravery without disciplined thought: such was the stereotype of barbarian courage, lacking any rational underpinning."

67. Tac. *Ann.* 14.37.2–3.

68. Tac. *Ann.* 14.37.1.

69. Cf. Zenobia, wife of Radamistus, king of Armenia, as another example of the self-sacrifice of women and the theme of death before dishonor (Tac. *Ann.* 12.51.2). Keitel (1978, 471–72) contrasts this relationship of conjugal love and the value of honor with that of Claudius and Agrippina.

Chapter 6

1. Tac. *Agr.* 15.5.

2. Dio 62.7.1.

3. E.g., Trow and Trow (2003, 144).

4. For Tanaquil, see Livy 1.34.4–9, 1.39.3, 1.41.1–5. Tullia perverts her model at Livy 1.47.6.

5. Livy 1.34.

6. Livy 1.39.

7. Hor. *Carm.* 3.30.8–10.

8. Tac. *Germ.* 8.2.

9. Ibid.

10. See Schuhmann (1999) on the origins of the names Aurinia ("golden") and Veleda, from the word for poet.

11. Tac. *Hist.* 4.17.6. See Lavan (2013, 142–46) on the issue of freedom in the revolt.

12. Cf. Brunt (1960, 501) on the connection with Tac. *Agr.* 13.1.

13. Brunt (1960, 499).

14. Tac. *Hist.* 4.14. Cf. Dyson (1971, 267) on the use of native customs and religion to rally the people behind him.

15. Tac. *Hist.* 4.61.2–3.

16. Tac. *Hist.* 4.65.

17. Tac. *Hist.* 5.25.2.

18. Tac. *Ann.* 12.40.3.

19. Tac. *Hist.* 5.23–24.

20. Tac. *Hist.* 5.24–25.

21. See Collingridge (2006, 237–38) on the spiritual significance of hares to the Britons. See Caes. (*BGall.* 5.12) on the hare used for divination.

22. Dio 62.6.1.

23. Dio 62.7.3.

24. See Linduff (1979); Aldhouse-Green (2003, 102–6).

25. See Green (1995) for an overview of women in religion. See Allason-Jones (2005, 142–63) on women in Roman Britain involved in classical cults, native cults, mystery cults, and the cult of the deified emperor. See Aldhouse-Green (2010, 210–30) on women in religion and the possibility of Druidesses.

26. See Hutton (2009) on the history of Druids in Britain. See Chadwick (1966), Beresford Ellis (1994), Green (1997), Aldhouse-Green (2010), and Ross (1999) for introductions to the Druids.

27. Tac. *Ann.* 14.30.3.

28. By comparison, Caesar forces his reluctant soldiers to cut down a sacred grove near Massilia in Lucan's *Pharsalia* (3.399–452).

29. Dudley and Webster (1962, 110–11). Cf. Bulst (1961, 499); Waite (2007, 144). Contra Dyson (1971, 260 and 266) for the suggestion that their political role has been exaggerated.

30. Creighton (1995, 297 and 300).

31. Creighton (1995, 300).

32. Creighton (1995, 300) argues for the nature of power in the southeast rather than the Roman conquest; contra J. Webster (1999, 11 and 16).

33. De la Bédoyère (2003, 56).

34. Caes. *BGall.* 6.13.11–12, 6.14.1. On Druids and life after death, cf. Pompon. 3.19.

35. Caes. *BGall.* 6.13.1–2.

36. E.g. Plin. *HN* 16.95, 30.4. See J. Webster (1999, 2–4) for a table of classical references to the Druids in Gaul and Britain.

37. Suet. *Claud.* 25.5. On the suppression of human sacrifice, cf. Plin. *HN* 30.13.

38. See Aldhouse-Green (2001) for an introduction to human sacrifice in Iron Age and Roman Europe. Cf. Aldhouse-Green (2010, 66–80); Rankin (1996, 285–88).

39. See Strabo 4.4.5 on human sacrifice via arrows, impalement, and wicker men.

40. See J. Webster (1994, 6–8). On the cessation of human sacrifice in Rome, see Plin. *HN* 30.4; Pompon. 3.2, 3.18. Eckstein (1982) discusses the instances of human sacrifice in Rome at significant moments of crisis, in 228 BC, in 216 BC after Cannae, and in 114/13 BC, linking the last two dates to scandals involving the Vestal Virgins. Cf. Livy 22.57.2–6; Plut. *Mor.* 284A–C.

41. E.g., in AD 213, Caracalla had four Vestals buried alive, one of whom he had debauched (Dio 78.16.1; cf. Hdn. 4.6.4).

42. Dio 48.14.4–5. The massacre is recalled by Propertius (1.22.1–10).

43. SHA *Sev.* 10.3. See Birley (1999, 125n14). After defeating Pescinnius Niger, Severus sent his head to Byzantium, and it was set up on a pole as a means to convince the Byzantines to join him (Dio 77[76].8.3). On the deprivation of senatorial property, see Dio 77[76].8.4.

44. Caes. *BGall.* 6.16.

45. Diod. Sic. 5.32.6.

46. Plin. *HN* 30.13.

47. On Lindow Man (Lindow II), see Brothwell (1987); Connolly (1985); Robins and Ross (1989); and Joy (2009). On Lindow Man and other bog bodies, see Stead, Bourke, and Brothwell (1986); Turner and Scaife (1995).

48. See Howarth (2008, 71–75) on his age and the sequence of death blows. Cf. C. D. Williams (2009, 162–63); Collingridge (2006, 158–59).

49. See Brothwell (1987) for Lindow Man as the member of a ruling class. See Robins and Ross (1989) on Lindow Man as a Druid.

50. Tac. *Ann.* 14.33.2. Braund (1996, 138) argues she is excessive in her vengeance and lacks reasoned forethought, a stereotypical failure of non-Roman leaders.

51. Lavan (2013, 124–25).

52. Dio 62.7.2.

53. Dio 62.7.3.

54. Allason-Jones (2005, 73).

55. Dio 62.9.1–2.

56. Dio 62.10.2.

57. Dio 62.11.4.

58. Sen. *De ira* 3.18–19; cf. Sen. *Ep.* 14.4–6.

59. Tac. *Ann.* 15.44.2–3.

60. Tac. *Ann.* 15.44.4.

61. Tac. *Ann.* 15.44.5.

62. Dio 62.11.1–5.

63. Dio 62.12.6.

64. See Carr (2007) on burial types in the Iron Age, and the shift from excarnation to cremation. Creighton (2000, 19–20) argues this was part of the Roman influence.

Chapter 7

1. Dyson (1971) compares the revolts of Vercingetorix, Bato, Arminius, Boudica, and the Batavian revolt.

2. Tac. *Ann.* 4.72.1–3. Similar rebellions arise when revenue is extracted in Thrace (Tac. *Ann.* 4.46) and Cappadocia (Tac. *Ann.* 6.41), in addition to Britain (Tac. *Ann.* 14.31–38).

3. Keitel (1978).

4. E.g., Tac. *Ann.* 3.18.4.

5. Tac. *Ann.* 12.11.2.

6. Keitel (1978, 467).

7. Tac. *Ann.* 12.2.2.

8. Dio 62.4.1.

9. Suet. *Tib.* 16.1.

10. See Dyson (1971, 250) for an overview of the area and Vell. Pat. (2.110.5) on their knowledge of Latin.

11. Dio (55.29.1–30.6, 56.11.1–17.3) is the lengthiest account of the rebellion. See Swan (2004, 195–203, 210–16, 221–22, and 235–60). Cf. Vell. Pat. 2.110.1–117.1; and Suet. *Tib.* 16.1–17.2, 20.

12. Dio 55.14.4.

13. Dio 56.15.2.

14. Dio 56.16.3.

15. Dio 62.5.6.

16. Swan (2004, 246) argues, "More than esteem for female nature, Dio's admiration for the wives of Arduba attests his scorn for men outdone by women in hatred of slavery."

17. The Varian disaster is told by Dio (56.18–24), among others. On Dio's account, see Swan (2004, 250–74).

18. Suet. *Tib.* 17.1.

19. Tiberius went to Germany to settle affairs and returned to celebrate his triumph over Bato after two years; Bato walked in his triumph and was eventually sent to Ravenna to live as an exile (Suet. *Tib.* 20.1). Bato may have arranged the capture of the Breucian Bato (Dio 55.34.4) and was rewarded with a life of relative comfort after Tiberius's triumph (Suet. *Tib.* 20; Dio 56.13.2–3, 56.16).

20. Dio 56.18.2–3.

21. Dio 56.18.3. Dyson (1971, 253–54) suggests the cultural impact was primarily an increase in trade that increased the wealth and power of the elite; problems arose with taxation. Cf. Vell. Pat. 2.117.3–4.

22. Tac. *Ann.* 2.10.3.

23. Tac. *Ann.* 2.9.3. See Adler (2011b, 130, 134, and 136) on echoes of Boudica in the speeches of Arminius and Civilis.

24. Tac. *Ann.* 2.45.2.

25. Dio 56.18.5.

26. Dio 56.24.3–5.

27. Simpson (1996, 386) notes that references to Victory statues may reflect a literary topos portending victory or defeat, rather than a historical reality. Cf. Standing (2005, 373–74).

28. Tac. (*Ann.* 12.27.3) mentions some of Varus's men were rescued from slavery forty years after the disaster.

29. Tac. *Ann.* 1.61.3.

30. Tac. *Ann.* 1.10.4.

31. Germanicus mentions his troops are willing to avenge the death of Varus and his three legions (Tac. *Ann.* 1.43.1).

32. Tac. *Ann.* 1.50–51.

33. Tac. *Ann.* 1.57.4.

34. Tac. *Ann.* 1.58.6.

35. Strabo 7.1.4.

36. Cf. Tac. *Ann.* 1.59.1, 2.10.1.

37. See Pagán (1999) on the narrative importance of the scene and its connection to actual battle scene motifs.

38. Tac. *Ann.* 1.61.5–6; Vell. Pat. 1.120.5. The practice is not unknown among Germanic tribes (Tac. *Germ.* 9.1–2), but it is not used often (Caes. *BGall.* 6.21.1–2).

39. Tac. *Ann.* 1.61–62.

40. Tac. *Ann.* 2.88.2.

41. Tac. *Ann.* 1.60.3, 2.25.1–2.

42. Tac. *Ann.* 2.41.1.

43. Dio 60.8.7.

44. Tac. *Ann.* 1.57.4.

45. Tac. *Ann.* 11.16.3.

46. The Varian disaster is recounted by Dio (56.18–24) and mentioned numerous times by Tacitus (*Ann.* 1.3.6, 1.10.4, 1.43.1, 1.55–71, 2.7.2, 2.41.1, 2.45.3, inter alia).

47. Tac. *Ann.* 2.88.2.

48. Tac. *Ann.* 1.11.4.

49. Cf. H. Benario (2003, 402).

50. Tac. *Agr.* 15.3.

51. Tac. *Ann.* 14.29.1.

52. Tac. *Ann.* 14.32.3, 14.33.2.

53. Suet. *Ner.* 39.1; Dio 62.1.1.

54. Tac. *Ann.* 14.37.3.

55. Tac. *Ann.* 14.38.2.

56. See de Filippis (2000) for a comparison of Agricola and Suetonius: Suetonius is too severe, although both have *virtus*. Orsi (1973) sees Tacitus's view as pro-Paulinus, while Dio is against. See further du Toit (1977).

57. Gambash (2012, 5) argues Classicianus was married to a noblewoman of a Gallic tribe, and perhaps was a Gaul himself.

58. Tac. *Ann.* 14.39.1–3.

59. Tac. *Ann.* 14.39.2.

60. Tac. *Ann.* 14.39.3.

61. Tac. *Ann.* 11.18–19.

62. Tac. *Ann.* 13.8.1.

63. Tac. *Ann.* 13.8.2.

64. Tac. *Ann.* 13.5–9, 13.34.2–41. Cf. Dio 61.30.4–6, 62.19–26.

65. Tac. *Ann.* 14.23–26.

66. Tac. *Ann.* 15.1–17. Cf. Suet. *Ner.* 39.1.

67. Tac. *Ann.* 15.18.1.

68. Tac. *Ann.* 15.24–31.

69. Dio 62.26.5, 63.6.3.

70. Dio 63.17.1–6.

71. See Gilmartin (1973).

72. Gilmartin (1973, 600).

73. Tac. *Ann.* 14.24.4.

74. Gambash (2012, 6).

75. See Griffin (1976–77, 145) on *Syll.* no. 23. Suetonius became consul in AD 66 (Tac. *Ann.* 16.14.1) but then disappears from the written record.

76. Gambash (2012, 7).

77. See Shotter (2004) for a history of the Romans in northwest England.

78. Rutledge (2000) argues Tacitus presents Calgacus as having a similar ideology and ideals as Rome. See Fick (1994) on Calgacus as a model of *virtus*; see Clarke (2001) on Calgacus as a representative of old Roman virtues. See Woodman (2014, 22) on Calgacus as a mirror for Rome and the lives of the Britons as similar to those of the senate under Domitian.

79. Tac. *Agr.* 30–32. On the speech of Calgacus, see Syme (1958, 528–29); Rutherford (2010). On the idea of freedom in Calgacus's speech, see Giua (1991).

80. Tac. *Agr.* 30.4.

81. Tac. *Agr.* 30.5.

82. Tac. *Agr.* 31.1.

83. Tac. *Agr.* 31.4.

84. Woodman (2014, 248) supports Wellesley's suggestion that Tacitus confused the *colonia* Camulodunum with the name of a fort in the land of the Brigantes (Wellesley 1969, 268).

85. Tac. *Agr.* 32.2.

86. Tac. *Agr.* 32.4.

87. Tac. *Agr.* 33.1.

88. See Campbell (2010) for details of the battle of Mons Graupius.

89. Tac. *Agr.* 38.1.

90. Woodman (2014, 282) cites Livy 21.14.4 (Saguntum) and 31.18.7 (Abydus) as comparanda.

91. Tac. *Hist.* 1.2.3. B. Jones (1992, 132) suggests this constituted a "massive withdrawal" of Roman forces, contra Woodman (2014, 18).

92. Tac. *Agr.* 3.1.

93. Dio 77.16.5.

Epilogue

1. Hingley and Unwin (2005, 111–221) comprises an extensive analysis of her afterlife. Cf. Macdonald (1987) for a summary of her later appearances and issues in the template she provides as a figure of British nationalism.

2. Hingley and Unwin (2005, 206).

3. See Hingley and Unwin (2005, 116–17) on Boudica as Voadicia in the *Anglica Historia*, published in 1534 by Polydore Vergil, and as Voada, sister of Caratak (Caratacus) in Hecter Boece's 1535 *Chronicles of Scotland* (*Historia Gentis Scotorum*).

4. See Hingley and Unwin (2005, 118–19) on Voadicia, alias Bonduica, who appears in Raphael Holinshed's *Chronicles of England, Scotland, and Ireland* (1577), and Stephen Gossom, who referred to Bunduica in his pamphlet, *School of Abuse* (1579), making a comparison between the warrior and Queen Elizabeth.

5. Crawford (1999).

6. Hingley and Unwin (2005, 145).

7. Cowper (1980, 432, lines 41–44)

8. Johnson (2012, 117) calls Boudica in the Victorian age "the legendary and larger-than-life warrior queen of *England*" (original italics). Hingley and Unwin (2005, 159) suggest, "In effect, an 'imperial cult of Boadicea' developed in late nineteenth- and early twentieth-century Britain that drew upon Cowper's poem for its inspiration."

9. Beard and Henderson (1999, 47) note the irony of the connection made between the two leaders, one a rebel and defender of native freedoms, the other a queen and empress of a world empire that sought to destroy such insurgents.

10. See Warren (2016).

11. Johnson (2012, 118) notes Tennyson was poet laureate, so the idea of a national poetry figures in this interpretation: "It is overly patriotic and firmly reflective of the empire under Victoria in terms of national pride, confidence and identity."

12. Tennyson (1875, 318, lines 83–86).

13. The third window commemorates kings of England, with Richard I at the center.

14. See Hingley and Unwin (2005, 162–67) on the history of the statue.

15. Cowper (1980, 431, lines 29–30).

16. Quoted by Hingley and Unwin (2005, 163).

17. Cf. Caes. *BGall.* 4.33.

18. Pompon. 3.52.1.

19. Hingley and Unwin (2005, 143–44).

20. See Futrell (2013, 214).

21. See Collingridge (2006, 353), Johnson (2012, 123–29), and Hingley and Unwin (2005, 175–77) on the suffragists' use of the statue.

22. Spence (1937) was one of the first scholarly studies of Boudica.

23. See Hingley and Unwin (2005, 189, fig. 41) for George Gale's cartoon from the *Daily Telegraph*, June 11, 1987. See further Aldhouse-Green (2006, 245) on connections made between Thatcher and Boudica as warrior women.

24. Holland (2016).

25. See Beard and Henderson (1999).

26. Thomson-Salo (2015).

Bibliography

Adler, E. 2008. "Boudica's Speeches in Tacitus and Dio." *Classical World* 101: 173–95.

Adler, E. 2011a. "Cassius Dio's Livia and the Conspiracy of Cinna Magnus." *Greek, Roman and Byzantine Studies* 51: 133–54.

Adler, E. 2011b. *Valorizing the Barbarians: Enemy Speeches in Roman Historiography.* Austin: University of Texas Press.

Aldhouse-Green, M. 2001. *Dying for the Gods: Human Sacrifice in Iron Age and Roman Europe.* Stroud: Tempus.

Aldhouse-Green, M. 2003. "Poles Apart? Perceptions of Gender in Gallo-British Cult-Iconography." In *Roman Imperialism and Provincial Art*, edited by S. Scott and J. Webster, 95–118. New York: Cambridge University Press.

Aldhouse-Green, M. 2004. "Gallo-British Deities and Their Shrines." In *A Companion to Roman Britain*, edited by M. Todd, 193–219. Malden, MA: Wiley-Blackwell.

Aldhouse-Green, M. 2006. *Boudica Britannia: Rebel, War-Leader and Queen.* New York: Pearson Longman.

Aldhouse-Green, M. 2010. *Caesar's Druids: Story of an Ancient Priesthood.* New Haven, CT: Yale University Press.

Allason-Jones, L. 2004. "The Family in Roman Britain." In *A Companion to Roman Britain*, edited by M. Todd, 273–87. Malden, MA: Wiley-Blackwell.

Allason-Jones, L. 2005. *Women in Roman Britain.* 2nd ed. York: Council for British Archaeology.

Allason-Jones, L. 2012. "Women in Roman Britain." In *A Companion to Women in the Ancient World*, edited by S. L. James and S. Dillon, 467–77. Oxford: Wiley-Blackwell.

Allen, D. F. 1970. "The Coins of the Iceni." *Britannia* 1: 1–33.

Allen, D. F. 1980. *Coins of the Ancient Celts.* Edinburgh: Edinburgh University Press.

Andrews, I. 1972. *Boudicca's Revolt.* London: Cambridge University Press.

Ash, R. 1999. *Ordering Anarchy: Armies and Leaders in Tacitus' Histories.* Ann Arbor: University of Michigan Press.

Baldwin, B. 1964. "The Death of Cleopatra VII." *The Journal of Egyptian Archaeology* 50: 181–82.

Baldwin, B. 1972. "Women in Tacitus." *Prudentia* 4: 83–101.

Barrett, A. A. 1979. "The Career of Tiberius Claudius Cogidubnus." *Britannia* 10: 227–42.

Barrett, A. A. 1990. "Claudius, Gaius and the Client Kings." *The Classical Quarterly* 40 (1): 284–86.

Barrett, A. A. 1991. "Claudius' British Victory Arch in Rome." *Britannia* 22: 1–19.

Barrett, A. A. 2002. *Livia: First Lady of Imperial Rome*. New Haven, CT: Yale University Press.

Bastomsky, S. 1992. "Tacitus *Annals* 14.64.1: Octavia's Pathetic Plea." *Latomus* 51 (3): 606–11.

Beard, M., and J. Henderson. 1999. "Rule(d) Britannia: Displaying Roman Britain in Museums." In *Making Early History in Museums*, edited by N. Merriman, 44–73. Leicester: Leicester University Press.

Benario, H. W. 1986. "Legionary Speed of March before the Battle with Boudicca." *Britannia* 17: 358–62.

Benario, H. W. 2003. "Teutoberg." *Classical World* 96: 397–408.

Benario, J. M. 1970. "Dido and Cleopatra." *Vergilius* 16: 2–6.

Benoist, S. 2015. "Women and *Imperium* in Rome." In *Women and War in Antiquity*, edited by J. Fabre-Serris and A. Keith, 267–88. Baltimore, MD: Johns Hopkins University Press.

Beresford Ellis, P. 1994. *A Brief History of the Druids*. London: Constable.

Birley, A. R. 1979. *The People of Roman Britain*. Berkeley: University of California Press.

Birley, A. R. 1999. *Tacitus: Agricola, Germania*. Oxford: Oxford University Press.

Birley, A. R. 2005. *The Roman Government of Britain*. Oxford: Oxford University Press.

Birley, A. R. 2008. "Britain: The Caesarian and Claudian Invasions." In *Die römischen Provinzen. Begriff und Gründung*, edited by I. Piso, 179–205. Cluj-Napoca: Mega Verlag.

Black, E. W. 2001. "The First Century Historians of Roman Britain." *Oxford Journal of Archaeology* 20: 415–28.

Blok, J. H. 1995. *The Early Amazons: Modern and Ancient Perspectives on a Persistent Myth*. Leiden: Brill.

Bogaers, J. E. 1979. "King Cogidubnus in Chichester: Another Reading of *RIB* 91." *Britannia* 10: 243–54.

Boissevain, U. P., ed. 1895–1969. *Cassii Dionis Cocceiani Historiarum Romanarum quae supersunt*. 5 vols. Berolini: Apud Weidmannos.

Braund, D. 1984a. "Observations on Cartimandua." *Britannia* 15: 1–6.

Braund, D. 1984b. *Rome and the Friendly King: The Character of Client Kingship*. London: Croom Helm.

Braund, D. 1996. *Ruling Roman Britain: Kings, Queens, Governors and Emperors from Julius Caesar to Agricola*. London: Routledge.

Brothwell, D. R. 1987. *The Bog Man and the Archaeology of People*. Cambridge, MA: Harvard University Press.

Brunt, P. A. 1960. "Tacitus on the Batavian Revolt." *Latomus* 19 (3): 494–517.

Brunt, P. A. 1980. "On Historical Fragments and Epitomes." *Classical Quarterly* 30 (2): 477–94.

Brunt, P. A. 1990. *Roman Imperial Themes*. Oxford: Oxford University Press.

Bryant, S. and R. Niblett. 1997. "The Late Iron Age in Hertfordshire and the North Chilterns." In *Reconstructing Iron Age Societies*, edited by A. Gwilt and C. Haselgrove, 270–81. Oxford: Oxbow.

Bulst, C. M. 1961. "The Revolt of Queen Boudicca in AD 60." *Historia* 10 (4): 496–509.

Buongiovanni, C. 2003. "Il lessico della storiographia: *dominatio* da Sallustio a Tacito." In *Tra strategie retoriche e generi letterari. Dieci studi di letteratura latina*, edited by V. Viparelli, 15–49. Naples: Liguori.

Campbell, D. B. 2010. *Mons Graupius AD 83*. Oxford: Osprey Publishing.

Carr, G. 2001. "'Romanisation' and the Body." In *TRAC 2000: Proceedings of the Tenth Annual Theoretical Archaeology Conference London 2000*, edited by G. Davies, A. Gardner, and K. Lockyear, 112–24. Oxford: Oxbow.

Carr, G. 2003. "Creolisation, Pidginisation and the Interpretation of Unique Artefacts in Early Roman Britain." In *TRAC 2002: Proceedings of the Twelfth Annual Theoretical Roman Archaeology Conference*, edited by G. Carr, E. Swift, and J. Weekes, 113–25. Oxford: Oxbow.

Carr, G. 2007. "Excarnation to Cremation: Continuity or Change?" In *The Later Iron Age in Britain and Beyond*, edited by C. Haselgrove and T. Moore, 444–53. Oxford: Oxbow.

Carroll, K. K. 1979. "The Date of Boudicca's Revolt." *Britannia* 10: 197–202.

Casson, T. E. 1945. "Cartimandua in History, Legend and Romance." *Transactions of the Cumberland and Westmorland Antiquarian and Archaeological Society* 44: 68–80.

Chadwick, N. 1966. *The Druids*. Cardiff: University of Wales Press.

Champlin, E. 1991. *Final Judgments: Duty and Emotion in Roman Wills, 200 BC–AD 250*. Berkeley: University of California Press.

Champlin, E. 2003. *Nero*. Cambridge, MA: Belknap Press.

Chaplin, J. 2000. *Livy's Exemplary Rome*. Oxford: Oxford University Press.

Cipriano, A. S. 1979. "Tacito fonte di Cassio Dione?" *Rendiconti dell'Academia di Archaeologia* 54: 3–18.

Clarke, C. 2001. "An Island Nation: Re-reading Tacitus' *Agricola*." *The Journal of Roman Studies* 91: 94–112.

Classen, C. J. 1988. "Tacitus: Historian between Republic and Principate." *Mnemosyne* 41 (1): 93–116.

Collingridge, V. 2006. *Boudica: The Life of Britain's Legendary Warrior Queen*. Woodstock: Overlook Books.

Collingwood, R. G. 1932. *Roman Britain*. 2nd ed. Oxford: Biblo and Tannen.

Collingwood, R. G., and R. Wright. 1965. *Roman Inscriptions of Britain*. Oxford: Clarendon Press.

Connolly, R. C. 1985. "Lindow Man: Britain's Prehistoric Bog Body." *Anthropology Today* 1 (5): 15–17.

Corbier, M. 1995. "Male Power and Legitimacy through Women: The *domus Augusta* under the Julio-Claudians." In *Women in Antiquity: New Assessments*, edited by R. Hawley and B. Levick, 178–93. New York: Routledge.

Cottam, E., P. de Jersey, C. Rudd, and J. Sills. 2010. *Ancient British Coins*. Chris Rudd: Aylesham.

Cowper, W. 1980. "Boadicea: An Ode." In *The Poems of William Cowper 1: 1748–82*, edited by J. D. Baird and C. Ryskamp, 431–32. Oxford: Clarendon Press.

Crawford, J. 1999. "Fletcher's 'Tragedie of Bonduca' and the Anxieties of the Masculine Government of James I." *SEL Studies in English Literature, 1500–1900* 39.2: 357–81.

Creighton, J. 1995. "Visions of Power: Imagery and Symbolism in Late Iron Age Britain." *Britannia* 26: 285–301.

Creighton, J. 2000. *Coins and Power in Late Iron Age Britain*. Cambridge: Cambridge University Press.

Creighton, J. 2006. *Britannia: The Creation of a Roman Province*. London: Routledge.

Crummy, N. 2013–14. "The Fenwick Treasure: The Jewellery." *The Colchester Archaeologist* 27: 22–27.

Crummy, P. 1997. *City of Victory: The Story of Colchester—Britain's First Roman Town*. Colchester: Colchester Archaeological Trust.

Crummy, P. 1999. "Colchester: Making Towns Out of Fortresses and the First Urban Fortifications in Britain." In "The Coloniae of Roman Britain: New Studies and a Review," edited by H. Hurst. Supplement, *Journal of Roman Archaeology* 36: 88–100.

Cuchet, V. S. 2015. "The Warrior Queens of Caria (Fifth to Fourth Centuries BCE): Archaeology, History, and Historiography." In *Women and War in Antiquity*, edited by J. Fabre-Serris and A. Keith, 228–46. Baltimore, MD: Johns Hopkins University Press.

Cunliffe, B. 1988. *Greeks, Romans, and Barbarians: Spheres of Interaction*. London: Batsford.

Cunliffe, B. 1991. *Iron Age Communities in Britain*. 3rd edition. New York: Routledge.

Cunliffe, B. 1998. *Fishbourne: Roman Palace*. Rev. ed. Stroud: Tempus.

Cunliffe, B. 2004. "Britain and the Continent: Networks of Interaction." In *A Companion to Roman Britain*, edited by M. Todd, 1–11. Malden, MA: Wiley-Blackwell.

Damon, C. 2012. *Tacitus: Annals*. London: Penguin.

Dauge, Y. 1981. *Le barbare. Recherches sur la conception romaine de la barbarie et de la civilisation*. Collection Latomus vol. 176. Brussels: Latomus.

Davies, J. and T. Williamson, eds. 1999. *The Land of the Iceni: The Iron Age in Northern East Anglia*. Studies in East Anglian History 4. Norwich: Centre of East Anglian Studies, University of East Anglia.

Davies, J. 1996. "Where Eagles Dare: The Iron Age of Norfolk." *Proceedings of the Prehistoric Society* 62: 63–92.

Davies, J. 1999. "Patterns, Power and Political Progress in Iron Age Norfolk." In *The Land of the Iceni: The Iron Age in Northern East Anglia*, edited by J. A. Davies and T. Williamson, 14–44. Studies in East Anglian History 4. Norwich: Centre of East Anglian Studies, University of East Anglia.

Davies, J. 2009. *The Land of Boudica: Prehistoric and Roman Norfolk*. Oxford: Oxbow.

Davies, J., ed. 2011. *The Iron Age in Northern East Anglia: New Work in the Land of the Iceni*. BAR British Series 549. Oxford: British Archaeological Reports.

Davies, J., and T. Gregory. 1991. "Coinage from a *Civitas*: A Survey of Roman Coins Found in Norfolk and Their Contribution to the Archaeology of the *Civitas Icenorum*." *Britannia* 22: 65–101.

De Filippis, C. 1978. "*Libido reginae et saevitia*: osservazioni sulla figura di Cartimandua in Tacito." *Rivista storica dell'Antichità* 8: 51–62.

De Filippis, C. 1979. "A proposito della partecipazione dei Trinovanti alla rivolta di Boudicca." *Rivista storica dell'Antichità* 9: 125–30.

De Filippis, C. 2000. "Ancora sulla rimozione di Suetonio Paolino. Uno considerazione storica." *Bollettino di studi latini* 30: 530–35.

De Jersey, P. 1996. *Celtic Coinage in Britain*. London: Shire Publications.

De la Bédoyère, G. 2003. *Defying Rome. The Rebels of Roman Britain*. Stroud: Tempus.

De la Bédoyère, G. 2015. *The Real Lives of Roman Britain: A History of Roman Britain through the Lives of Those Who Were There*. New Haven, CT: Yale University Press.

Dent, J. 1985. "Three Cart Burials from Wetwang, Yorkshire." *Antiquity* 59: 85–92.

Devillers, O. 1994. *L'art de la persuasion dans les* Annales *de Tacite*. Collection Latomus vol. 223. Brussels: Latomus.

Dickinson, B., and B. Hartley. 1995. "Roman Military Activity in First-Century Britain: The Evidence of Tacitus and Archaeology." In *Papers of the Leeds International Latin Seminar*, Vol. 8, edited by R. Brock and A. J. Woodman, 241–55. Leeds: Francis Cairns.

Drinkwater, J. F. 1975. "The Trinovantes: Some Observations on Their Participation in the Events of A.D. 60." *Rivista storica dell'Antichità* 5: 53–57.

Du Toit, L. A. 1977. "Tacitus and the Rebellion of Boudica." *Acta Classica* 20: 149–58.

Ducos, M. 1977. "La liberté chez Tacite: Droits de l'individu ou conduit individuelle." *Bulletin de l'Association Guillaume Budé* 1 (2): 194–217.

Dudley, D. R., and G. Webster. 1962. *The Rebellion of Boudicca*. New York: Routledge.

Dudley, D. R., and G. Webster. 1965. *The Roman Conquest of Britain AD 43–57*. London: Batsford.

Dyson, S. 1971. "Native Revolts in the Roman Empire." *Historia* 20 (2): 239–74.

Eckstein, A. M. 1982. "Human Sacrifice and Fear of Military Disaster in Republican Rome." *American Journal of Ancient History* 7: 69–95.

Edwards, C. 1993. *The Politics of Immorality in Ancient Rome*. Cambridge: Cambridge University Press.

Edwards, C. 1994. "Beware of Imitations: Theatre and the Subversion of Imperial Identity." In *Reflections of Nero: Culture, History and Representation*, edited by J. Elsner and J. Masters, 80–97. Chapel Hill: University of North Carolina Press.

Erim, K. T. 1982. "A New Relief Showing Claudius and Britannia from Aphrodisias." *Britannia* 13: 277–81.

Evans, E. C. 1935. "Roman Descriptions of Personal Appearance in History and Biography." *Harvard Studies in Classical Philology* 46: 43–84.

Evans, R. 2003. "Containment and Corruption: The Discourse of Flavian Empire." In *Flavian Rome: Culture, Image, Text*, edited by A. J. Boyle and W. J. Dominik, 255–76. Leiden: Brill.

Ferris, I. M. 1994. "Insignificant Others: Images of Barbarians on Military Art from Roman Britain." In *TRAC 94: Proceedings of the Fourth Annual Theoretical Roman Archaeology Conference, Durham 1994*, edited by S. Cottam, D. Dungworth, S. Scott and J. Taylor, 24–31. Oxford: Oxbow.

Ferris, I. M. 2000. *Enemies of Rome: Barbarians through Roman Eyes*. Stroud.

Fick, N. 1994. "Calgacus, héros breton." In *Mélanges François Kerlouégan*, Annales Littéraires de l'Université de Besançon 515, edited by D. Conso, N. Fick, and B. Poulle, 235–48. Paris: Les Belles Lettres.

Fischler, S. 1994. "Social Stereotypes and Historical Analysis: The Case of Imperial Women at Rome." In *Women in Ancient Societies*, edited by L. S. Archer, S. Fischler, and M. Wyke, 115–32. Hampshire: Routledge.

Flory, M. B. 1988. "The Meaning of Augusta in the Julio-Claudian Period." *American Journal of Ancient History* 13 (2): 113–38.

Fomin, A. 2016. "Speeches in Dio Cassius." In *Cassius Dio: Greek Intellectual and Roman Politician*, edited by C. H. Lange and J. M. Madsen, 217–37. Leiden: Brill.

Forcey, C. 1997. "Beyond 'Romanization': Technologies of Power in Roman Britain." In *TRAC 96: Proceedings of the Sixth Annual Theoretical Roman Archaeology Conference*, edited by K. Meadows, C. Lemke, and J. Heron, 15–21. Oxford: Oxbow.

Fraser, A. 1986. *The Warrior Queens: Boadicea's Chariot*. London: Anchor.

Freeman, P. W. M. 1997. "Mommsen through to Haverfield: The Origins of Romanization Studies in Late 19th c. Britain." In "Dialogues in Roman Imperialism: Power, Discourse and Discrepant Experiences in the Roman Empire," edited by D. Mattingly. Supplement, *Journal of Roman Archaeology*, 23: 27–50.

Frere, S. 1999. *Britannia: A History of Roman Britain*. 4th rev. ed. London: Folio Society.

Freyburger-Galland, M. L. 1992. "Tacite et Dion Cassius." In *Présence de Tacite*, edited by R. Chevalier and R. Poignault, 127–39. Tours: Centre de Recherches A. Piganiol.

Fuhrer, T. 2015. "Teichoskopia: Female Figures Looking on Battles." In *Women and War in Antiquity*, edited by J. Fabre-Serris and A. Keith, 52–70. Baltimore, MD: Johns Hopkins University Press.

Fulford, M. 2008. "Nero and Britain: The Palace of the Client King at Calleva and Imperial Policy towards the Province after Boudicca." *Britannia* 39: 1–14.

Futrell, A. 2013. "Love, Rebellion and Cleavage: Boadicea's Hammered Breastplate in *The Viking Queen* (1967)." In *Screening Love and Sex in the Ancient World*, edited by M. S. Cyrino, 211–25. New York: Palgrave Macmillan.

Gambash, G. 2012. "To Rule a Ferocious Province: Roman Policy and the Aftermath of the Boudican Revolt." *Britannia* 43: 1–15.

Gillespie, C. 2014. "Agrippina the Younger: Tacitus' *Unicum Exemplum*." In *Valuing the Past in the Greco-Roman World. Proceedings from the Penn-Leiden Colloquia on Ancient Values VII*, edited by J. Ker and C. Pieper, 269–93. Leiden: Brill.

Gillespie, C. 2015. "The Wolf and the Hare: Boudica's Political Bodies in Tacitus and Dio." *Classical World* 108 (3): 403–29.

Gilmartin, K. 1973. "Corbulo's Campaigns in the East: An Analysis of Tacitus' Account." *Historia* 22: 583–626.

Ginsburg, J. 1981. *Tradition and Theme in the* Annals *of Tacitus*. New York: Arno Press.

Ginsburg, J. 1993. "*In maiores certamina*: Past and Present in the *Annals*." In *Tacitus and the Tacitean Tradition*, edited by T. J. Luce and A. J. Woodman, 86–103. Princeton: Princeton University Press.

Ginsburg, J. 2006. *Representing Agrippina: Constructions of Female Power in the Early Roman Empire*. Oxford: Oxford University Press.

Giua, M. A. 1991. "Paesaggio, natura, ambiente come elementi strutturali nela storiografia di Tacito." *Aufstieg und Niedergang der römischen Welt* 2.33.4: 2879–902.

Gould, J. 2004. "Boudica—Yet Again." *London Archaeologist* 10 (11): 300.

Gowing, A. M. 1990. "Tacitus and the Client Kings." *Transactions of the American Philological Association* 120: 315–31.

Gowing, A. M. 1992. *The Triumviral Narratives of Appian and Cassius Dio*. Ann Arbor: University of Michigan Press.

Gowing, A. M. 1997. "Cassius Dio on the Reign of Nero." *Aufstieg und Niedergang der römischen Welt* 2.34.3: 2556–99.

Gowing, A. M. 2009. "The Roman *Exempla* Tradition in Imperial Greek Historiography: The Case of Camillus." In *The Cambridge Companion to the Roman Historians*, edited by A. Feldherr, 332–47. Cambridge: Cambridge University Press.

Green, M. J. 1995. *Celtic Goddesses: Warriors, Virgins and Mothers*. London: George Braziller.

Green, M. J. 1997. *The World of the Druids*. New York: Thames & Hudson.

Gregory, A. K. 1991. *Excavations at Thetford, 1980–82, Fisons Way*. East Anglian Archaeological Report 53. Norwich: Oxbow.

Griffin, M. T. 1976–77. "Nero's Recall of Suetonius Paullinus." *Scripta Classica Israelica* 3: 138–52.

Griffin, M. T. 2000. *Nero: The End of a Dynasty*. Rev. ed. London: Routledge.

Halfmann, H. 2002. "Zu Tacitus' *Agricola* als Dokument römischer Herrschaftsauffassung." In *Widerstand—Anpassung—Integration: Die griechische*

Staatenwelt und Rom: Festschrift für Jürgen Deininger zum 65. Geburtstag, edited by N. Ehrhardt and L.-M. Günther, 255–63. Stuttgart: Franz Steiner Verlag.

Hälikkä, R. 2002. "Discourses of Body, Gender and Power in Tacitus." In *Women, Wealth and Power in the Roman Empire*, edited by P. Setälä, R. Berg, R. Hälikkä, M. Keltanen, J. Pölönen, and V. Vuolanto, 75–104. Rome: Institutum Romanum Finlandiae.

Hallett, J. P. 2015. "Fulvia: The Representation of an Elite Roman Woman Warrior." In *Women and War in Antiquity*, edited by J. Fabre-Serris and A. Keith, 247–65. Baltimore, MD: Johns Hopkins University Press.

Hammond, M. 1963. "*Res olim dissociabiles: Principatus ac Libertas*: Liberty under the Early Roman Empire." *Harvard Studies in Classical Philology* 67: 93–113.

Hanson, W. S., and D. B. Campbell. 1986. "The Brigantes: From Clientage to Conquest." *Britannia* 17: 73–89.

Hardie, P. 1993. *The Epic Successors of Virgil: A Study in the Dynamics of a Tradition.* Cambridge: Cambridge University Press.

Hardwick, L. 1990. "Ancient Amazons—Heroes, Outsiders or Women?" *Greece and Rome* 37 (1): 14–36.

Hartog, F. 1988. *The Mirror of Herodotus: The Representation of the Other in the Writing of History.* Translated by J. Lloyd. Berkeley: University of California Press.

Haselgrove, C. 1982. "Wealth, Prestige and Power: The Dynamics of Late Iron Age Political Centralization in South-East England." In *Ranking, Resource and Exchange*, edited by A. C. Renfrew and S. Shennan, 79–88. Cambridge: Cambridge University Press.

Haselgrove, C. 1984. "Romanization before the Conquest: Gaulish Precedents and British Consequences." In *Military and Civilian in Roman Britain*, edited by T. F. C. Blagg and A. C. King, 1–64. *BAR* British Series 136. Oxford: British Archaeological Reports.

Haselgrove, C. 1987. *Iron Age Coinage in South-East England.* BAR British Series 174. Oxford: British Archaeological Reports.

Haselgrove, C. 2004. "Society and Polity in Late Iron Age Britain." In *A Companion to Roman Britain*, edited by M. Todd, 12–29. Malden, MA: Wiley-Blackwell.

Haselgrove, C., ed. 2016. *Cartimandua's Capital? The Late Iron Age Royal Site at Stanwick, North Yorkshire, Fieldwork and Analysis 1981–2010.* CBA Research Report 175. York: Council for British Archaeology.

Haselgrove, C., and M. Millett. 1997. "Verlamion Reconsidered." In *Reconstructing Iron Age Societies*, edited by A. Gwilt and C. Haselgrove, 282–96. Oxbow Monograph 71. Oxford: Oxbow.

Haselgrove, C., and T. Moore. 2007. "New Narratives of the Later Iron Age." In *The Later Iron Age in Britain and Beyond*, edited by C. Haselgrove and T. Moore, 1–15. Oxford: Oxbow.

Häussler, R. 1999. "Architecture, Performance and Ritual: The Role of State Architecture in the Roman Empire." In *TRAC 98: Proceedings of the Eighth Annual Theoretical*

Roman Archaeology Conference, Leicester 1998, edited by P. Baker, C. Forcey, S. Jundi, and R. Witcher, 1–13. Oxford: Oxbow.

Haverfield, F. 1923. *The Romanization of Roman Britain*. 4th ed. Oxford: Clarendon Press.

Henderson, J. 1989. "Tacitus, the Wor(l)d in Pieces." *Ramus* 18: 167–210.

Henig, M. 1995. *The Art of Roman Britain*. Ann Arbor: University of Michigan Press.

Heubner, H. P., ed. 1994. *P. Cornelii Taciti libri qui supersunt: Tom. I. Ab Excessu Divi Augusti*. Stuttgart: Teubner.

Hill, J. D. 1997. "'The End of One Kind of Body and the Beginning of Another Kind of Body'? Toilet Instruments and 'Romanization' in Southern England during the First Century AD." In *Reconstructing Iron Age Societies*, edited by A. Gwilt and C. Haselgrove, 96–107. Oxford: Oxbow.

Hill, J. D. 2001a. "A New Cart/Chariot Burial from Wetwang, East Yorkshire." *PAST* 38: 2–3.

Hill, J. D. 2001b. "Romanisation, Gender and Class: Recent Approaches to Identity in Britain and Their Possible Consequences." In *Britons and Romans: Advancing an Archaeological Agenda*, edited by S. James and M. Millett, 12–18. York: Council for British Archaeology.

Hill, J. D. 2004. *Later Iron Age Norfolk: Metalwork, Landscape and Society*. BAR British Series 361. Oxford: British Archaeological Reports.

Hill, J. D. 2007. "The Dynamics of Social Change in Later Iron Age Eastern and South-Eastern England c. 300 BC–AD 43." In *The Later Iron Age in Britain and Beyond*, edited by C. Haselgrove and T. Moore, 16–40. Oxford: Oxbow.

Hind, J. G. F. 2007. "A. Plautius' Campaign in Britain: An Alternative Reading of the Narrative in Cassius Dio (60.19.5–21.2)." *Britannia* 38: 93–106.

Hingley, R., and C. Unwin. 2005. *Boudica: Iron Age Warrior Queen*. London: Hambledon and London.

Hingley, R. 1997. "Resistance and Domination: Social Change in Roman Britain." In "Dialogues in Roman Imperialism. Power, Discourse and Discrepant Experience in the Roman Empire," edited by D. J. Mattingly. Supplement, *Journal of Roman Archaeology* 23: 81–100.

Hingley, R. 2000. *Roman Officers and English Gentlemen: The Imperial Origins of Roman Archaeology*. London: Routledge.

Hölkeskamp, H.-J. 1996. "Exempla und mos maiorum: Überlegungen zum kollektiven Gedächtnis der Nobilität." In *Vergangenheit und Lebenswelt: Soziale Kommunikation, Traditionsbildung und historisches Bewusstsein*, edited by H.-J. Gehrke and A. Möller, 301–38. Tübingen: Narr.

Holland, T. 2016. "When the Barbarous Brits First Quit Europe." *The New York Times*, May 29.

Hornblower, S. A., A. Spawforth, and E. Eidinow, eds. 2012. *Oxford Classical Dictionary*. Fourth Edition. Oxford: Oxford University Press.

Howarth, N. 2008. *Cartimandua: Queen of the Brigantes*. Stroud: The History Press.

Hunt, R. 2003. *Queen Boudicca's Battle of Britain*. Kent: Spellmount.

Hutcheson, N. 2007. "An Archaeological Investigation of Later Iron Age Norfolk: Analysing Hoarding Patterns across the Landscape." In *The Later Iron Age in Britain and Beyond*, edited by C. Haselgrove and T. Moore, 358–70. Oxford: Oxbow.

Hutton, R. 2009. *Blood and Mistletoe: The History of the Druids in Britain*. New Haven, CT: Yale University Press.

Ireland, S. 1986. *Roman Britain: A Sourcebook*. New York: Routledge.

Isaac, B. 1990. *The Limits of Empire: The Roman Army in the East*. Oxford: Oxford University Press.

Isaac, B. 2004. *The Invention of Racism in Classical Antiquity*. Princeton, NJ: Princeton University Press.

Jackson, K. 1979. "Queen Boudicca?" *Britannia* 10: 255.

Jackson, R. 1985. "Cosmetic Sets from Late Iron Age and Roman Britain." *Britannia* 16: 165–92.

James, S. 1999. "*Perdomita Britannia . . .*': Roman and Indigenous Strategies and Their Outcomes from Caesar to Domitian and Beyond." In *Fines imperii—imperium sine fine?*, edited by G. Moosbauer and R. Wiegels, 87–105. Osnabrükker Forschungen zu Altertum und Antike-Rezeption 14. Rahden: Verlag Marie Leidorf.

Johns, C. 1996. *The Jewelry of Roman Britain: Celtic and Classical Traditions*. London: Routledge.

Johnson, M. 2012. *Boudica*. London: Bristol Classical Press.

Jones, B. W. 1992. *The Emperor Domitian*. London: Routledge.

Jones, B., and D. Mattingly. 1990. *An Atlas of Roman Britain*. Oxford: Oxbow.

Jones, M. 2004. "Cities and Urban Life." In *A Companion to Roman Britain*, edited by M. Todd, 162–92. Malden, MA: Wiley-Blackwell.

Joshel, S. R. 1992. "The Body Female and the Body Politic: Livy's Lucretia and Verginia." In *Pornography and Representation in Greece and Rome*, edited by A. Richlin, 112–30. Oxford: Oxford University Press.

Joy, J. 2009. *Lindow Man*. London: British Museum Press.

Jundi, S., and J. D. Hill. 1998. "Brooches and Identities in First Century AD Britain: More than Meets the Eye?" In *TRAC 97: Proceedings of the Seventh Annual Theoretical Roman Archaeology Conference Nottingham 1997*, edited by C. Forcey, J. Hawthorne and R. Witcher, eds., 125–37. Oxford: Oxbow.

Kampen, N. B. 1996. "Gender Theory in Roman Art." In *I Claudia: Women in Ancient Rome*, edited by D. E. E. Kleiner and S. B. Matheson, 14–25. New Haven: Yale University Press.

Kaplan, M. 1979. "Agrippina *Semper Atrox*: A Study in Tacitus' Characterization of Women." In *Studies in Latin Literature and Roman History I*, edited by C. Deroux, 410–17. Collection Latomus 164. Brussels: Latomus.

Kehne, P. 2001. "Cartimandua, Boudica und Veleda: Auswärtige 'Frauenmacht' in der römischen Historiographie." *Eos* 88: 267–84.

Keitel, E. 1978. "The Role of Parthia and Armenia in Tacitus *Annals* 11 and 12." *American Journal of Philology* 99 (4): 462–73.

Keitel, E. 2009. "'Is Dying so Very Terrible?' The Neronian *Annals*." In *The Cambridge Companion to Tacitus*, edited by A. J. Woodman, 127–44. Cambridge: Cambridge University Press.

Keitel, E. 2010. "The Art of Losing: Tacitus and the Disaster Narrative." In *Ancient Historiography and Its Contexts: Studies in Honour of A. J. Woodman*, edited by S. Kraus, J. Marincola, and C. Pelling, 331–53. Oxford: Oxford University Press.

Kleiner, D. 2005. *Cleopatra and Rome*. Cambridge, MA: Harvard University Press.

Koestermann, E., ed. 1957. *P. Cornelii Taciti libri qui supersunt: Tom. II. Fasc. 2. Germania, Agricola, Dialogus de Oratoribus*. Stuttgart: Teubner.

Koestermann, E., ed. 1963–68. *Cornelius Tacitus: Annalen*. 4 vols. Heidelberg: Carl Winter.

Kolb, A. 2010. "*Augustae* - Zielsetzung, Definition, prosopographischer Überblick." *Augustae: Machtbewusste Frauen am römischen Kaiserhof? Herrschaftsstruckturen und Herrschaftspraxis II. Akten der Tagung in Zürich 18.- 20.9.2008*, edited by A. Kolb, 11–35. Berlin: Akademie Verlag.

Kotula, T. 2001. "*Iam domiti, ut pareant . . .* [?] (Tac. *Agric.* 13). Rom et ses sujets au Ier siècle de l'empire." *Antiquitas* 25: 55–65.

Krebs, C. B. 2011. "Borealism: Caesar, Seneca, Tacitus, and the Roman Discourse about the Germanic North." In *Cultural Identity in the Ancient Mediterranean*, edited by E. S. Gruen, 202–21. Los Angeles: Getty Research Institute.

Lavan, M. 2011. "Slavishness in Britain and Rome in Tacitus' *Agricola*." *Classical Quarterly* 61: 294–305.

Lavan, M. 2013. *Slaves to Rome: Paradigms of Empire in Roman Culture*. Cambridge: Cambridge University Press.

Laurence, R. 2001. "Roman Narratives: The Writing of Archaeological Discourse—A View from Britain." *Archaeological Dialogues* 8 (2): 90–101.

Lepper, F., and S. S. Frere. 1988. *Trajan's Column: A New Edition of the Chicorius Plates*. Gloucester: Sutton.

Levene, D. S. 1999. "Tacitus' Histories and the Theory of Deliberative Oratory." In *The Limits of Historiography: Genre and Narrative in Ancient Historical Texts*, edited by C. S. Kraus, 197–216. Leiden: Brill.

Levene, D. S. 2009. "Speeches in the *Histories*." In *The Cambridge Companion to Tacitus*, edited by A. J. Woodman, 212–24. Cambridge: Cambridge University Press.

Levi, A. C. 1952. *Barbarians on Roman Imperial Coins and Sculpture*. New York: American Numismatic Society.

L'Hoir, F. S. 1992. *The Rhetoric of Gender Terms: "Man," "Woman" and the Portrayal of Character in Latin Prose*. Leiden: Brill.

L'Hoir, F. S. 1994. "Tacitus and Women's Usurpation of Power." *Classical World* 88 (1): 5–25.

L'Hoir, F. S. 2006. *Tragedy, Rhetoric, and the Historiography of Tacitus'* Annals. Ann Arbor: University of Michigan Press.

Liebeschuetz, W. 1966. "The Theme of Liberty in the *Agricola* of Tacitus." *Classical Quarterly* 16: 126–39.

Linduff, K. M. 1979. "Epona: A Celt among the Romans." *Latomus* 38 (4): 817–37.

Luce, J. V. 1963. "Cleopatra as *Fatale Monstrum* (Horace, *Carm*. 1.37.21)." *Classical Quarterly* 13: 251–57.

Luce, T. J. 1991. "Tacitus on 'History's Highest Function': *Praecipuum Munus Annalium* (Ann. 3.65)." *Aufstieg und Niedergang der römischen Welt* 2.33.4: 2904–27.

Macdonald, S. 1987. "Boadicea: Warrior, Mother and Myth." In *Images of Women in Peace and War*, edited by P. Holden Macdonald and S. Ardner, 40–61. London: Macmillan Education.

Manley, J. 2002. *AD 43: The Roman Invasion of Britain. A Reassessment*. Stroud: The History Press.

Mann, J. C. 1985. "Two 'Topoi' in the *Agricola*." *Britannia* 16: 21–24.

Manuwald, B. 1978. *Cassius Dio and Augustus*. Wiesbaden: Steiner.

Marincola, J. 1999. "Genre, Convention and Innovation in Greco-Roman Historiography." In *The Limits of Historiography: Genre and Narrative in Ancient Historical Texts*, edited by C. S. Kraus, 281–324. Leiden: Brill.

Marshall, A. J. 1984. "Ladies in Waiting: The Role of Women in Tacitus' *Histories*." *Ancient Society* 15–17: 167–84.

Mattern, S. P. 1999. *Rome and the Enemy: Imperial Strategy in the Principate*. Berkeley: University of California Press.

Mattingly, D. 2006. *An Imperial Possession: Britain in the Roman Empire*. London: Penguin.

Mattingly, D. 2013. *Imperialism, Power, and Identity: Experiencing the Roman Empire*. Princeton, NJ: Princeton University Press.

Mayor, A. 2014. *The Amazons: Lives and Legends of Warrior Women Across the Ancient World*. Princeton, NJ: Princeton University Press.

McDonnell, M. 2006. *Roman Manliness: Virtus and the Roman Republic*. Cambridge: Cambridge University Press.

Millar, F. 1964. *A Study of Cassius Dio*. Oxford: Clarendon Press.

Millett, M. 1990a. "Romanization: Historical Issues and Archaeological Interpretation." In *The Early Roman Empire in the West*, edited by T. Blagg and M. Millett, 35–41. Oxford: Oxbow.

Millett, M. 1990b. *The Romanization of Britain: An Essay in Archaeological Interpretation*. Cambridge: Cambridge University Press.

Millett, M. 1995. *Roman Britain*. London: Batsford.

Milne, G. 1995. *Roman London*. London: Batsford.

Milnor, K. 2005. *Gender, Domesticity, and the Age of Augustus: Inventing Private Life*. Oxford: Oxford University Press.

Mitchell, S. 1978. "Venutius and Cartimandua." *Liverpool Classical Monthly* 3: 215–19.

Mommsen, T. 1886. *The Provinces of the Roman Empire: From Caesar to Diocletian*. Translated by W. P. Dickson. New York: Charles Scribner's Sons.

Moore, T. 2011. "Detribalizing the Later Prehistoric Past: Concepts of Tribes in Iron Age and Roman Studies." *Journal of Social Archaeology* 11 (3): 334–60.

Morford, M. P. O. 1985. "Nero's Patronage and Participation in Literature and the Arts." *Aufstieg und Niedergang der römischen Welt* 2.32.3: 2003–31.

Morford, M. P. O. 1991. "How Tacitus Defined Liberty." *Aufstieg und Niedergang der römischen Welt* 2.33.5: 3420–50.

Mossop, H. R., and D. F. Allen. 1979. "An Elusive Icenian Legend." *Britannia* 10: 258–59.

Nash, D. 1987. *Coinage in the Celtic World*. London: Numismatic Fine Arts Intl.

Nash Briggs, D. 2011. "The Language of Inscriptions on Icenian Coinage." In *The Iron Age in Northern East Anglia: New Work in the Land of the Iceni*, edited by J. A. Davies, 83–102. *BAR* British Series 549. Oxford: British Archaeological Reports.

Niblett, R. 1992. "A Catuvellaunian Chieftain's Burial from St Albans." *Antiquity* 66: 917–29.

Niblett, R. 1999. *The Excavation of a Ceremonial Site at Folly Lane, St Albans*. Britannia Monograph 14. London: Society for the Promotion of Roman Studies.

Niblett, R. 2000. "Funerary Rites in Verulamium during the Early Roman Period." In *Burial, Society and Context in the Roman World*, edited by J. Pearce, M. Millett, and M. Struck, 97–104. Oxford: Oxbow.

Niblett, R. 2001. *Verulamium: The Roman City of St Albans*. Stroud: Tempus.

Niblett, R. 2004. "The Native Elite and their Funerary Practices from the First Century BC to Nero." In *A Companion to Roman Britain*, edited by M. Todd, 30–41. Malden, MA: Wiley-Blackwell.

Nice, A. 1993. "Superstition and Religion in Tacitus' and Dio's Accounts of the Boudican Revolt." *Pegasus* 36: 15–18.

Oakley, S. P. 2009. "*Res olim dissociabiles*: Emperors, Senators and Liberty." In *The Cambridge Companion to Tacitus*, edited by A. J. Woodman, 184–94. Cambridge: Cambridge University Press.

Ogilvie, R. M., and I. A. Richmond, ed. 1967. *Cornelii Taciti de vita Agricolae*. Oxford: Oxford University Press.

O'Gorman, E. 1993. "No Place like Rome: Identity and Difference in the *Germania* of Tacitus." *Ramus* 22: 135–54.

Orsi, D. P. 1973. "Sulla rivolta di Boudicca." *Annali della Facoltà di Lettere e Filosofia* 16: 529–36.

Overbeck, J. C. 1969. "Tacitus and Dio on Boudicca's Rebellion." *American Journal of Philology* 90: 129–45.

Pagán, V. E. 1999. "Beyond Teutoburg: Transgression and Transformation in Tacitus *Annales* 1.61-62." *Classical Philology* 94: 302–30.

Pagán, V. E. 2000. "Distant Voices of Freedom in the *Annales* of Tacitus." In *Studies in Latin Literature and Roman History* Vol. 10, edited by C. Deroux, 358–69. Collection Latomus 254. Brussels: Latomus.

Paul, G. M. 1982. "*Urbs Capta*: Sketch of an Ancient Literary Motif." *Phoenix* 36 (2): 144–55.

Percival, J. 1980. "Tacitus and the Principate." *Greece and Rome* 27: 119–33.

Perring, D. 2015. "Recent Advances in the Understanding of Roman London." In *The Towns of Roman Britain: The Contribution of Commercial Archaeology since 1990*, edited by M. Fulford and N. Holbrook, 20–43. Britannia Monograph Series 27. London: Society for the Promotion of Roman Studies.

Philpott, R. 1991. *Burial Practices in Roman Britain: A Survey of Grave Treatment and Furnishing AD 43–410.* BAR British Series 219. Oxford: British Archaeological Reports.

Plass, P. 1988. *Wit and the Writing of History: The Rhetoric of Historiography in Imperial Rome.* Madison: University of Wisconsin Press.

Potter, T. W., and C. Johns. 1992. *Roman Britain.* Berkeley: University of California Press.

Raaflaub, K. A., and R. J. A. Talbert, eds. 2010. *Geography and Ethnography: Perceptions of the World in Pre-Modern Societies.* Malden, MA: Wiley-Blackwell.

Rankin, D. 1996. *Celts and the Classical World.* 2nd ed. London: Routledge.

Reed, N. 1974. "The Sources of Tacitus and Dio for the Boudiccan Revolt." *Latomus* 33: 926–33.

Reinhold, M., and P. M. Swan. 1990. "Cassius Dio's Assessment of Augustus." In *Between Republic and Empire: Interpretations of Augustus and his Principate*, edited by K. Raaflaub and M. Toher, 155–73. Berkeley: University of California Press.

Revell, L. 2009. *Roman Imperialism and Local Identities.* Cambridge: Cambridge University Press.

Revell, L. 2010. "Romanization: A Feminist Critique." In *TRAC 2009: Proceedings of the Nineteenth Annual Theoretical Roman Archaeology Conference*, edited by A. Moore, G. Taylor, E. Harris, P. Girdwood, and L. Shipley, 1–10. Oxford: Oxbow.

Revell, L. 2016. *Ways of Being Roman: Discourses of Identity in the Roman West.* Oxford: Oxbow.

Richardson, J. S. 2008. *The Language of Empire: Rome and the Idea of Empire from the Third Century BC to the Second Century AD.* Cambridge: Cambridge University Press.

Richmond, I. A. 1954. "Queen Cartimandua." *The Journal of Roman Studies* 44: 43–52.

Richmond, I. A. 1955. *Roman Britain.* Harmondsworth: Penguin.

Rivet, A. L. F. 1983. "The First Icenian Revolt." In *Rome and Her Northern Frontiers*, edited by B. Hartley and J. Wacher, 202–9. Gloucester: Sutton.

Roberts, M. 1988. "The Revolt of Boudicca (Tacitus, *Annals* 14.29–39) and the Assertion of *Libertas* in Neronian Rome." *American Journal of Philology* 109 (1): 118–32.

Robins, D., and A. Ross. 1989. *The Life and Death of a Druid Prince: The Story of Lindow Man.* New York: Touchstone.

Roddaz, J. M. 1983. "De César à Auguste: L'image de la monarchie chez un historien du Siècle des Sévères. Réflexions sur l'oeuvre de Dion Cassius, à propos d'ouvrages récents." *Revue des études anciennes* 85: 67–87.

Rodgers, R. 2003. "Female Representation in Roman Art: Feminising the Provincial "Other"." In *Roman Imperialism and Provincial Art*, edited by S. Scott and J. Webster, 69–94. Cambridge: Cambridge University Press.

Rogers, A. 2015. *The Archaeology of Roman Britain: Biography and Identity.* New York: Routledge.

Roller, D. W. 2010. *Cleopatra: A Biography.* Oxford: Oxford University Press.

Roller, M. 2004. "Exemplarity in Roman Culture: The Cases of Horatius Cocles and Cloelia." *Classical Philology* 99: 28–50.

Roller, M. 2009. "The Exemplary Past in Roman Historiography and Culture." In *The Cambridge Companion to Roman History*, edited by A. Feldherr, 214–30. Cambridge: Cambridge University Press.

Romm, J. S. 1992. *The Edges of the Earth in Ancient Thought: Geography, Exploration, and Fiction.* Princeton, NJ: Princeton University Press.

Rose, C. B. 1991. "'Princes' and Barbarians on the Ara Pacis." *American Journal of Archaeology* 94: 453–67.

Ross, A. 1999. *Druids.* Stroud: Tempus.

Rothe, U. 2013. "Whose Fashion? Men, Women and Roman Culture as Reflected in Dress in the Cities of the Roman North-West." In *Women and the Roman City in the Latin West*, edited by E. A. Hemelrijk and G. Woolf, 243–68. Leiden: Brill.

Rutherford, R. B. 2010. "Voices of Resistance." In *Ancient Historiography and its Contexts: Studies in Honour of A. J. Woodman*, edited by C. S. Kraus, J. Marincola, and C. Pelling, 312–30. Oxford: Oxford University Press.

Rutland, L. W. 1978. "Women as Makers of Kings in Tacitus' *Annals*." *Classical World* 72: 15–29.

Rutledge, S. H. 2000. "Tacitus in Tartan: Textual Colonization and Expansionist Discourse in the *Agricola*." *Helios* 27: 76–95.

Said, E. 1978. *Orientalism.* London: Vintage.

Salway, P. 1982. *Roman Britain.* 2nd ed. Oxford: Oxford University Press.

Sánchez, P. 2004. "Les prêts de Sénèque aux Bretons et la révolte de Boudicca: calomnie ou cas exemplaire de romanisation forcée?" *Museum Helveticum* 61 (1): 32–63.

Schuhmann, R. 1999. "*Aurinia* und *Veleda*: zwei germanische Seherinnen? Personennamen im Sprachkontakt." *Beiträge zur Namenforschung* 34: 131–43.

Sealey, P. R. 1997. *The Boudican Revolt against Rome.* Princes Risborough: Shire Publications.

Sharrock, A. 2015. "Warrior Women in Roman Epic." In *Women and War in Antiquity*, edited by J. Fabre-Serris and A. Keith, 157–78. Baltimore: Johns Hopkins University Press.

Shotter, D. 1978. "Principatus ac Libertas." *Ancient Society* 9: 235–55.

Shotter, D. 1998. *Roman Britain.* 2nd ed. London: Routledge.

Shotter, D. 2004. *Romans and Britons in North-West England.* 3rd edition. Lancaster: University of Lancaster.

Shumate, N. 2006. *Nation, Empire, Decline: Studies in Rhetorical Continuity from the Romans to the Modern Era*. London: Bloomsbury.

Simpson, C. J. 1996. "The Statue of Victory at Colchester." *Britannia* 27: 386–87.

Sinclair, P. 1995. *Tacitus the Sententious Historian: A Sociology of Rhetoric in Annales 1–6*. University Park: Pennsylvania State University Press.

Smith, J. T. 1978. "Villas as a Key to Social Structure." In *Studies in the Romano-British Villa*, edited by M. Todd, 149–73. Leicester: Leicester University Press.

Smith, R. R. R. 1987. "The Imperial Reliefs from the Sebasteion at Aphrodisias." *Journal of Roman Studies* 77: 88–138.

Smith, R. R. R. 2002. "The Uses of Images: Visual History and Ancient History." In *Classics in Progress: Essays on Ancient Greece and Rome*, edited by T. P. Wiseman, 59–102. Oxford: Oxford University Press.

Späth, T. 1994. *Männlichkeit und Weiblichkeit bei Tacitus. Zur Konstruktion der Geschlechter in der römischen Kaiserzeit*. Frankfurt am Main: Campus.

Spence, L. 1937. *Boadicea, Warrior Queen of the Britons*. London: R. Hale.

Standing, G. 2005. "The Varian Disaster and the Boudiccan Revolt: Fabled Victories?" *Britannia* 36: 373–75.

Stead, I. M., J. Bourke, and D. Brothwell. 1986. *Lindow Man: The Body in the Bog*. London: British Museum Publications.

Stevens, C. E. 1951. "Britain between the Invasions (BC 54–43 AD): A Study in Ancient Diplomacy." In *Aspects of Archaeology in Britain and Beyond*, edited by W. F. Grimes, 332–44. London: H. W. Edwards.

Stewart, A. 1995. "Imag(in)ing the Other: Amazons and Ethnicity in Fifth-Century Athens." *Poetics Today* 16 (4): 571–79.

Straub, J. 1977. "Imperium-Pax-Libertas (Rom und die Freiheit der Barbaren)." *Gymnasium* 84: 136–48.

Strunk, T. E. 2016. *History after Liberty: Tacitus on Tyrants, Sycophants, and Republicans*. Ann Arbor: University of Michigan Press.

Swan, P. M. 2004. *The Augustan Succession: An Historical Commentary on Cassius Dio's Roman History, Books 55–56 (9 BC–AD 14)*. Oxford: Oxford University Press.

Syme, R. 1958. *Tacitus*. 2 vols. Oxford: Clarendon Press.

Syme, R. 1988. "Rome and the Nations." In *Roman Papers*, edited by R. Syme, 62–73. Oxford: Clarendon Press.

Talbot, J., and I. Liens. 2010. "Before Boudicca: The Wickham Market Hoard and the Middle Phase Gold Coinage of East Anglia." *The British Numismatic Journal* 80: 1–23.

Tennyson, A. L. 1875. *Poetical Works of Alfred Lord Tennyson*. vol. II. London: Henry S. King and Co.

Terrenato, N. 1998. "The Romanization of Italy: Global Acculturation or Cultural Bricolage." In *TRAC 97: Proceedings of the Seventh Annual Theoretical Roman Archaeology Conference*, edited by C. Forcey, J. Hawthorne, and R. Witcher, 20–27. Oxford: Oxbow.

Thomson-Salo, F. 2015. "Boadicea, Warrior Queen: A Baby's Perspective and an Analysand's Perspective." In *Myths of Mighty Women: Their Application in Psychoanalytic Psychotherapy*, edited by A. K. Richards and L. Spira, 99–108. London: Karnac Books.

Todd, M. 2004. "The Claudian Conquest and Its Consequences." In *A Companion to Roman Britain*, edited by M. Todd, 42–59. Malden, MA: Wiley-Blackwell.

Tomlin, R. S. O. 2016. *Roman London's First Voices: Writing Tablets from the Bloomberg Excavations 2010–14*. MoLAS Monograph 72. London: Museum of London.

Toynbee, J. M. C. 1962. *Art in Roman Britain*. London: Phaidon Press.

Toynbee, J. M. C. 1964. *Art in Britain under the Romans*. Oxford: Clarendon Press.

Trow, M. J., and T. Trow. 2003. *Boudicca: The Warrior Queen*. Stroud: History Press Ltd.

Turnbull, P., and L. Fitts. 1988. "The Politics of Brigantia." In *Recent Researches in Roman Yorkshire*, edited by J. Price and P. R. Wilson, 377–86. BAR British Series 193. Oxford: British Archaeological Reports.

Turner, R. G., and R. C. Scaife, eds. 1995. *Bog Bodies: New Discoveries and New Perspectives*. London: British Museum Press.

Van Arsdell, R. D. 1989. *Celtic Coinage of Britain*. London: Spink & Son Ltd.

Veyne, P. 1993. "*Humanitas*: Romans and Non-Romans." In *The Romans*, edited by A. Giardina, 342–69. Chicago: University of Chicago Press.

Von Bothmer, D. 1957. *Amazons in Greek Art*. Oxford: Clarendon Press.

Vout, C. 2007. *Power and Eroticism in Imperial Rome*. Cambridge: Cambridge University Press.

Waite, J. 2007. *Boudica's Last Stand: Britain's Revolt Against Rome AD 60–61*. London: The History Press.

Warner, M. 1985. *Monuments and Maidens: The Allegory of the Female Form*. New York: Atheneum.

Warren, R. 2016. "Henry Courtney Selous' Boadicea and the Westminster Cartoon Competition." In *Graeco-Roman Antiquity and the Idea of Nationalism in the 19th Century*, edited by T. Fögen and R. Warren, 175–98. Berlin: De Gruyter.

Watts, D. 2005. *Boudicca's Heirs: Women in Early Britain*. London: Routledge.

Webster, G. 1978. *Boudica: The British Revolt against Rome AD 60*. Totowa, NJ: Rowman and Littlefield.

Webster, G. 1980. *The Roman Invasion of Britain*. London: Routledge.

Webster, G. 1993. *Rome against Caratacus: The Roman Campaigns in Britain AD 48–58*. London: Routledge.

Webster, J. 1994. "The Just War: Graeco-Roman Texts as Colonial Discourse." In *TRAC 94: Proceedings of the Fourth Annual Theoretical Roman Archaeology Conference*, edited by S. Cottam, D. Dungworth, S. Scott, and J. Taylor, 1–10. Oxford: Oxbow.

Webster, J. 1999. "At the End of the World: Druidic and Other Revitalization Movements in Post-Conquest Gaul and Britain." *Britannia* 30: 1–20.

Webster, J. 2001. "Creolizing the Roman Provinces." *American Journal of Archaeology* 105: 209–25.

Webster, J., and J. Cooper, eds. 1996. *Roman Imperialism: Post-Colonial Perspectives.* Leicester: University of Leicester.

Wellesley, K. 1969. "Review of Ogilvie and Richmond." *Journal of Roman Studies* 59: 266–69.

Whitmarsh, T. 2006. "'This In-between Book': Language, Politics and Genre in the *Agricola*." In *The Limits of Ancient Biography*, edited by B. McGing and J. Mossman, 305–33. Swansea: Classical Press of Wales.

Wild, J. P. 1968. "Clothing in the North-West Provinces of the Roman Empire." *Bonner Jahrbücher* 168: 166–240.

Wild, J. P. 1985. "The Clothing of Britannia, Gallia Belgica and Germania Inferior." *Aufstieg und Niedergang der römischen Welt* 2.12.3: 362–422.

Williams, C. A. 2000. *Roman Homosexuality.* 2nd ed. Oxford: Oxford University Press.

Williams, C. D. 2009. *Boudica and Her Stories: Narrative Transformations of a Warrior Queen.* Newark: University of Delaware Press.

Williams, J. 2000. "The Silver Coins from East Anglia Attributed to King Prasutagus of the Iceni—A New Reading of the Obverse Inscription." *Numismatic Chronicle* 160: 276–81.

Williams, J. 2001. "Coin Inscriptions and the Origins of Writing in Pre-Roman Britain." *British Numismatic Journal* 71: 1–17.

Williams, J. 2007. "New Light on Latin in Pre-conquest Britain." *Britannia* 38: 1–12.

Willis, S. 1997. "Settlement, Materiality and Landscape in the Iron Age of the East Midlands: Evidence, Interpretation and Wider Resonance." In *Reconstructing Iron Age Societies*, edited by A. Gwilt and C. Haselgrove, 205–15. Oxford: Oxbow.

Wirszubski, C. 1950. *Libertas as a Political Idea at Rome during the Late Republic and Early Principate.* Cambridge: Cambridge University Press.

Wiseman, T. P. 2013. *The Death of Caligula: Josephus Ant. Iud. XIX 1–273, Translation and Commentary.* Liverpool: Liverpool University Press.

Woodman, A. J., ed., with contributions from C. S. Kraus. 2014. *Tacitus: Agricola.* Cambridge: Cambridge University Press.

Woolf, G. 1998. *Becoming Roman: The Origins of Provincial Civilization in Gaul.* Cambridge: Cambridge University Press.

Woolf, G. 2011. *Tales of the Barbarians: Ethnography and Empire in the Roman West.* Malden, MA: Wiley-Blackwell.

Wyke, M. 1992. "Augustan Cleopatras: Female Power and Poetic Authority." In *Roman Poetry and Propaganda in the Age of Augustus*, edited by A. Powell, 98–104. London: Bristol Classical Press.

Index

Dio, Lucius Cassius
  biography and style of, 5–7
  Boudica in, 1–2, 69–72, 74 (see also
    Boudica)
  Caledonians in, 81–82, 132
  campaigns of Caesar in, 16
  critique of imperial family members
    in, 84–87
  female speeches in, 77–81
  revolt of Bato in, 119–21
Dionysius of Halicarnassus, 22, 78
dominatio, 59–60, 60n27, 60n28, 60n29
Domitian (emperor AD 81–96), 4, 43, 115,
    129, 131
Druids, 17, 29, 92, 105–12, 134
Drusus (Nero Claudius Drusus, Livia's
    son, Germanicus's father), 122
Drusus (Drusus Julius Caesar, Tiberius's
    son), 100
dux femina, meaning of, 12, 91–92, 98

Edward the Elder, 135
Elizabeth I, 133
Epona, 109, 109 (figure 6.1)

Fenwick treasure, 51
Fishbourne Palace, 48–49, 49 (figure 2.3)
Fulvia, 97–98, 111

Gallus, Aulus Didius, 27
Gauls
  chariots of, 137
  comparisons between Britons and, 17,
    22–23, 56, 71
  religion and rituals of, 109–112
  resistance to Rome of, 16
  in Roman army, 59, 130
  trade with, 17–18
Germanicus (Germanicus Julius
    Caesar), 98–100, 120, 123–24
Geta, Publius Septimius (emperor AD
    209–211), 81
Gildas, 133
governor, Roman, 21, 27, 42, 56–57. See
    also Suetonius Paulinus

Hadrian (emperor AD 117–138), 76,
    82, 131
Herodotus, 83, 95

Hersilia, 78, 94–95, 114
Heyman, Francis, 137
hillforts, 46, 46 (figure 2.1)
Homer, 94
Horace, 19, 37–38, 106
hostages (obsides), 19, 94, 122, 124,
    127, 130
humanitas, 23–24, 23n59, 24n61
Hypsicratea, 89. See also Amazons

Iceni
  archaeological finds of, 25, 48–49
    (see also torc)
  Caesar and, 25
  centers of habitation of (see Saham
    Toney; Snettisham; Thetford; Venta
    Icenorum)
  Claudius's alliance with, 26
  coins of, 25, 26 (figure 1.3, figure 1.4),
    27 (figure 1.5), 44–45
  culture and lifestyle of, 35–36,
    46–48, 62–63
  first revolt of, 27, 41–42
  leadership of, 44–45
  See also Boudica; Iron Age;
    Prasutagus
Icilius, 65–66
imperium, 67–68, 87, 97, 101, 104, 130
Iron Age
  burial practices in, 89–90
  coins of, 18
  culture of, 8–10, 17–18, 46–47
  dress and ornamentation in,
    71–73, 73n19
  religious practices in, 63, 110–11
    (see also ritual)
  settlements in, 46–47 (see also
    hillforts; roundhouses)
  trade in, 17–18

James I, 133
Julia Domna, 81, 84n74, 132

legions, 16, 19–21, 33, 39, 93, 99–100, 108,
    111, 120, 123–24
  Fourteenth Legion, 30–32
  Ninth Legion, 30–32, 101 (see also
    Petillius Cerialis)
  Twentieth Legion, 24, 30, 32

Made in the USA
Monee, IL
09 January 2022